# *The Audience*
# *The Message*
# *The Speaker*

# The Audience
# The Message
# The Speaker

**EIGHTH EDITION**

## JOHN HASLING

Professor Emeritus
*Foothill College*

**Higher Education**

Boston   Burr Ridge, IL   Dubuque, IA   New York   San Francisco   St. Louis
Bangkok   Bogotá   Caracas   Kuala Lumpur   Lisbon   London   Madrid   Mexico City
Milan   Montreal   New Delhi   Santiago   Seoul   Singapore   Sydney   Taipei   Toronto

# Higher Education

THE AUDIENCE, THE MESSAGE, THE SPEAKER
Published by McGraw-Hill, a business unit of The McGraw-Hill Companies, Inc., 1221 Avenue
of the Americas, New York, NY 10020. Copyright © 2010 by The McGraw-Hill Companies, Inc.
All rights reserved. No part of this publication may be reproduced or distributed in any form or
by any means, or stored in a database or retrieval system, without the prior written consent of
The McGraw-Hill Companies, Inc., including, but not limited to, any network or other electronic
storage or transmission, or broadcast for distance learning.
Some ancillaries, including electronic and print components, may not be available to customers
outside the United States.

3 4 5 6 7 8 9 0 QFR/QFR 1 5 4 3 2 1

ISBN: 978-0-07-338504-4
MHID: 0-07-338504-2

Vice president and editor-in-chief: *Michael Ryan*
Publisher: *Frank Mortimer*
Sponsoring editor: *Katie Stevens*
Director of development: *Dawn Groundwater*
Development editor: *Meghan Campbell*
Editorial coordinator: *Erika Lake*
Marketing manager: *Pamela Cooper*
Marketing Specialist: *Rebecca Saidlower*
Senior production editor: *Mel Valentín*
Production assistant: *Rachel J. Castillo*
Production service: *Matrix Productions Inc.*

Design manager: *Preston Thomas*
Designer: *Margarite Reynolds*
Cover designer: *Margarite Reynolds*
Photo researcher: *Poyee Oster*
Media project manager: *Thomas Brierly*
Production supervisor: *Tandra Jorgensen*

The text was set in 10.5/12 Palatino by Laserwords Private Limited, and printed on acid-free 45#
New Era Matte by Quebecor-World.

Because this page cannot legibly accommodate all acknowledgements for copyrighted material,
credits appear at the end of the book, and constitute an extension of this copyright page.

**Library of Congress Cataloging-in-Publication Data**

Hasling, John.
   The audience, the message, the speaker / John Hasling.—8th ed.
       p. cm.
   Includes bibliographical references and index.
   ISBN-13: 978-0-07-338504-4 (alk. paper)
   ISBN-10: 0-07-338504-2 (alk. paper)
   1. Public speaking.   I. Title.
   PN4129.15.H38 2009
   808.5′1—dc22

                                                    2008051894

*J*ohn (Jack) Hasling earned the title of Professor Emeritus after teaching for 27 years at Foothill College in Los Altos Hills, California. He received his MA in 1963 from Sacramento State University, where he later taught and coached the debate team. He came to Foothill College in 1966 to teach public speaking and serve as faculty adviser for the college radio station. In the years following, he contributed to the speech curriculum by writing and developing courses in group discussion, interpersonal communication, and broadcast journalism. Teaching was his second career, his first being broadcasting. From 1952 to 1961 he worked as an announcer and engineer for several radio stations in northern California. In 1980 he published a book with McGraw-Hill entitled *Fundamentals of Radio Broadcasting*.

During his years at Foothill College, Jack was actively involved in faculty affairs at the state and local levels. He served as chair of the Improvement of Instruction committee and later as president of the Academic Senate. He is a former member of the Commission on Instruction for the California Association of Community Colleges and is a charter member of the Bay Area Speech Teachers Association. He has also served as parliamentarian at conventions of the California State Academic Senate.

Since his retirement Jack has extended his interest in writing to include adult fiction and children's literature. He has published two novels, both concerning social issues in recent history, and two children's books. He reads his works to third- and fourth-grade classes and speaks to adult groups on the importance of reading aloud to children.

P A R T **I**     *The Audience*    **9**

PART **II** *The Message* 65

## 6    *Organizing and Outlining*                          *89*

## 7    *The Speech to Inform*                              *103*

# P A R T III    *The Speaker*    *147*

*I*t never occurred to me that this text would be read by anyone other than English-speakers. But this year it will be translated into and published in Chinese so that it can be used in colleges and universities in Asia. It was selected, I have learned, because of its emphasis on overcoming cultural differences and addressing the relationship that the speaker has with the audience. I am especially pleased about that because those thoughts tie in nicely with the new material I have added to this edition on finding common ground.

In recent years we have seen a growing climate of polarization in the public dialogue on social issues. Presidential campaigns contribute to that condition as candidates make every effort they can to distinguish themselves from other contenders. The result has been to encourage speakers to highlight differences at the expense of unity. The challenge to today's speaker is to break down the walls that divide us and bring people together in supporting a common cause.

Students of public speaking need to distinguish between a general audience and a political rally. Candidates for public office can address selected groups that consist of like-minded people. The speaker at a rally can pretty much count on the crowd favoring the policies that are expressed and cheering on cue at the applause lines. That will not be the case when a student gives a speech in class or to a general audience. Most of the time a speaker can expect that there will be people in the audience with different points of view and with cultural backgrounds that give them different perspectives. Speakers need to consider how they can reach those who might not understand their references, and how they can connect with those who may have fundamental disagreements.

In Chapter 3, "Finding Common Ground," I have elaborated on the practice of framing a thought in language that is inclusive rather than divisive. Too often we rely on standard expressions such as "pro-life" or "pro-choice" that separate people into categories that carry unnecessary baggage. I like to point out that there are other ways of expressing beliefs on issues such as family planning that do not generate and exacerbate alienation. A meeting of minds cannot occur when speaker and audience are on opposite sides of a fence. Somewhere in between there is common ground that does not require one side to yield to the other, but offers an alternative that both can accept. Finding that ground is not so much a matter of compromise as of thinking creatively about collective interests and unexplored possibilities.

I believe that inclusiveness in public speaking has not been given the attention it deserves. In recent years we have had too many debates and not enough healing discussions. We have come to regard good public speaking as effectively attacking the opposition rather than seeking common ground that may bring two sides together. My hope is that this text will encourage readers to place more stock in reconciliation.

When the first edition of this textbook was published in 1971, there was little need to pay attention to the challenges of speaking to a diversified audience. At Foothill College, where I taught for 27 years, almost all of my students had the same cultural and ethnic background and were familiar with the literary, historical, and political references I made. But as the years went by, the picture began to change. Students came to our college from all parts of the world. In the past decade, men and women from over 70 different nations have enrolled. No longer can instructors assume that everyone in their classes will understand the implications of historical events that all of us in my generation and culture were taught in school.

In subsequent editions of the text, and in my lectures, I included considerations pertaining to cultural diversity when I wrote or spoke about audience analysis. The first rule for the speaker is to reach the people in the audience from *where they are,* rather than from the place where you want them to be. I would be pleased if all my students or people in my audience were in the same political party as I am. I would be delighted if they all enjoyed theater and poetry, had traveled to places where I have been, had seen the same plays that I had seen and read the same books. I would like it if they all studied geography, rode bicycles, and belonged to environmental protection organizations and peacemaking groups as I do. But I know that's not always going to be the case. I can speak of those things and convey my own enthusiasm, but I must recognize that my experience is not necessarily going to be the same as theirs. Somehow I have to be able to relate what I know to something similar in their own frame of reference.

The foundation of this text is based upon the writings of Aristotle, who had a profound effect upon the way people in the Western world have structured their society. That is not something that everyone in this country would acknowledge. For the most part, the average person in America knows very little about Aristotle and would find it difficult to cite an example of how his or her behavior was affected by any of the early Greek philosophers. Nevertheless, that influence is there. I suspect that the Chinese regard their philosophers in the same way. How many people in China would be able or willing to say that Lao-tse or Confucius has played an important role in the way they think or act?

In considering the translation of this text from English to Chinese, I had to wonder if it would be possible to find common ground between Eastern and Western thinking. Is there any comparison that can be made between the wisdom of Lao-tse and that of Aristotle? One lived three hundred years before the other and on the opposite side of the globe. Aristotle professed control of the environment to meet the needs of human beings, while Lao-tse believed in the acceptance of things the way they are to achieve peace of mind. Can we reconcile those differences? How does a controlling philosophy equate with an accepting one? I think both philosophers could agree that the pursuit of wisdom begins with understanding one's self, taking responsibility for one's own actions, and accepting the reality of the physical world. Both might also agree that things of the physical world need to be defined and classified. With that foundation I think we can build a case to show the value that the art of public speaking and persuasion has in both worlds.

Another commonality present in all cultures is the need for ethical standards. A chapter on that element of public speaking has been included in most editions of this text, but in this current edition I have expressed the concepts in contemporary language rather than in the words of the philosophers. In the 1960s students themselves came up with a phrase that summarizes the essence of rhetorical ethics—"Tell it like it is." That's what I have tried to do.

My area of study includes all aspects of oral communication. Public speaking is, perhaps, the most clearly defined division of the speech arts. It is the course I recommend for those who want to develop their skills of persuasion and teaching. But it may not be the best discipline for those students interested in problem solving and decision making. The difference is that the former deals with *professing* the best solution, while the latter addresses the process of *seeking* it. My course in small-group discussion relies upon a student's ability to listen to the thoughts expressed by others, to weigh their value, and incorporate the best ideas into solutions that work for the good of all. The goal is to reach consensus rather than to persuade others to accept the conclusion of the leader.

The speech curriculum in many colleges includes interpersonal communication. This division of the discipline examines the motives, perceptions, and expectations of senders and receivers. It recognizes that all face-to-face communication is *transactional*, meaning that messages flow in both directions. It is an effort to help people understand each other at the emotional as well as the cognitive level, to set aside inclinations to control or to be judgmental, and to form honest and accepting relationships. It is not part of the rhetorical tradition but leans heavily upon the behavioral sciences.

While public speaking is the primary focus of this text, the well-rounded student should have some exposure to the broader theories of communication. When standing on a podium, a speaker needs to be aware and sensitive to the way the audience is receiving the message. There are very real hazards ahead for those who do not.

In the past decade the common ground between China and the United States has been technology. The city where I teach in California is in the heart of Silicon Valley. It is similar in many ways to the "special economic zones" that were responsible for the growth of cities like Shenzhen. The development of the

Internet and cell phone technology has made tremendous strides in bridging the gap between our two cultures. Young people in particular have mastered the terminology of the digital world. Now that we have the *means* to communicate, what are we going to say to one another? The progress made by scientific minds in providing instruments of communication must now be matched by the intelligent thought and articulation of those who study the rhetoric of the social sciences and humanities.

## Supplements

The supplements for the eighth edition will include an Instructor's Manual for instructors, and Chapter Quizzes, Progress Management Checklists, and Internet Exercises for students. All of these resources were prepared by Delois V. Medhin of Milwaukee Area Technical College and can be found on the Online Learning Center at www.mhhe.com/hasling8e.

# The Audience
# The Message
# The Speaker

# *Theory of Oral Communication*

*O*ur Constitution guarantees our rights to freedom of speech, and we must never take that privilege for granted. We could lose our right to free speech in a very real sense by not exercising it. If we become content to have others speak for us and to allow the positions and interests of the few to dominate public policy and law, we might just as well not have it at all. An important dimension of the First Amendment is that we also have the right to *listen,* if we will, and to evaluate what we hear. What *free speech* means is that we will be exposed to all kinds of viewpoints. We will hear false information as well as truth, and we must learn to separate one from the other. That is not always easy and requires that we keep informed on significant issues. Truth is never self-evident; if it were, there would be no need for us to study the art of persuasion. Our Constitution can guarantee that we have the right to speak our minds, but it cannot guarantee that anyone will listen. Although what we say may be true, there is no assurance that it will be accepted and believed. If we want to have influence over other people, our government officials, and those who control our institutions, we must be able to make our perception of the truth sound plausible. The capability for this comes more easily to some than to others, but the opportunity is available to all, regardless of sex, religion, nationality, or economic status. It is denied only to those who choose to remain silent.

We have been speaking and listening our whole lives. How effectively we have been doing these things may depend to some extent on our natural ability and inclinations, but it has a lot to do with the speaking and listening skills that we acquire.

1

Traditionally the speaker's art is known as *rhetoric,* and it was Aristotle who provided us with the best definition. He said that the study of rhetoric is to observe in any given case the *available means of persuasion.*[1] In other words, the art has subject matter of its own. Learning *how* to explain and persuade is a function separate from the body of knowledge that is central to any particular discipline. It is for this reason that public speaking is taught as an individual subject.

"Available means of persuasion" refers primarily to the power of words to create mental images, to provide explanations and argumentation, to introduce concepts, to organize ideas, and to offer supporting evidence. In the context of public speaking, "available means of persuasion" also refers to vocal inflection, gesticulation, and every other aspect of oral delivery.

Aristotle's definition suggests that rhetoric is an applied art. It can add a practical dimension to your academic pursuits because it will help you use the information you learn in other subject areas. In applying the art of rhetoric, you have an opportunity to pull together the principles inherent in the arts, human-ities, and sciences so that you can see their interrelationships and how the ideas are interconnected. In the process of learning how to express what you know and how to influence other people, you will find that your education will begin to take on new significance.

## THE FUNDAMENTALS OF COMMUNICATION

A writer, a book, and a reader provide a communication model. It is a basic and fairly simple model, but it is one that is useful to examine. It consists of a sender, a message, and a receiver—the three elements that are essential for human communication to take place. As the writer of the message, I am the sender. Your task as the receiver is to interpret what I write. The model is a simple one because I am not getting any immediate response from you. If we were in the same room, there would be another dimension, because messages would be flowing in both directions. Even if you were not saying anything, I would be getting feedback that would tell me something about the way you were reacting.

When people relate to one another face-to-face, we say that the communi-cation is *transactional:* That means there are messages flowing in both directions simultaneously; you and the other person are both senders and receivers.[2] The term *transactional* does not mean that each person is *talking* at the same time; messages do not have to be *verbal.* A great deal of the meaning that we convey

---

[1]Aristotle, *On Rhetoric,* trans. George A. Kennedy (New York: Oxford University Press, 1991) pp. 36–37.
[2]Sylvia Moss and Stewart L. Tubbs, *Human Communication,* 6th ed. (New York: McGraw-Hill 1991), pp. 6–7.

to other people is in the form of *nonverbal* messages. When you smile and nod your head you are saying, "I hear you, and I like what you say," just as clearly as you would be if you were to speak the words. Often, we forget that when we are in the presence of another person we are sending messages, whether we intend to or not; in fact, it is impossible for us *not* to communicate. When we bring this simple observation to the level of awareness, we have a better chance of knowing how to be intentional in what we do and say.

## Making Ourselves Understood

If I speak or write to you without being able to hear you or see you, I have no way of knowing whether or not my message is being received. You might be reading the words on this page right now and understanding everything I mean; on the other hand, you could be staring at the words, with your thoughts a million miles away. In communication theory, anything that is causing you to be distracted from the message is called *noise*.

### Noise

The interference we call *noise* can be of a physical nature or a psychological nature. If it's physical, in a private situation it might be something such as a smoky room that is causing you discomfort or a television program that you can see out of the corner of your eye while you are trying to read. In a public speaking situation it might be distractions caused by members of the audience who are rattling chairs, or a faulty sound system that squeals when the volume is turned up. Noise can also be of a psychological nature. For example, you may resent the fact that you have been assigned to read this chapter when there are other things you would much rather be doing, or there may be references in the book that remind you of experiences that are difficult for you to put out of your mind. Psychological noise could be any emotional feeling that competes with the cognitive reception of the message. Both the sender and the receiver could be aware of physical noise, but only the receiver would be affected by psychological noise.

### Feedback

If I were in the same room with you and were trying to explain what I mean, we would have *two-way communication*. I would be able to observe physical noise distractions that might be interfering with your reception of the message, and I would be able to receive your verbal and nonverbal feedback. You might just nod your head as I talk, or you could respond verbally and say, "I know what you mean." If you had any difficulty in comprehending, you could say, "I don't understand that." Feedback is a very important part of the communication process because it enables the sender to correct for error or to clarify the message.

## Meaning

When I write I use words to convey my meaning, and my assumption is that you as the reader will have an understanding of those words. But even if we both speak the same language I can never be sure that we attach the same meaning to the words. For example, I may talk about the *folklore* of the Hollywood movie industry, meaning the popular stories that describe its development and the people who played the principal roles. The dictionary says that *folklore* is "a body of widely accepted but *specious* notions about a place, a group, or an institution." We look up the word *specious,* and we find that the definition is "seemingly fair, attractive, sound, or true, but actually not so." My intention is to say that we can learn to understand an institution by studying its folklore; however, you might perceive the message to be that folklore obscures the reality of what actually happened, because the stories are untrue. Observations of this kind remind us that words can mean different things to different people. In other words, one meaning is contained in the mind of the person who initiates the message, but a different meaning may reside in the mind of the receiver. Lewis Carroll relates how the self-centered Humpty-Dumpty says, "When I use a word, it means just what I choose it to mean—neither more nor less." What we (and the foolish egg) need to understand is that our attempts to communicate would be pointless if we did not consider the way the message is received.

## Communication Models

The two-person model is fairly easy to understand, but models become complex when we add more people and vary the structure and purpose of the communication. When we do that, we are changing the *dynamics* of the event. That term could refer to the way people relate to one another, their communication skills, their attitude toward the topic, the intensity of their emotions, the physical environment, or anything else that influences what they say and do. Again, we can look at models to help us in our analysis.

### Conversation Model

In an ordinary conversation, we say that the communication is *unstructured*—there are no formalized requirements placed upon any of the individuals to conform to any particular style, topic, or sequence of expressed thought. The only rules or guidelines imposed on people in a conversational model are those that social convention and common courtesy require, and the interaction is often more important than the content of the message (Figure P–1). The dynamics become more complex, of course, as we introduce more people to the circle. In the case of a larger group, there may be one person to whom you relate differently, and that variation may affect the way the others relate to you. From your own experience in groups, you are probably aware that what others do and

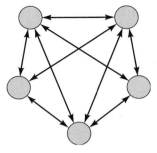

**FIGURE P-1.**   In unstructured communication personal contact may be more important than message retention.

what they say have a strong influence on your own behavior. If you perceive that people are interested and are listening to your ideas, you may elaborate more fully; if you believe they are bored or are disapproving, you might hold back some ideas or even say nothing at all. Probably the best conversations you have are those in which the participants regard each other as equals. When one person attempts to introduce structure to the conversation by leading or directing the flow of communication, the dynamics change and the model begins to take a different shape.

### Group Discussion Model

The model changes when people get together for a specific task. A group with an identified purpose might be called a *committee* or a *task force,* and it probably would have an *agenda* so that members stick to the topic that they are supposed to be addressing. An agenda puts limitations on the subject matter and gives focus and direction to the discussion (Figure P–2). At such gatherings there is usually a specified time for the meeting to start and end, goals that the group is expected to accomplish, and probably a summary statement to review the decisions that have been made. Participants might make some preparation for a discussion of this kind, but they speak in an *impromptu* fashion—that is, they do not plan their remarks in advance, and they do not expect to speak in any particular order.

### Public Speaking Model

We have a much different kind of model when one person has the attention of many people for an extended period of time. This is the one we call the *public speaking* model. A number of characteristics distinguish this model from the others we have mentioned.

First is *structure.* This means the speaker has some sort of organizational framework in mind and has given thought to how the message will start, how

**FIGURE P–2.**    An agenda gives focus to a group discussion.

the ideas will be developed, and what conclusion will be drawn at the end. The speaker will make an effort to focus on a central theme and not drift off onto tangents. Also, there is probably an expectation that audience members will hear the message all the way through to the end before asking questions or making their own remarks. These are characteristics that would not be appropriate in a social conversation or group discussion.

Second is *purpose*. Speakers need to maintain consistency in the main idea they express. If they are advocating a particular point of view, they should defend that position even if they get objections from members of the audience. It is inappropriate for a speaker to make structural modifications of a thesis while standing on the podium. Qualifications that need to be made in a speaker's main purpose should be thought of before the speech begins, rather than after.

Third is *posture*. In public speaking we *stand* when we speak. Assuming this posture may be the very thing you dislike most when you have to make a presentation, but there is a very good reason for doing so: When you address an audience you want to be the focus of attention. Standing is a nonverbal message that means "I have the floor and I want you to listen until I am finished." Sitting down is an invitation for others to speak. There is an expectation on the part of the audience that the person who is standing wants to be heard and has something to say that is worthy of attention (Figure P–3).

Fourth is *motivation*. This is one of the most important differences between public speaking and conversation. You converse with your friends because you enjoy the experience. You are not doing it for *their* benefit; you are doing it for your own. When you make a presentation you may still be enjoying the experience (certainly you want your audience to believe that you are), but it's the *audience's* interest that you serve more than your own. You don't stand up in front of a group of people because you have a burning desire to give a speech. You do it because you believe you have information that will be useful to those who hear it. That may be an important notion for you to keep in mind on those occasions when you really don't want to subject yourself to the anxiety of addressing an audience.

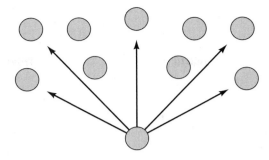

**FIGURE P–3.**   In the public speaking model, receivers allow the sender to "have the floor."

The elements of communication are interconnected. We'll be looking at each one individually, but we must keep in mind that they are all essential parts of a complete package. The principles of Aristotle provide the basis for just about everything that has been written on the subject of rhetoric since his time, and a great many textbooks, including this one, borrow heavily from his fundamental model of the audience, the message, and the speaker.

# The Audience

# *Communication Begins with an Audience*

AFTER READING THIS CHAPTER, YOU SHOULD BE ABLE TO DO THE FOLLOWING:

- Describe the three basic elements of speech communication.

- Understand the common courtesies of a speaker and the audience.

- Appreciate the value of learning public speaking.

- Start the process of preparing a speech by recognizing the criteria for evaluation.

**W**hat you are going to do in this course is learn how to talk to people. That doesn't sound hard, does it? You've been doing it most of your life. But now you're going to learn to speak to more than three or four people at a time in a way that will help them understand what you mean, benefit from the information you give, and perhaps even be influenced by what you say. We call that process *public speaking*. It has an intimidating ring to it, but it needn't have. Its nasty reputation has been exaggerated. We're going to tame the monster by breaking it down into its component parts and coming to friendly terms with each one.

## THE COMMUNICATION PROCESS

The first thing to remember is that public speaking is *not* an adversarial relationship between the speaker and the audience. It is a *cooperative* arrangement that leads to a mutually gratifying experience for all parties. People in the audience know that what you are doing is not easy. Many of them have probably faced an audience just as you are doing. They *want* you to succeed. They *want* to hear your message and understand what you say. They *want* you to feel good about what you are doing. Most important, they *want* to have the benefit of learning what you have to tell them. If that were not true, they wouldn't have come to hear you speak. When you can accept and internalize that notion, you will have taken a big step toward overcoming your fear of public speaking.

### The Audience

Understand that no communication process begins until you have an audience. Someone has to receive the message that you send. You probably would not bother to talk in an empty room unless you were practicing your delivery. Only when someone else is present do we have the *potential* for communication, and even then we know that it might not occur unless the person is listening and has some capacity for understanding. Sometimes speakers believe that what they say will be replicated in the listener's mind, but that is not always the case. You need to be realistic about your ability to communicate and understand that the *message is the message received*. What you intend your message to be is the way it is for you, but the message *received* is the way it is for the listener.

### The Message

When people take courses in public speaking, they often feel that the most difficult part will be (1) conquering their fears of facing an audience and (2) learning the skills of delivery. While those two elements may initially be students' significant concerns, the most important consideration in speechmaking is the quality of the message. As students begin to understand what public address is all about, they learn that the most fundamental and most difficult part is gathering the information and putting it together in a well-organized fashion.

## Content

In classical rhetoric the process of developing the content of speech is called the *inventio*. In contemporary language you could say it's *preparing the substance*. This is the time when you examine your resources to discover what information you want to include in the message. What you say should be something that you, yourself, have found to be interesting and significant, but, most important, it must be a message that will be useful in some way to the audience. The best source of material for a speech is the information that is already in your head, but that should be substantiated with ideas and evidence that you gather from your research. Take as much time as you need in the planning stage. Don't be motivated by what is the easiest thing to say; instead, think in terms of what will be of the greatest value to the audience.

## Structure

As noted earlier, public speaking is a *structured* form of communication—the progression of thought forms a pattern and the ideas move in a logical sequence from the beginning to the end. These characteristics may not be prevalent in other forms of oral communication. In ordinary conversation, for example, we may ramble, go off on tangents, and perhaps never reach any kind of conclusion because we don't prepare for conversations as we prepare for speeches. Consequently, conversations may contain a limited amount of factual information, cumbersome expression of ideas, and many digressions to trivialities. The advantage in prepared and structured communication is that it is a faster and more comprehensible means of transmitting the message to the listener. Conversation can be fun and is often informative, but it is very time-consuming. Class discussion can also be stimulating and enjoyable, but, in terms of efficiency, a professor can cover more material in a shorter period of time by delivering a well-prepared lecture.

## *The Speaker*

Seeking opportunities to speak in public may not be something that occupies a great deal of your time. However, even without looking for them, you will find that such occasions occur frequently, and they present you with a chance to give expression to beliefs or experiences you would like to share. Some occasions at which you could speak might be a graduation ceremony, a business meeting, a memorial service, or a town-hall gathering. The setting could be in a school, a church, a home, a conference room, or an auditorium. One excellent opportunity for developing proficiency in public speaking is to become a member of Toastmasters International. You probably will be able to find a local chapter by looking in your telephone directory.

But why would a person volunteer to give a speech in the first place? Sitting in the audience is much more comfortable than standing on a speaker's platform. What is it that causes people to accept the risk of criticism and rejection for the sake of expressing their ideas in a public forum? Do these people suffer less from speech fright than most people do? Not necessarily. They probably have the same anxieties as everyone else. Are they people who are smarter or better informed than others? Maybe, but maybe not. You might know just as much as they do. The difference is that they are *willing* to do it.

## Value to the Speaker

Willingness is an important factor in the process of developing public speaking skills. In order to make any progress at all, you must be able to set aside negative attitudes you might have and convince yourself that there is real value in the effort you will be called upon to expend. Your willingness to speak may develop as a result of your perception that something needs to be said; however, that might not be sufficient motivation for you if you perceive the task to be greater than the reward. What do you have to gain by exposing your ideas to the scrutiny of an audience?

1. You have a chance to clarify your thinking and gain a firmer grasp on what you believe by organizing your ideas in a way that makes them understandable to you and your audience and useful to others.

2. You may succeed in motivating other people to support a cause that is important to you.

3. You demonstrate leadership capabilities and show others that you are able and willing to take responsibility.

4. You build your self-confidence and raise your self-esteem by learning to defend the positions you take on controversial issues.

5. You enrich your life with new relationships by attracting people who share your interests and points of view.

There is, perhaps, one more personal value connected to the study of public speaking skills, and that is an appreciation for rational thought. The student who takes the art seriously becomes part of a tradition that goes back thousands of years. Aristotle said, "It is absurd to hold that a man ought to be ashamed of being unable to defend himself with his limbs, but not of being unable to defend himself with speech and reason, when the use of rational speech is more distinctive of a human being than the use of his limbs."[1]

---

[1]Aristotle, *On Rhetoric*, trans. George A. Kennedy (New York: Oxford University Press, 1991), pp. 36–37.

In a society that seems to value physical prowess over effective articulation, we may wonder how much impact Aristotle's assertion has had. It is unlikely that a debate tournament will ever draw as many spectators as a football game will. Yet, it is certainly true that in a civilized culture, we rely more heavily on our verbal abilities than on our physical strength to defend our lives, our property, and our principles.

## Speaker–Audience Relationship

While we study public speaking, we should also be developing our listening skills because we know that, as members of the audience, we can either enhance or jeopardize the success of the speech. Nothing productive is ever accomplished by heckling a speaker. I know there are some who will say that heckling has been refined to an art form at Hyde Park in London, and that encouraging it is regarded as an acceptable strategy of debate in the Oxford Union. It is also quite common in the British Parliament; nevertheless, it is a practice that impedes reasoned discourse. If you disagree with what a speaker is saying, wait for your turn before you advance your refutation. Heckling is a form of censorship, and all too frequently it silences the views of those who are less aggressive and suppresses ideas that may need to be heard.

The question period that comes after a presentation is a time when the speaker–audience relationship is clearly illustrated. When you are the one on the podium, you hope that there will be questions; that's the way you find out whether the audience has been interested and whether your words have been understood. As a member of the audience, you will want to take advantage of the opportunity to add your own thoughts and concerns to the dialogue. You may be required to stand when you ask your question, which means that you will have to employ the rhetorical skills of a speaker. Be sure to use enough volume so that the whole audience can hear you. As a general rule, you want to keep your question short; it is a discourtesy to begin making a speech of your own from the floor.

Your job as a speaker is to make your message clear even if you know that what you have to say is controversial and may draw criticism from the audience. If you use language that is intentionally obscure, and you jeopardize the relationship of trust that a speaker must have with the audience, you violate your ethical contract. Sometimes we use the term *hidden agenda* to refer to a covert motive that a speaker may have. For example, let's say an accountant of a business firm is speaking to a group of its investors. The company has had a series of financial setbacks and is on the verge of bankruptcy; the management does not want the investors to know that. Therefore, instead of making a clearly articulated presentation, the accountant deliberately speaks in abstract language, using technical jargon that no one in the audience understands. The hidden agenda in this case is to go through the motions of providing an explanation but to conceal the real information from the listeners. As another example, political figures sometimes find themselves in "hot water" when a story breaks that suggests their involvement in an indiscretion or scandal of some kind. At such times a spokesperson who is skillful at handling the press may be brought in to minimize the criticism and keep the story from doing too much damage to the politician's image or cause. This procedure is called *damage control* or *spin*. The terms refer to the practice of answering questions in such a way as to give as little information as possible and to justify the role that the politician played in the incident.

## GETTING STARTED

There is much to learn about the preparation and delivery of a good speech. As you proceed in reading this text you will get some insight into the basic theory, and as you begin to give speeches in class you will discover that experience is the best teacher. Here is a brief checklist of what you need to know to get started:

1. *Content.* Your first step is to pick a topic that meets the requirements of the assignment you are given. Choose one that interests you and contains examples that the audience will find significant and relevant. Start by thinking of topics about which you already have some knowledge or with which you are somewhat familiar.

2. *Organization.* The information must be arranged in some sort of logical sequence, so plan on making an outline. Give thought to your organizational structure, and stick to that pattern when you present the material. Make sure you have a statement of purpose, clearly phrased main contentions, specific information that is relevant to your main ideas, and a conclusion to reinforce what you have said.

3. *Language.* Don't write the speech out word for word; plan on delivering it extemporaneously from your outline. When you speak, choose language that effectively communicates your meaning. Pronounce words correctly, and use proper and appropriate grammar.

4. *Voice.* Use enough volume so that you can be heard by everyone in the room, and enunciate your words and syllables clearly. Employ vocal inflection to place emphasis on key words and phrases.

5. *Timing and Pacing.* Be sure to start and end the speech on time. Speak fast enough to keep your audience alert and to ensure that you have time to cover all your material, but not so rapidly that you run words together.

6. *Attitude.* Before you begin to give the speech, develop a positive attitude toward the subject matter and toward the audience. Convey a sense of interest and enthusiasm for what you are saying, and let the audience know that you think it's important for them to listen.

7. *Appearance.* Project an air of confidence to the audience; stand up straight and maintain eye contact with your listeners. Your posture, gestures, and facial expressions should reinforce the message. Be sure to dress appropriately for the occasion.

8. *Integrity.* Honesty and sincerity are the hallmarks of effective public speaking. Never attempt to deceive your listeners or exploit them in any way. Maintain a high ethical standard for your own sake, as well as for theirs.

These are the criteria that will probably be used for evaluation when you give your speeches in class. Your fellow students in the audience may make observations about what they saw and heard, and, of course, your instructor will give you a grade. But rather than relying entirely on the feedback you get from other people, learn to be your own critic. Keep these criteria in mind as you prepare your speech and as you deliver it, and afterward make your own evaluation of how well you did. Try to discover for yourself what worked and what didn't work, and never let a public speaking opportunity go by without learning something from the experience.

## EXERCISE

Much of the history of the world can be told in the words of great orators who spawned or guided significant social, political, or religious movements. The causes they advocated may not always have been the most beneficial to humanity or civilization; nevertheless, we have all been profoundly influenced by them. Look up one of the following names in a reliable reference book and give a short biographical talk on one of them:

| | | |
|---|---|---|
| Pericles | Wendell Willkie | Margaret Thatcher |
| Demosthenes | William Jennings Bryan | Nelson Mandela |
| Cicero | Jonathan Edwards | Benazir Bhutto |
| Mark Antony | Harry Emerson Fosdick | Indira Nehru Gandhi |
| Patrick Henry | Theodore Roosevelt | George C. Marshall |
| Daniel Webster | Huey Long | Barbara Jordan |
| Edmund Burke | Adolf Hitler | John F. Kennedy |
| Abraham Lincoln | Winston Churchill | Martin Luther King Jr. |
| Susan B. Anthony | Franklin D. Roosevelt | |
| Clarence Darrow | Harry S. Truman | |

- Start by telling the person's name, title, nationality, and period in history.
- Describe briefly the significant social conditions that prevailed in his or her time.
- Relate the point of view expressed in one or more of the person's speeches.
- Quote at least one line of what the person said.
- Conclude with the results that the person's oratorical efforts achieved.

## QUESTIONS FOR DISCUSSION AND REVIEW

1. Can a speaker's message ever be completely replicated in the listener's mind? What is meant by the phrase "The message is the message received?"
2. What is the advantage of structured communication over casual conversation? How do you react to people who start making speeches during casual conversation?

3. What personal values can students gain by developing their skills of public speaking? What do you think are the most important of those values?

4. How do you feel about heckling a speaker? Are there any occasions when you would do that?

5. What are the criteria for evaluating speeches and speakers? Which of those criteria do you think are the most important?

6. What do you think will be the most difficult part about giving your first speech?

# PROGRESS MANAGEMENT CHECKLIST

### *How can you tell if you are making progress?*

_____ 1. In a conversation you can make yourself heard and can hold the attention of five or more people.

_____ 2. You can believe that people in an audience want to hear what you have to say and want you to succeed in delivering your message.

_____ 3. You understand that the way the audience hears your message is the way it is for them, even though what they hear is not exactly what you mean.

_____ 4. You understand that strong content and good organization are the most important criteria for effective public speaking, although smooth delivery is also a significant factor.

_____ 5. You understand that effective public speaking begins with willingness, and there is more to the art than just overcoming anxiety.

_____ 6. You perceive the rewards of public speaking:
   • Clarifying what you know and believe.
   • Achieving a nod of agreement.
   • Being asked to take a leadership role.
   • Feeling good about yourself for having contributed to a conversation.
   • Making new friends.

_____ 7. You observe common courtesies as a speaker or as a member of the audience.

_____ 8. You understand the criteria for evaluating your own speeches.

 *Visit the book's Web site at www.mhhe.com/hasling8 for study tools such as practice quizzes, activities, and Web links.*

# Preparing to Meet the Audience

AFTER READING THIS CHAPTER, YOU SHOULD BE ABLE TO DO THE FOLLOWING:

- Know what to do when you receive an invitation to speak; understand the importance of logistics and demographics.

- Adapt your speech topic to the interests of the people in the audience; allow for differences in culture, attitudes, political perspectives, and religion.

- Recognize the gaps in your own listening behavior; understand the obstacles to listening that you will have to overcome when you are speaking to an audience.

- Apply public speaking techniques that are designed to ease the difficulties people have in receiving and retaining messages.

- Have respect and appreciation for the rights of the audience and the rights of the speaker.

*T*he more you know about the people to whom you are speaking, the better prepared you will be to adapt your presentation to their needs. When your audience is a group of your friends or members of an organization with which you are affiliated, the task of planning what you need to say is somewhat simplified. You would already have some understanding of how much they know about the topic and how much technical detail you could include. You would also have a certain amount of insight into their feelings and attitudes toward the subject matter that you plan to cover. If some part of your presentation is controversial, you would know when and where you might encounter opposition. But when you are speaking to a group of strangers, your task is more difficult. Suppose you receive an invitation from the program chairperson of a local service club to speak at its weekly luncheon meeting—what do you do?

## RECEIVING AN INVITATION TO SPEAK

Before you do anything in the way of preparing a speech, *listen* to what is being said by the people who have invited you. They have picked you as a speaker because they believe you can tell them something they need to know. The message you present must accommodate that need in some way. You'll have to make a quick assessment of your own background to see if you can give them what they want and if you have the time to prepare.

### Logistics

Make sure you are clear about the *logistics* of the speaking occasion—that means the date and the time, the size of the group, the location, and the physical arrangements. Certainly, you want to know how long you are expected to speak and if there is to be a question period afterward. You should also know if other speakers are on the program, and if so, what their topics will be. If you plan to use visual aids, find out what facilities are available. Don't expect that any organization will have all the equipment you need, particularly if it is something specialized like PowerPoint. You may want an easel for charts, a whiteboard, or perhaps a projector and screen. Double-check to make sure those details have been arranged—such equipment is not always provided unless you request it, even if you are a prominent person. President Clinton had to make a quick adjustment when he spoke to a joint session of Congress on health care. In a major address with full press coverage and the whole nation watching, he discovered to his consternation that the speech on the teleprompter was the wrong one. With the remarkable agility that comes from many years of experience, he was able to extemporize until the right speech was found and slipped into place. There are two messages here: Be familiar enough with your material so you will know when mistakes like that have been made, and be prepared to deal with them.

## Demographics

Find out from the person who invited you as much as you can about the *demographics* of the audience: What is the median age and the ratio of men to women? What is their economic status and educational level? Where are they on the political scale between conservative and liberal? What is their ethnic, cultural, and religious background? What else might affect their beliefs, attitudes, and perceptions? That information does not have to be scientifically gathered; it can be based simply on casual observations made by someone who is familiar with the group you will be addressing. Knowing just a few specific characteristics about your listeners will help you plan a speech that is relevant to their needs and interests. The people who serve as program directors for large organizations that invite speakers on a regular basis often distribute questionnaires to their audiences to collect demographic information that they can use for planning purposes. Be sure to ask if such a survey has been taken and if the results would be available to you.

Read your daily newspaper. There is much you can learn on a day-to-day basis about the population trends in the vicinity where you live. Is employment up or down? Is traffic becoming congested? Is there a shortage of housing or rental units? Are more children starting school, and are they coming from other countries of the world? Do the schools offer courses in English as a second language? Are local merchants stocking more ethnic foods than before? Knowing the answer to some of these questions will start you thinking about the kind of audience you might face if you are invited to speak.

## ADAPTING YOUR SPEECH TO THE AUDIENCE

Let's say, for example, that you have been invited to speak to the Junior Chamber of Commerce in your community. You can probably expect an audience of men and women in their late 20s and early 30s who are college-educated and career-oriented. Their affiliation with the Junior Chamber tells you that they probably have a concern for social issues, particularly those that affect the local economy. Knowing this about them makes it possible for you to select examples that are within their frame of reference.

### Particular Interests

Suppose you have been asked to speak because of your association with the local college or university. That gives you some idea of what interests the audience has, but the subject area is still pretty broad. You want to address the concerns of your audience, so you need still more information about them. It may be that you have been invited so that a particular group of high school students could hear you. In this case you might orient your remarks to those who are considering enrollment in the college. You could talk about the courses that are offered; scholarships and financial aid; and the social activities, athletics, and other aspects of college life that would be of interest to incoming students. What if you were addressing the business executives of the community—the ones who pay the taxes that support the college? Here your approach would be quite different. You might discuss the funding of programs, the financial health of the institution, the research that the college is doing that will benefit business and industry, and the cultural offerings. If your audience were made up of graduate students and prospective teachers, you might talk about academic freedom in the classroom, the quality of education, the opportunity for tenure, or the role that the faculty plays in the governance of the college. These are just some examples of entirely different speeches in the same subject area, each designed for the interest of a specific audience.

In terms of the subject matter itself, I believe you can adapt just about any topic to suit the interest and the understanding of the audience. The people in the Junior Chamber of Commerce, for example, would probably be just as concerned about Social Security as would be members of the American Association of Retired People (AARP). The difference might be that the younger people would want to know about new taxation laws and the AARP members would be more interested in benefits. But that's just a difference in your emphasis. One word of caution: Be very careful about making generalized assumptions based on conventional stereotypes. Older people are not always conservative, and young folks are not necessarily progressive; a great many women have an interest in science, and there are a lot of men who enjoy cooking. Avoid the mistake of allowing people in the audience to believe that you have classified them into restricted categories.

## Possible Opposition

Try to understand the particular orientation of the audience you plan to address and make an informed guess as to the members' willingness to agree with you. This advice does not imply that you must always try to appease your listeners; there will be times when you may have to say things that they don't want to hear. A good example of this occurred when Colin Powell faced a largely conservative Republican audience and said, "You all know that I believe in a woman's right to choose, and I strongly support affirmative action." There was a murmur of boos from the crowd, as Powell had known there would be, but he regained the listeners' goodwill by adding, ". . . we are a big enough party—and a big enough people—to disagree on individual issues and still work together for our common goal." Powell was not trying to change anyone's mind on the issues of abortion and civil rights; his objective was to make his own position clear and commend the party for its willingness to accept differences.

### Public Opinion Polls

Trying to analyze how listeners might react to your position on a complex issue is not an easy task. Even if you ask people what they believe, you can't always count on their answers being an accurate reflection of their thinking. For example, poll takers might pose the question, "Do you favor the continuation of affirmative action in hiring policies?" It's impossible to give an intelligent yes or no answer to a question like that. A considered response might be something like this: "I favor having companies make every effort they can to seek out qualified minorities to fill job vacancies, but I don't think preference should be given solely on the basis of race." So, does that mean "yes" or "no"? The point is that complex issues are never entirely true or false even though poll takers will try to make you think that they are. If a lot of yes or no answers are given to questions such as that one, public opinion might appear to be very different from what it really is.

Another factor that makes analysis difficult is that public opinion is never firmly fixed. This can be illustrated by the changes that occur every month in the responses people make to questions pertaining to the president's performance. Apparently, thousands of people change their minds periodically about how well the president is doing his job. Presidential advisers are kept guessing as to what particular event caused the shift in opinion.

**Descriptive Labels**

Analyzing expected audience reaction is uncertain even when you have access to demographic information, because over the years labels that were used to describe political inclinations have become blurred. You might be able to make broad generalizations about groups that are said to be "conservative" or "liberal," but these categories are unreliable when it comes to making predictions regarding the way individual audience members will respond. Contrary to what you might think, there are conservatives who favor the legalization of marijuana and liberals who vote to put restrictions on welfare payments. How can you predict audience reaction under those circumstances? The answer is that regardless of who your audience may be, the presentation you make must be reasonable and supportable. If it is, even those who disagree will be obliged to respect you. When you are speaking on a controversial issue, you never want to assume that you will have 100 percent approval. And conversely, it's not a good idea to expect complete disapproval, either; if you do, you may find yourself sounding defensive.

## Political Perspectives

A good way to get experience in audience analysis is to work as a volunteer for a political candidate. You will develop an understanding of the extent to which politicians will go in order to discover the best approaches for gaining the voters' attention and favor. Large political organizations at the national level try to hone their campaign techniques to a science by compiling massive amounts of data that reveal which particular issues are of concern to every demographic profile in each section of the country. Speeches given by politicians and their supporters can then be tailored to fit a specific audience.

In recent years it has become increasingly difficult to predict the voting patterns of the American people. For one thing, there are a great many independent voters who do not align themselves with any particular political party. And even those who do choose a party often do not feel a sense of loyalty to it. There was a time when you could be fairly certain which side of a controversial issue people who described themselves as Democrats or Republicans would take, and you could discover what they believed by reading the platforms drawn up by the party leaders. But election analysts have a much more difficult time now because candidates themselves do not always agree with the planks written into their own party's platform. Also, there are a great many people who have become *single-issue voters*—people who will vote for a candidate only if he or she has taken the "correct" stand on one particular issue. It may have to do with capital punishment, gun control, abortion, or taxes—but whatever it is, the single-issue voter will disregard all other matters or personal characteristics and focus only on that one item.

If you are giving a speech in support of a political candidate, your best strategy would be to describe the accomplishments and the qualifications of the person rather than attempt to interpret his or her policies. Surveys have indicated that people often decide to vote for someone on the basis of personal characteristics that they like, even though they disagree with the candidate on policy matters. Arnold Schwarzenegger became governor of California because of his fame as an actor even though voters knew little about the specifics of his political program. If it seems that candidates are putting a lot of emphasis on "image," it's because they know that the persona they project may have more to do with their getting elected than their policies.

## Religious Influences

According to the most recent census, 76 percent of the people in the United States regard themselves as Christian. The next largest bloc, 13 percent, indicated they had no religious affiliation. That does not mean that Christians have a lock on political thought, however. Minority religions have powerful voices and are able to gain support from the broader population.

Debates on topics such as abortion, homosexuality, prayer in public schools, teaching the biblical theory of creation, and the phrase "under God" in the Pledge of Allegiance to the flag are commonly related to religious beliefs, but in recent years even more issues have come into play. The very principle of separation of church and state is on the table. Under the Faith Based Initiatives Act, churches are receiving federal funds to carry out social programs. Ministers are more inclined than ever before to relate their sermons to social and political causes.

## Cultural Differences

Failure to communicate effectively from the podium may occur when the audience believes that the speaker does not understand or does not appreciate the values and the attitudes of those who are being addressed. Cultural differences may sometimes interfere with your ability to gain the respect of the audience—for example, if you are perceived as a person whose perspective on life is significantly different from those of the listeners. If you were reared in a middle-class neighborhood, it may be difficult for you to relate to the experience of people who were brought up in a ghetto. There is much to be gained in a college classroom when there is some measure of cultural diversity—particularly in a speech class where students have the opportunity to share their experiences and talk about their beliefs, attitudes, values, and feelings. One subject area that is frequently discussed in the classroom involves social welfare. Opposition to such programs as subsidized housing generally comes from people who have spent their entire lives in middle-class, suburban neighborhoods and have never known anyone who was living on welfare. For the most part, attitudes are formed by mental pictures of welfare recipients as being lazy, irresponsible, and probably dishonest. It can be beneficial to have someone in the class who is able to dispel the image by revealing that he or she was reared in a subsidized housing unit by a parent receiving welfare. The effect is better still when the person who has had that experience is intelligent and articulate and can testify to the critical support that social welfare programs can provide. The study of public speaking fosters the development of a broad perspective on life. People who are the most effective speakers are those who are able to recognize that the point of view they are expressing is not the only one that exists. Speakers who do not learn this are going to be confronted by questions they did not anticipate, coming out of attitudes they never considered.

## The Relevance Factor

One of the most important things you need to know about your audience is the *relevance factor*. How directly are your listeners affected by the subject matter of your speech? To obtain close attention, the relevance factor should be high. If what you are talking about is only remotely connected to their lives, they may listen politely but not really be engaged in what you are saying. You could probably develop a fairly good speech on the receding glaciers in the northern regions of Canada, but for people in the southwestern states, that's a long way away. Closer to home would be a discussion of the diminishing water table in their own county. It may be that the two are related. If that's the case, be sure to point it out.

Personal relevance is an even stronger factor, particularly when it comes to health and economic well-being. The high cost of medical care at the national level may be of some general concern, but the closing of a local hospital or an increase in insurance premiums is more likely to gain and hold attention.

Don't let yourself get blind-sided by addressing an abstract issue that may have important implications at a local level. For example, giving a speech on the practice of offering stock options to employees without calling the certificates an expense to the company may seem like an academic matter and not closely related to your own life. But to members of your audience who work in Silicon Valley it could be extremely relevant. If companies were not permitted to do that, they would have to pay higher salaries and might choose to export jobs to other countries where wages are lower.

Studies have shown that when the relevance factor is high, speakers need to be prepared with strong and specific information. If the relevance factor is low, they can probably get by on anecdotal support and the credibility of their own personal style.

## STEPPING INTO THE LISTENER'S SHOES

Some studies say that 70 percent of our waking hours are spent in some form of verbal communication, and almost half of that time is spent in listening. With all that practice, you might think that the receptive skills of an audience would be highly developed, but don't count on it. Even though listening is an extremely important skill, not much instruction on it is given in our public schools because it is very difficult to teach. We know how to teach people to speak—we can provide them with methods and guidelines, let them try it, observe their behavior, and critique their performance. Speaking is an observable art, but listening is not. We can't know for sure if people are listening just by watching their reactions. We can make some guesses based on their facial expressions and eye contact, but nonverbal feedback often proves to be inaccurate. In a classroom, of course, the instructor can give students a quiz to test their comprehension of a lecture, but you do not have that opportunity in an average speaking situation. The fact is that an audience may stop listening without your ever knowing it.

You can get some insight into the listening habits of the average audience by reflecting on your own listening behavior patterns. You may regard yourself as someone who is able to pay attention to a speaker most of the time, but chances are that you have the same obstacles to overcome as everyone else. Let's say, for example, that you've had plenty of sleep, the time is midmorning, the environment is comfortable and attractive, and the topic is one that interests you. Even under those ideal circumstances, are you going to be able to hear and retain everything?

- Do you normally start listening from the very beginning of the speech?
- Are you generally able to construct a clear picture of the speaker's main idea?
- Are you able to recognize all the points that are really important, and can you grasp new information as well as that which you have heard before?
- Can you connect the specific information to the generalizations?
- Do you make a practice of giving the speaker your undivided attention without allowing your thoughts to drift away to other matters that concern you?

- Are you able to sustain your attention when a speaker is tedious, hard to hear, or has mannerisms that annoy you?

- Do you never allow prejudices based on age, race, sex, or ethnic origin to get in the way of your hearing a speaker's message?

- Do you listen all the way through to the end to hear how the speaker's conclusion reinforces the main idea of the approach?

If you can answer "yes" to all those questions, you are truly remarkable. But if your listening habits fall short of being perfect, you can understand that the average person is going to have difficulties as well.

## SPEAKING SO THAT PEOPLE WILL LISTEN

Public speaking would be a lot easier if we could select for our audience only those people who are skilled and highly motivated listeners. But, alas, we can't do that. We have to take whatever audience we get and do what we can to gain and hold the audience members' attention. The challenge of the speaker is to ease the task of the listeners and overcome whatever obstacles impede the reception of the message. We have a better chance of doing that if we know what those obstacles are.

### Gain the Audience's Attention

In order to listen effectively, the audience needs to be *ready* to listen, and that readiness may not always coincide with the beginning of the speaker's message. Communication breakdowns often occur at the very start of a presentation if the listener is thinking about something else when the speaker is providing orientation to the message.

*Solution:* The speaker must say something that will gain the attention of the audience before launching into the main idea of the message. We call this the *attention statement.* It might consist of a humorous anecdote, a quotation, a rhetorical question, a reference to the occasion, or just a word of welcome, but it is as important to an audience as a starter is to an automobile.

### Have a Clear Purpose Statement

If the audience fails to understand your main idea, the thrust of your speech will be lost. People will become confused, frustrated, and perhaps even antagonistic. They should not have to guess at your purpose or position, and they should not have to sort through a maze of obscure language to find it.

*Solution:* As soon as you are sure you have gained the attention of the audience, make a clearly phrased statement that provides orientation to the topic and to your point of view. The statement should be sufficiently qualified so that it focuses on what you want to say and excludes any tangential aspects of the topic that you do not plan to cover.

## Emphasize Key Words and Important Points

It's easy for people to listen to what they already know; it's much more difficult for them to expand their fund of knowledge. They may find it difficult to perceive the value of a specific piece of information and may fail to retain the key words or important points.

*Solution:* Identify in your own mind what is important for the audience to remember; then think of ways to emphasize those items. For example, if you are going to use a key word that you think listeners might be hearing for the first time, you have to say it more than once. *Repetition* is the most effective means you have for facilitating audience retention. You could also *write the word* on a whiteboard or flip chart; you could use *vocal emphasis*—modulating your pitch or volume. A very easy device to use is a *pointer phrase* such as "It's important to remember that . . . ." Such a phrase calls attention to the fact that what follows is a significant part of your message.

## Provide Connecting Phrases

It's not just the retention of specific information that is difficult, but also the ability to see connections. The audience needs to understand how the specifics relate to the main idea and how they support the thesis. Here again, the speaker must not rely upon listeners being able to tie everything together by themselves.

*Solution:* Help the audience see the significance of the information by using *connecting phrases* to link the data to the generalizations. The listening process is greatly enhanced when the speaker uses such expressions as "What we can see from this fact is that . . ."

## Build Attention Features into the Speech

You may believe that what you want to tell your listeners is the most important thing they need to know; however, there are going to be other matters on their minds. One listener is concerned about the unfavorable evaluation he has just received from his supervisor; another has remembered that he is double-parked; and a third person has just found out that she is pregnant. All these things are on the minds of the people who you believe should primarily be interested in your speech on, say, the possible extinction of the spotted owl.

*Solution:* Build into your presentation features of interest that are designed to capture and hold the attention of the audience. These *interest* or *attention features* need to be woven into the speech so that they contribute to the content rather than interrupt the flow. *Humor* is one of the best features to use—not jokes, necessarily, but humorous phrases and references. When you are researching your topic, look for *unusual examples* that will grab the listeners' attention and try, if you can, to *tailor the example* to an interest of the audience.

Visual aids such as slides, transparencies, or computer graphics can also be interest features; more will be said about them in a later chapter.

## Ease the Strain of Listening

What we know about listening is that it is not easy, and people who are not highly motivated to pay attention may tune out if they are given an excuse to do so. Certainly it is true that they should not give up on you even if your volume is a bit low or your voice is a monotone, but the fact is that they often do. If listening to you becomes too difficult, or if they perceive something about you that they don't like, they may conclude that it's not worth the effort, regardless of how important the message may be.

*Solution:* Don't give the audience a reason to stop listening. Speak loud enough and clearly enough so that you can be heard, and modulate your voice so that you are not talking in a monotone. Dress appropriately for the occasion. Learn what behaviors are distracting to an audience and make an effort to avoid them. Don't try to put on airs by bragging and showing off your knowledge, and don't "talk down" to people by speaking as though they were inferior to you.

## Penetrate Stereotyped Notions

People in the audience should not reject the message because of stereotypes they have formed about the race, nationality, age, or sex of the speaker, but sometimes they do. You can't always count on listeners being tolerant and free of prejudices. You certainly have a right to object if you experience intolerance or prejudice, but complaining does not help the audience get the message. What can you do if you perceive that your listeners are rejecting you because of something over which you have no control?

*Solution:* Don't react in anger. You have nothing to gain by expressing hostility to an audience; in fact, doing that may reinforce audience members' prejudices. Try, if you can, to penetrate the stereotype by projecting yourself as a person who is different from their preconceived notions. If you speak intelligently and convey a sense of reason and responsibility, you may succeed in overcoming their biases and in gaining their respect in the long run.

Are we making progress in this area? Let's hope so. There was a time when black people could not even vote, let alone run for office; in many states women were not permitted to sit on a jury; long-haired men were not moved into corporate executive positions; and homosexuals were forced to resign from public service jobs. These conditions began to change when articulate people who belonged to such groups were able to break through the barriers of prejudice and convince those in positions of power that race, gender, hairstyle, and sexual orientation had nothing to do with a person's character or ability.

# The Audience's Bill of Rights

We, the people of the audience, in order to form a more perfect speaking environment, establish clarity, ensure attention and interest, provide common understanding, promote communication, and secure the blessings of reason and logic for ourselves and our fellow listeners, do ordain and establish this Bill of Rights for the Public Forums of the United States.

## ARTICLE I

No speaker shall come to the podium unprepared. The speaker shall have given thought to the issue and shall be equipped with notes and visual aids as required.

## ARTICLE II

The information contained in the speech shall be significant and useful. No excessive trivialities shall prevail on the podium.

## ARTICLE III

The speaker shall tell the truth and nothing but the truth, and shall not intentionally deceive the audience by omitting necessary information.

## ARTICLE IV

The speaker shall be punctual and not unnecessarily delay the audience. The speech shall begin and end on time.

## ARTICLE V

The speaker shall articulate clearly and speak in a voice loud enough for all to hear. Attention shall be given even to those in the back of the room.

## ARTICLE VI

The speaker shall be courteous to the audience at all times during the main address and during the question period.

## THE SPEAKER'S RIGHTS

In accordance with this Bill, the speaker's rights shall not be abridged by the audience. Members of the audience shall not heckle or create distractions that interfere with the speaker's thoughts. The audience shall listen attentively even though they might disagree with the speaker's viewpoint. They shall participate during the question period with directness and brevity. They shall not make speeches of their own from the floor.

## *Observe the Time Limit*

Any person in show business will tell you that timing is one of the most essential ingredients of a successful performance; the same is true of public speaking. If your speech runs long, the audience members may stop listening before you reach your conclusion. Even though they may politely remain in their seats, nothing is getting through to them after they have shut off their auditory receptors. Studies tell us that the attention of an audience peaks in the first 20 minutes of a presentation and begins to taper off after that. Does that mean that speeches should never be longer than 20 minutes? No. But you may have to work harder for attention if you are demanding a lot of the audience's time. Regardless of how vital your information may be, there is no point in talking if no one is listening.

*Solution:* Never go beyond the time that has been scheduled for you. Keep the speech as tight as you can; if you have a lot to say, you may have to talk at a fairly brisk rate. Don't go into so much detail that members of the audience miss the main point; they will listen better if your material is concentrated. The more time you consume, the greater your risk of losing their attention.

## RESPECT FOR THE AUDIENCE

Keep in mind that your function as a speaker is to meet the needs of the audience members. You are on the platform for their benefit, not for your own. You may be getting certain rewards from the experience—it may be gratifying and fulfilling—but basically your purpose is to provide information that your audience can use. If your listeners value your assertions, you can take satisfaction for having achieved your objective; however, if they don't, you must remember that they have the right to disagree. There is no way you can force your message upon them. You have an opportunity to be heard, but there is no guarantee that your message will succeed in persuading them. People will listen as long as they believe it is in their interest to do so. If you try to demand attention, you will probably meet with resistance. Recognize the fact that communication is a shared experience and can be accomplished only when the rights of both the speaker and the listener are acknowledged and respected.

## EXERCISE

Survey the class members and gather demographic information that will provide a statistical profile of the audience you will be addressing. Find out the average age, ratio of men to women, the nationalities represented, number of married people, and the average amount of time students spend working for pay. In your survey ask how many students voted in the last election and in what political party they are registered. You might also want to inquire about religious affiliations by having them check one of the predominant categories: Catholic, Protestant, Jewish, Muslim, Hindu, Buddhist, other, or none. After this information has been compiled, conduct a class discussion and speculate about the generalizations a speaker could make about the possible reactions the class might have to various topics and points of view.

## Questions for Discussion and Review

1. What do we mean by the *demographics* of an audience?
2. What do we mean by the *logistics* of the speaking occasion?
3. How might age differences between the speaker and the audience affect the way a speaker's message is received?
4. What is meant by the *relevance factor?* What does the speaker have to do if the relevance factor is high? Explain.
5. What is meant by a *single-issue* voter? What effect do single-issue voters have on political candidates?
6. What are some of the bad habits that interfere with good listening?
7. What does a speaker need to do before launching into the main idea of the message?
8. What do we mean when we say the purpose statement should be *qualified?*
9. What are several ways to emphasize key words and important points?
10. What are some ways of holding the listener's attention?
11. What do we mean by *stereotypes?* How can they be overcome?
12. What might be the consequences of speaking beyond your time limit?

## Progress Management Checklist

### *How can you tell if you are making progress?*

_____ 1. You are willing to say "yes" when you receive an invitation to speak.

_____ 2. You begin to think about the demographics of your audience and what information would be the most useful to them.

_____ 3. You consider possible opposition you might receive when you are speaking on a controversial issue.

_____ 4. You act on the awareness that descriptive labels such as "liberal" and "conservative" don't always tell you what views an individual might hold.

_____ 5. Your mind becomes open to points of view you had not considered before.

_____ 6. You know how to make your subject matter relevant to the needs of your listeners.

_____ 7. You can step into the listeners' shoes and understand how your words are going to sound to them.

_____ 8. You can emphasize your message well enough to overcome obstacles to listening.

_____ 9. You recognize and respect the rights of the audience.

 *Visit the book's Web site at www.mhhe.com/hasling8 for study tools such as practice quizzes, activities, and Web links.*

# CHAPTER 3

# Finding Common Ground

AFTER READING THIS CHAPTER, YOU SHOULD BE ABLE TO DO THE
FOLLOWING:

- Frame your topic in a way that connects with the interests and values of
  your audience.

- Understand how finding common ground differs from compromising,
  yielding, or giving up something you really want.

- Separate specific *positions* from common *interests.*

- Talk to friends and family members about issues on which you strongly
  disagree.

- Discover stereotypes you might
  have of others and recognize
  those that others might have
  of you.

- Appreciate the advantages
  of living in a pluralistic
  society; understand
  how cultural diversity
  has enriched the
  lives of people in the
  United States.

*A*ristotle's teachings emphasize that the central task for the speaker is to find or make common ground with the audience. To be an effective speaker you need to convey to the audience a sense of understanding for their concerns. You have to let them know that you are aware of their needs and interests, that you are connected in some way to their cultural beliefs and attitudes, and that you can empathize with their feelings. That's a lot to ask of you as a speaker, but it will move you in the direction of becoming *audience oriented*. You will start thinking about the way the speech is going to sound to the listeners.

When it comes to giving a speech to your classmates, you can probably think of several common denominators such as getting an education and earning a degree, planning a career, considering a family, applying new technology, taking a trip, participating in sports, listening to music, becoming involved in social causes, meeting new people, and learning about the customs of other cultures. It's likely that everyone you know wants health, happiness, economic security, and justice for themselves and others, so use those platforms as a starting point.

## CONNECTING WITH THE AUDIENCE

When selecting the subject matter for your speech, choose a topic that will address the interests of your audience and make them want to listen. In order for them to be receptive, they must be able to *connect* what you are saying to something that is relevant to their lives and congruent with their values. It has to hold their attention and contribute to their thinking. In some cases you may be able to add to their knowledge and even alter their point of view. That becomes challenging as you progress into more serious and controversial areas of discussion.

You can disconnect yourself from your audience very quickly if you begin with opening remarks that are antagonistic and outside their zone of tolerance. This can happen even when you are giving a speech to inform if the topic pertains to something that has multiple dimensions. For example, speaking on a subject like the pleasure and recreational value of driving a Hummer in a wilderness area may seem safe enough for a select group of off-road enthusiasts, but it might not be well received by an audience concerned about environmental protection. It could be that the audience is divided in their thinking. If you know that, or think that to be the case, always phrase your thesis in such a way as to reach out and connect with the ones who might find the activity offensive.

Sometimes issues are so divisive that there is little chance of finding common ground at all. Take, for example, a highly charged controversy such as the impeachment of a president. Advocates have to consider whether or not the end result would compensate for the stress of the debate. In such cases the leader of a party might say that the issue is "off the table." There is no point in even talking about it when the dialogue itself could be more damaging than the prevailing conditions. You may be able to relate to this: It's not uncommon for family members to come to a silent agreement that they are just not going to discuss matters that they know will cause hard feelings and perhaps even alienation.

As a speaker you need to be aware that the possibility for finding common ground can be jeopardized if a sensitive issue is raised unnecessarily with the wrong words at the wrong time with the wrong audience. On those occasions when a controversial point cannot be avoided and needs to be introduced, there are ways of *framing* what you say so that it has a better chance of being received without hostility.

## Framing an Issue

Framing refers to choosing words and phrases that convey the point of view of your thought. The way an audience reacts depends to a large extent on the way the message is framed. George Lakoff explains: "Political framing is really applied cognitive science. Frames facilitate our most basic interactions with the world—they structure our ideas and concepts, they shape the way we reason, and they even impact how we perceive and how we act."[1] He goes on to say that usually the framing of our words is done unconsciously. We may not try deliberately to manipulate the audience's reaction, but we do. We would prefer to think that we are just giving them facts and that they will arrive at the same conclusion we do, but it's not as simple as that. "The facts," says Lakoff, "must be framed in a way to make sense in order to be accepted as a basis for further reasoning."[2] Thus, an issue that is framed as a "death tax" will be viewed by the audience much differently than one that is framed as an "inheritance tax."

It may occur to you that framing can be used in a positive, or ethical, way as well as in a negative, or manipulative, way. That's true, and your personal biases may blind you to which one you are choosing. Ethical speakers will select language that is the most neutral and allow the evidence and argumentation to determine which side the audience favors. It is particularly important for speakers to avoid unnecessarily antagonizing an audience by using a frame that reveals an obvious bias and cuts the common ground out from under them. For example, when trying to find common ground on establishing a national health care program, you would not label it "socialized medicine" if you have a sincere desire to reach a meeting of the minds.

## Avoiding Divisiveness

One of the most divisive domestic issues today is that of abortion. The frame commonly used by those who oppose the legalization of abortion is *pro-life.*

---

[1]George Lakoff and The Rockridge Institute, *Thinking Points* (New York: Farrar, Straus, and Giroux, 2006), p. 25.
[2]Ibid, p. 40.

That has a nice ring to it. Who could not be in favor of choosing life over death? On the other side are those who have selected as their frame *pro-choice.* That also sounds good. Who could be opposed to allowing a woman the right to choose when or if she wants to become a mother? The trouble is that the language is polarizing because we understand the implications of those frames. The challenge to the speaker is to find a way to talk about hot topics that will gain the respect and hold the attention of both sides. Senator Hillary Clinton attempted to do that when she said to an audience, "We should all be able to agree that we want every child born in this country and around the world to be wanted, cherished, and loved. The best way to get there is do more to educate the public about reproductive health, about how to prevent unsafe and unwanted pregnancies."[3] Taken by itself there is no reason for the statement to be offensive to anyone. Nothing is said about abortion or the right to choose. Disagreement may occur over the details and the plan to achieve the goal, but at least common ground is established as a base.

Sometimes the best a speaker can do is to *seek* common ground until it is found. In his speech at Arlington, Virginia, Senator John McCain knew he did not have the complete support of his Republican colleagues in his presidential campaign. He said, "On the issue of illegal immigration, a position which provoked the outspoken opposition of many conservatives, I stood my ground aware that my position would imperil my campaign. I respect your opposition, for I know that the vast majority of critics to the bill based their opposition in a principled defense of the rule of law."[4] Acknowledging disagreement and expressing awareness of why the differences exist always works better than dogmatically pursuing a point of view that the audience is not willing to accept.

In the 2008 presidential campaign, Barack Obama was faced with the task of dealing with racial discrimination in a way that would be healing and not divisive. The speech he gave in March of that year titled "A More Perfect Union" was delivered at the National Constitution Center in Philadelphia. The purpose of his message was to answer criticism of his connection to a controversial minister who had made scathing charges against the United States. Referring to the fact that in 1787 our Constitution was signed by men calling for all citizens to be equal, yet permitting some to be slaves, Obama said we must "narrow the gap between the promise of our ideals and the reality of their time . . . Race is an issue our nation cannot afford to ignore . . . it is a part of our union that we have not yet made perfect."[5] He appealed to our common belief that people have the right to dissent even when it's unpopular to do so, and challenged Americans to lift higher our standards of equality.

[3]Hillary Rodham Clinton, speech to NYS Family Planning Providers, Jan. 24, 2005.
[4]John McCain, speech to CPAC, Arlington, Virginia, Feb. 7, 2008.
[5]Barack Obama, "A More Perfect Union," speech at the National Constitution Center, Philadelphia, Mar. 18, 2008.

## Basic Agreement

The term *common ground* can be applied to several areas of the communication arts. In group dynamics, for example, it would refer to the starting point for a negotiated settlement. In order for two opposing parties even to begin deliberations, there must be at least a minimal area of accord. In some cases it might be nothing more than a desire to avoid mutual destruction. Labor and management, for example, might find common ground in acknowledging that the company must be able to survive in a competitive market.

For a speaker, finding common ground with the audience is not an easy thing to do, nor is it always regarded as desirable. It can be construed as meaning that you must compromise on what you really want to say, or modify your principles in order to accommodate the opposition. You may believe you are the one standing on the common ground and become impatient with those who don't join you. It may also be that your desire to find common ground causes you to yield in areas that you later regret. In the same manner, you could be the one who coerces someone else into reluctantly accepting an agreement that they really don't want. If we are going to regard the finding of common ground as being a desirable objective, we must establish some criteria for what it means.

## The Qualified Meaning of Common Ground

Common ground does not mean that everyone has to agree on all aspects of the issue. During the civil rights movement, for example, there were many people who believed in school integration but opposed the busing of students to achieve it. In the same way, you can find common ground among most Americans who believe we should support our troops but not continue to occupy Iraq. People can stand on common ground without having to agree with everyone around them. The fact that they are there makes further communication possible.

"Finding common ground is not the same as settling for the lowest common denominator—it's generating a new 'highest common denominator.'"[6] The nonprofit organization Search for Common Ground works to improve the way the world deals with conflict. It currently has representatives in 17 different countries mediating, facilitating, training, and organizing. One of their key practices is to distinguish between positions and interests. *Positions* refer to the opinions that people hold regarding a particular plan for solving a problem. *Interests,* on the other hand, are broader and pertain to such things as security, health, and the well-being of the society. As a speaker you are not restricted to addressing only positions. Frame your thesis in a way that speaks to the interests of your audience. For example, you may want to take the position that automobile exhaust emissions should be controlled by federal standards. Before

[6]"Finding Common Ground," www.sfcg.org/sfcg/sfcg_intro.html#1 (retrieved Aug. 1, 2008).

you do that, however, there must first be agreement that the common interest of the whole society is to reduce the causes of global warming.

If common ground is not yielding, compromising, or coercing others to join you, how do you achieve it? You do it by finding a new way to frame the issue. That's when public speaking becomes a creative art. Speakers who rely on standard phrases to define their point of view confine their meaning to a limited dimension; they fail to reach out and include people who might be brought in if the circle were wider.

Radio and television moderators are generally very good at identifying the political position of a guest, but are often guilty of trying to attach a label to the person that will put him or her in a box. When guests try to qualify their positions, they find themselves limited by time constraints. The media have little time or patience for nuanced answers.

As a speaker, you have more control over the content of your speech than does a guest on an interview program. You get to ask the questions yourself, and you can control the agenda. Take advantage of that opportunity by not framing your issue in a way that alienates the audience. You don't have to choose between the simplistic labels of *pro-life* or *pro-choice*. You don't have to define your immigration program as *amnesty*. There is a way to find common ground among people of goodwill by using language that is inclusive and respectful.

### Positive Results

What evidence is there to show that trying to find common ground is realistic? Matt Miller in his book *The 2% Solution* selected health care as an issue to see if two opposing politicians, Democrat Jim McDermott of Seattle, Washington, and Republican Jim McCrery of Shreveport, Louisiana, could find common ground. They did after a two-hour session on neutral ground. A key factor was that they were separated from their constituents and the press, forces that are often responsible for encouraging polarization. They started with the premise that spending for health care should be as low as possible but consistent with a *just* society. That was enough for them to build on and form a policy. Miller explains why so many other attempts to find agreement on this issue have failed. "The debate is never framed this clearly. Instead it proceeds issue by issue . . . the battles are isolated from any broader framework defining the common good."[7]

### Common Ground Begins at Home

The search for common ground is not for everyone or for every occasion. If you are fighting for a cause and want to win; if you think you can rally enough support, overcome the odds, and convince other people that they should accept your position; if you want to demonstrate that you are a strong and courageous

---

[7]Matthew Miller, *The 2% Solution* (New York: *PublicAffairs*, 2003), p. 90.

leader; if you are prepared to accept responsibility for maintaining dominance over those you have defeated, then use your persuasive skills and go for it. But be sure you recognize the consequences.

Seeking common ground is for those occasions when you need to preserve relationships and the goodwill of the parties involved. It is also for those times when continued conflict is destructive to both sides. And contrary to that cautionary phrase regarding hazardous practices, DO try this at home. Practice on your friends and family using the following guidelines:

1. Start by talking about *interests* rather than specific *positions*. Don't move on to talking about controversial positions until you have first established that you have common interests. It might be something like, "Morality must include the good of society."

2. Frame the issue using words that both parties can accept. Don't use clichés and expressions that ridicule people or ideas embraced by the other party. Never bait the other person by using terminology that you know will be antagonistic.

3. Don't think of the dialogue as being a debate where you have to refute everything the other person says. Let go of the idea that you have to *win* the argument. If you end the discussion with different opinions, that's OK. Winning is being able to talk about the subject without hostility.

4. Modify your vocal inflection. Anger is more likely to be generated by the *sound* of your voice than by the words themselves.

5. Listen. Make sure that each of you hears and understands the other.

### The Ears of the Audience

How do you know when you are on common ground? You don't know unless you get feedback from the people you are addressing. If you are not on common ground, they will tell you. Examine your position to see if there are reasons why other people might not be there with you. *Listen to what you are saying with the ears of the audience.* You may never be able to find common ground for driving a Hummer in the wilderness, for example. You might have to settle for restricting your audience to those who share with you the pleasure of that sport. To acquire broader common ground you would have to claim that there is a need to make the wilderness area accessible to those who could not get there otherwise. Perhaps you could say that a Hummer is less damaging to the environment than other off-road vehicles when access is necessary. If you can't make that case, maybe you'd better give up on it as a speech topic.

### Who Gains and Who Loses?

A good way to examine the objectivity of your thesis is to give yourself a reality check. Who gains by the position you are taking and who is hurt by it? Are there legitimate reasons for opposing parties not to accept your position? What are the advantages or disadvantages to a general audience if your position is accepted? Is your position based on fundamental principles of decency and fairness?

### Chances of Achieving Common Ground

On highly polarizing issues such as abortion, immigration, and race relations, the chances of being able to achieve common ground are not good. The task would be much easier if we were a more homogeneous society. The United States, however, is a mosaic of races, nationalities, tribes, religions, and cultures. Just about every ethnic group in the world is represented within our borders. This did not happen by accident, but by design. At the base of our Statue of Liberty in New York Harbor are inscribed the words of Emma Lazarus:

> Give me your tired, your poor,
> Your huddled masses yearning to breathe free,
> The wretched refuse of your teeming shore.
> Send these, the homeless, tempest-tost to me,
> I lift my lamp beside the golden door.

## THE AUDIENCE IN A PLURALISTIC SOCIETY

Given the fact that we are a culturally diverse nation, what kind of assumptions can a speaker make about the probable reactions of a general audience, particularly when the topic of the speech deals with a social issue? We must be aware that not everyone perceives our cultural traditions or even our historical events in the same way. The attitude that members of the audience have toward episodes in American history such as the winning of the West, the defense of the Alamo, and the use of Chinese labor for building the railroads may vary, depending on their individual ethnic origins. As a speaker you need to recognize that the perspective you have will not necessarily be shared by all the members of your audience. With that in mind, it's good practice to act on the assumption that there is someone in the audience who represents an ethnic group that might be offended by a callous and insensitive remark. Rather than relying on "rules to be followed by public speakers," a better plan would be to work on changing any personal attitude or inclination you might have that denigrates others for their age, sex, race, or national origin. If those thoughts are running through your mind, they will be revealed through your vocabulary or tone of voice—perhaps without your knowing it. Consider an extreme case: Senate Majority Leader Trent Lott was forced out of office for making a casual remark he thought would be perceived as humorous when he said the country would be better off if more people had voted for Strom Thurmond. Senator Thurmond had run for president as a segregationist and many people interpreted Mr. Lott's remark to be an endorsement of that policy. Even if you think that Senator Lott's accusers overreacted, you have to remember that the message is the message *received*. If listeners perceive it as a racist remark, that's the way it is for them.

Equally important is avoiding careless remarks of a sexist nature. A Colorado football coach was addressing reporters during a nationwide press conference after charges were brought against his team that male players had raped a female goal kicker. Instead of expressing an apology for the incident, he made matters worse by claiming that she was a "lousy player." Somehow he managed to ignore the sensitivity training he might have received in a speech class.

## Diverse Perceptions of Communication Skills

You can probably tell from what I have said so far that this text is written by someone whose cultural orientation has been configured by the influences of the Western world. Literature on the subject of communication coming from Asia, Africa, the Middle East, or the Pacific Islands would have a much different perspective. In Micronesia, for example, a speaker might be taught to begin a speech by saying, "Please excuse me for speaking when I have nothing of significance to say. . . ." That is not a recommendation that I would ever make in any of my classes.

Public speaking in a pluralistic society can be daunting, not only because of differences in language and cultural references, but also because of variations in styles of communication. In Nigeria it is customary for a speaker to give you all the facts but not offer you anything in the way of an interpretation. You are expected to understand what the speaker means and draw the conclusion yourself.

Having conveyed this example to you, I'm not sure that I can give you a good solution to the dilemma that it poses. All of us—from all cultures—must understand that these differences exist. I'm sure some of you reading this text feel frustrated because what this course advocates conflicts with the manners and customs that your family has taught you. The challenge for those of you in that situation is to hold on to the patterns of behavior that are serving you well, but adapt your style to accommodate the methods of communicating that are prevalent in the society where you live. Remember that those of us in the Western world follow Aristotle, which leads us to a problem-solving methodology; if we had been influenced instead by Lao-tse we might have taken a Taoist approach to public speaking, accepting things as they are.

### Principal Attitudes

Principal attitudes that are common among students of rhetoric who have had a Western education may strike someone from an Eastern culture as being self-centered, disrespectful, patronizing, inconsistent, and rude. They are not intended to be so. They are the reflections of people who desire to become effective in the art of persuasion. Consider the following examples:

1. "I have individual differences and I do not want to be regarded as being the same as everyone else in the society. I don't want to feel that I have to accept the ideas of other people for the sake of conforming."
2. "My information is important, and even older people can learn something from what I have to say. I have no reason to sound humble or apologetic."

3. "I want you to understand my point, so I'm going to tell you directly what I mean. I will relate to you all the details, but at the end I will tell you what conclusion I have drawn."

4. "I may make mistakes, but I do not regard that as being shameful. I am willing to accept criticism and change my position if the evidence shows that I am wrong."

5. "If we have a task that needs immediate attention, let's begin to analyze it right away without devoting valuable time to irrelevant formalities."

If you would have a problem making any of the above assertions, talk it over with your instructor. Those values are basic to the instruction you will receive in the rest of this text.

Even if all five statements seem perfectly acceptable to you, consider the possibility that everyone in your audience may not agree.

### Assertiveness

Assertiveness is something we prize in this country, but it is not necessarily embraced by people of all nations. In my class assignments I ask students to gather evidence on a controversial subject and then stand up and declare their point of view. That's very hard for some of them who have been taught always to agree with their elders and people of authority. However, the nature of a speech class is to teach you to make your own thoughts and ideas known to others. Those who choose to pursue a college education need to recognize that their lives are going to be transformed in the process. They may learn things that conflict with what they have previously been taught, and once something is learned, it can't be unlearned. Education necessarily makes cultural values subject to scrutiny.

## *Learning about Yourself and Others*

If you are in a multicultural class, you are fortunate, because you have an opportunity to talk with people of different backgrounds and get a broader perspective on the world. You might even discover that some of the preconceived notions you had about people of other races or nationalities are inaccurate, and if you are serious about your education, you will make adjustments in your thinking accordingly. There is also much to be gained by developing an awareness of the way you are perceived by others.

All of us have a cultural background that influences the way we speak and act. But we tend to regard ourselves as individuals first, and we may not be aware of the way our racial, ethnic, or national characteristics are perceived by others. We are probably more cognizant of the stereotypes we have of people from different cultures than of the ones they might have of us. As an exercise in dealing with stereotypes, get together with three or four members of your class who represent ethnic groups that are different from yours, and conduct your own multicultural study. Before you pursue this activity, it is important that you establish healthy solidarity among the members of the group. Begin by having everyone make an affirming observation about each of the others. This may be difficult if you are not a person who is used to relating in this fashion, but it is a good communication exercise. If you can't think of anything positive to say, find out from each person what kind of affirming comment he or she would like to have you make. This kind of validation of one another is important, because we cannot be completely candid with others unless they know that we have goodwill toward them and that our motives are sincere. When you have done this, identify what each person in the group regards as his or her culture. After that, proceed by asking questions that pertain only to those cultures that are represented in your group. Examples of some questions follow:

- *What are the common stereotypes that are associated with the people in your culture?* Now, remember, these are generalizations that we know are not going to apply to every individual in the category. Nevertheless, there had to be some basis for them even though the origin may have been misguided. For example, if you are talking to someone who came from Ireland, you and the other people in the group might identify the following stereotypes: Good sense of humor, poetic, musical, somewhat superstitious, heavy drinkers, quick to lose their tempers. Are those fair generalizations to make, and would anyone of Irish descent be offended?

- *Which of those stereotypes are positive and which are negative?* The answer to that is going to vary depending upon whom you ask. An Irish alcoholic, or perhaps one who abstains entirely from hard liquor, might not like the suggestion that people in his or her nation tend to be heavy drinkers. On the other hand, one who enjoys the camaraderie of the pub might view that characteristic with fondness.

- *Which of the stereotypes do you, as an individual in that culture, regard as applying to you?* We can do a little "reverse engineering" here. Ask the student of Irish descent to describe some personal characteristics and see if they translate into the stereotypes of his or her culture. It may be that this particular student is not the least bit superstitious, but might be willing to agree that it's a fair generalization to make of the Irish.

- *Which of the stereotypes have become obsolete?* Perhaps historically the Irish could have been described as superstitious, but maybe that generalization is no longer valid. Are there other descriptive terms that more accurately pertain to the new generation of Irish people?

- *Are you as an individual influenced in any way by a stereotype that has been applied to your culture?* For example, if you are an Irish American person and are inclined to lose your temper a lot, do you justify it on the grounds that you are Irish? Even if that does not apply to you, do you believe that it might happen to others of Irish descent?

- *Which of the stereotypes do you believe are unfair and wrongfully applied?* Answers to this question can be useful to the public speaker. What you learn from one person of Irish extraction will not tell you everything you need to know, but it could help you dispel some misconceptions that might otherwise get you into trouble.

## Common Characteristics

The word *stereotype* has negative connotations, and we generally regard stereotypes as being building blocks of prejudiced thinking. We say, "Don't believe that; it's just a stereotype." On the other hand, there are such things as common characteristics, or cultural traits, that are often viewed in a positive way by those who share them. They can and do have a bonding effect on people to whom they are applied. Individuals who identify closely with their own particular ethnic group or culture feel a sense of community when they believe that they share with others a range of special qualities. They will cheer when a speaker who is one of them pays tribute to their common values, and they may scorn an outsider who doesn't comprehend what they stand for. An English politician, for example, is likely to have a difficult time rallying the support of an Irish audience.

# THE CULTURAL EFFECTS OF DIVERSITY

Because of our cultural diversity we have a rich opportunity in this country to broaden our perspectives and improve the quality of our lives. There would probably be no disagreement with this claim when it comes to art, science, literature, music, and food. It's hard to imagine our society without the contributions made by the talented artists, writers, scientists, musicians, and culinary masters from countries all over the world that have graced every neighborhood in the United States.

## Diversity in the Workplace

In public and private corporations all over the country, sensitivity training classes are being held to teach employees at all organizational levels how to relate to people in a pluralistic society. Large companies such as Colgate-Palmolive and many others of the Fortune 500 companies have full-time *cultural diversity managers* whose job it is to facilitate communication among and between members of a workforce who may have vastly different cultural backgrounds. There are practical reasons for doing this, of course, because a business will function more efficiently if the workers feel a community spirit. There will be fewer misunderstandings and work-related errors; there will not be as many interpersonal conflicts; there will be a higher degree of loyalty to the company and a greater sense of security among workers. But there is also a legalistic factor: A cultural diversity manager can help a business corporation stay within the scope of the laws that protect employees from racial or sexual discrimination. In effect, the people participating in these sensitivity courses are studying audience analysis in much the same way that a student of public speaking does. They are learning about the reaction they can expect to what they do and say.

## Social Implications of Diversity

Respecting differences does not mean that all customs from every culture are acceptable. For example, we are critical of parents who put their children to work in the fields and factories rather than sending them to school. We do not permit people to train animals to engage in mortal combat. We do not allow the practice of having multiple spouses, nor do we let husbands beat their wives with impunity. We scorn the caste system that creates untouchables and locks members of the society into social or economic levels. We reject the practice of forcing women to undergo female circumcision. I cite these examples to express my belief that we are selective in this country about the kinds of customs and practices we are and are not willing to accept. Speakers need to know that there are limits to the range of notions that an audience will applaud.

*Martin Luther King Jr. was able to find the common ground shared by all races and all nations.*

## The Speaker's Dilemma

How does knowing that differences exist help speakers to understand what they have to do when they step onto the podium with a topic that has racial overtones? For one thing, speakers may at least recognize the obstacles and perhaps adjust their expectations accordingly. Persuasion is possible when there is some common ground, and the task of the speaker is to find out what that is. But trying to reverse a fundamental belief by turning up the pressure is just not going to work, no matter how firmly you believe that you are right and others are wrong.

There is an expression that applies to people who do not understand the strength of the resistance against what they are doing. It is often applied to men who use sexist language and don't realize that their behavior is offensive to women. We say, "He just doesn't get it!" It's important to heed the meaning of that expression, because the more the behavior persists, the more the problem is aggravated. I remember how hard it was for many white students in the 70s to learn not to say to a black person during class discussion, "What is it that *you people* want, anyway?" The failure to recognize the offensiveness of that phrase did much to exacerbate the hostility between the races. If speakers have a sincere intent to make race or gender relationships better, they need to avoid saying things that will, by nature, make them worse.

Try to recognize how firmly entrenched a belief may be in the minds of the people you are addressing. For example, there is some leeway in an issue such as affirmative action because of its highly complex nature. Even those who support the policy may be willing to consider modifications in its implementation. On the other hand, the belief that racism is pervasive in the society is a conviction that is not likely to be adjusted on the basis of rational argumentation. There are no techniques, psychological ploys, or clever phrases that will reverse this kind of fundamental perception. This is not an issue that is going to be resolved by persuasive rhetoric. Don't expect that what you say in a speech is going to have a more powerful influence on people's thinking than what they experience directly in the real world. Change has to come from the way people treat each other on a day-to-day basis.

## Overcoming Cultural Barriers

Certainly we have evidence of cultural barriers being overcome. The best example is the one we see every four years at the Olympics. Athletes from all nations come together to compete, but also to draw strength from one another and to live by the common set of rules that govern the contests. For the period of time they are together, they set aside any cultural differences that may separate them and celebrate the remarkable capabilities of the human body. The respect they have for each other has nothing to do with race or creed; it comes out of their shared experiences. All of them know how much dedication, commitment, physical pain, and love for the sport was involved in the training necessary to measure up to the standards of the Olympics.

There is an important message here for speakers to observe: Set aside the differences that you know cannot be changed, and find the common ground.

## The Challenge of Pluralism

To speak from a position of strength but at the same time lay the foundation for peace and reconciliation takes a truly exceptional orator. Such a person was Martin Luther King Jr. It is proper, of course, that we honor the man for who he was, but, for the sake of rhetorical analysis, we also need to examine what he did and how he did it. The crowd that gathered in Washington, D.C., on August 28, 1963, resembled salt and pepper to many observers—it was more than 25 percent white. King was surprised by the mix, but not dismayed. Certainly, all 200,000 of the people in the audience would not be of the same mind, but that didn't matter. His message was tailored for all segments of the civil rights movement, rather than for a select few. His purpose was to find a common ground upon which all could stand. His strategy was not to narrow the focus of the issue, but to broaden it; to embrace everyone in the cause, not just those who had suffered injustices. He did not call for a change of purpose and direction, but for living out the true meaning of this nation's creed. Thus, he succeeded in pulling down the walls that separated one faction from another and in building bridges instead.

The legacy of Martin Luther King Jr. has been felt by ethnic minorities of every kind, not just by African Americans. And our nation is stronger because of it. Whenever we feel discouraged about our failure to resolve differences between the many cultures that are represented within our borders, we would do well to think about the challenge of the task. No other country of our size in the world has opened its doors as wide as we have. Whether we have a melting pot, a mosaic, or a salad bowl, the concept of ethnic inclusion is something that all of us can celebrate. Cultural diversity is our common ground.

## EXERCISE

Prepare a short (three- to five-minute) talk that you can give to the class, telling what you would like people to know about the social contributions that have been made by the nationality or ethnic group (or groups) that you represent. You can use either current or historical examples. Your purpose is to promote respect for the people you are describing. Don't use a problem-solving format: You are not identifying social injustices, and you don't need to make any recommendations. Focus on the positive characteristics of your roots and not on the negative qualities of others. Be friendly and not angry; build bridges and not walls.

## QUESTIONS FOR DISCUSSION AND REVIEW

1. What does it mean to *connect* with an audience, and how is that achieved?
2. What is meant by "framing an issue"? How can framing affect the way a message is received by an audience?

3. Why is establishing common ground a good way to start negotiations?
4. How is finding common ground different from settling for the lowest common denominator? How is it different from compromising or yielding?
5. How do specific *positions* differ from common *interests*?
6. Under what circumstances is it desirable to find common ground? When might you *not* want to seek common ground?
7. What are the guidelines to follow when talking to close friends or family members who strongly disagree with you on a particular issue?
8. What is meant by a *pluralistic society,* and what are its implications?
9. What are the principal attitudes toward public speaking among people influenced by Western culture? How might they differ from attitudes in other cultures?
10. What is meant by the word *stereotype?*
11. What is meant by the word *prejudice?*
12. What effect has cultural diversity had upon the world of business and manufacturing?
13. What function does a cultural diversity manager serve in a business organization?
14. What was the rhetorical strategy Martin Luther King Jr. used in his address on August 28, 1963?

## Progress Management Checklist

### *How can you tell if you are making progress?*

_____ 1. You will begin to include in your thinking the way your audience might respond to what you say.

_____ 2. You will be less likely to make insensitive or callous remarks that antagonize the people to whom you relate.

_____ 3. You will become aware that the way you communicate is related closely to the values of your culture, and that others may see things differently.

_____ 4. You will begin to develop assertiveness and learn to cope with the consequences of making your thoughts and ideas known to others.

_____ 5. You will develop an awareness of the way others see you.

_____ 6. You will be able to recognize and identify stereotypes you have of others and those that they might have of you.

_____ 7. You will learn to appreciate cultural diversity and the richness it adds to your life.

_____ 8. You will become consciously aware of the need to find some way to connect your point of view with the opposing ideas that others may have.

*Visit the book's Web site at* **www.mhhe.com/hasling8** *for study tools such as practice quizzes, activities, and Web links.*

# CHAPTER 4

# Listening and Reacting

**AFTER READING THIS CHAPTER, YOU SHOULD BE ABLE TO DO THE FOLLOWING:**

- Recognize that effective listening is a communication skill that can be learned through instruction; that speakers rely upon the verbal and nonverbal feedback they receive; that to be a good listener means you must listen actively, rather than passively.

- Become familiar with the eight common obstacles to listening and not allow them to interfere with your reception of a message.

- Recognize the fallacies of logic; know how critical listening is related to critical thinking.

- Understand how semantics is involved in the reception of messages; know what is meant by *operational meaning* and *semantic reactions;* know that words can be high or low on the scale of abstraction and that euphemisms can obscure meaning.

*I*f you were to read this out loud to someone, clipping along at a brisk pace, you might be able to read at the rate of 175 to 200 words per minute. But on the average, college students should be able to read the same pages for themselves at about 300 words per minute—faster if they have taken a speed reading course. In other words, your audience can comprehend your message in about two-thirds of the time it takes you to say it. So, wouldn't it be easier and less time-consuming to pass out copies of your speech to the audience and let them read it for themselves? Not really. There are important advantages to hearing the message spoken. The United States Supreme Court decided many years ago that even though oral arguments took up a great deal more time than simply reading an attorney's brief, it was necessary for the judges to have face-to-face dialogue with the presenters on each side of the case in order to ask questions and clarify the finer points of argumentation. While a well-written paper might be persuasive, it lacks the vocal qualities that effective speakers can impart to their listeners. When facing an audience, speakers can emphasize specific details, call attention to important concepts, offer additional evidence, retract a mistake, expand on a thought, clarify information that may have been misinterpreted, and repeat or rephrase something that was not understood.

In the previous chapter we observed that good speakers can compensate for a certain amount of poor listening, but regardless of how skillful those speakers may be, they cannot get their message across to people who choose not to listen.

## Choosing to Listen

Is listening a choice? Maybe and maybe not. When neighbors are shouting at each other with all the windows wide open on a summer night, you don't have much of an alternative—the sound is imposed upon you. Of course, you might be *hearing* the sounds but not *listening* to what is being said. We need to make that distinction. Listening implies cognitive reception and some degree of retention. It's possible to hear a voice but not *listen* to the meaning. Some research studies suggest that we actually listen to only about 30 percent of the words we hear, and we retain even less. But if you have normal hearing capacity and the ability to think, you have more choice that you might realize in most everyday situations to listen or not to listen. You can choose to go or not to go to a lecture. When you're there you can choose to listen or not to listen. In that respect public speaking is similar to broadcasting in the sense that transmission can only be received if listeners have their radios turned on. Just as you can dial to whatever station you want to hear on the radio, you can select when and to whom you want to listen.

### Listening Models

The simple truth is that we learn to speak the language as children by listening to adults. Even now, we continue to learn effective speaking skills from other people who use the language in ways we try to emulate. A good deal of our success depends not just on *whom* we listen *to*, but also on *what* we listen *for*. Certainly we want to develop our vocabularies so we are able to understand the spoken message as accurately as possible, but we also want to learn how to listen for *strings* of words that guide our comprehension. When *New York Times* columnist Thomas Friedman says he'd like to be able to " . . . huff and puff about outsourcing jobs to India . . ." we know that he is criticizing pundits who pretend to understand the issue.[1] Effective listening means you have to pay attention to the phrases that connect the thought to the meaning of the words. In *The Power of Words* the authors observe, "In rhetorical scrabble, one's target is not words but *strings* of words and their ability to *prime* categories of audience experience."[2] They point out that to be skilled speakers students must learn to listen for words that are used as *priming* tools—words that give the audience a sense of where the speaker is going with the thought.

## LEARNING TO LISTEN

Studies indicate that people who are good listeners score higher on academic achievement tests than do those who do not listen well.[3] That being the case, it seems as though we should make a course in listening a prerequisite for all students in their first year of college. The fact is that some schools do require a class in oral communication, and listening is generally a part of the course content. Many institutions offer speech as an elective, but others do not put it in the curriculum at all, believing that students already know how to communicate by the time they get to college.

### Forming Good Listening Habits

Nobody is born with good listening habits. Like anything else, good listening is a learned behavior. Michael Purdy makes the following recommendations:

- Make eye contact with the speaker.
- Be attentive to the speaker's verbal and nonverbal behavior.
- Be patient. Wait for the speaker to finish.
- Be responsive by using verbal and nonverbal expressions.
- Ask questions in a nonthreatening tone.
- Paraphrase, restate, and summarize what the speaker says.
- Provide constructive feedback.
- Be empathic. Work to understand the speaker.

[1]Thomas Friedman, "The Jobs-Go-Round," *San Jose Mercury News*, Feb. 27, 2004, p. 9C.
[2]David Kaufer, et al., *The Power of Words* (Mahwah, NJ: Lawrence Erlbaum Associates, 2004), p. 8.
[3]Carolyn Coakley and Andrew Wolvin, "Listening in the Educational Environment," in Deborah Borisoff and Michael Purdy (eds.), *Listening in Everyday Life: A Personal and Professional Approach* (Lanham, MD: University Press of America, 1991), pp. 163–164.

- Show interest in the speaker as a person.
- Demonstrate a caring attitude.
- Don't be judgmental.
- Be open-minded.[4]

## Feedback to the Speaker

But why should we be concerned about listening when the focus of this text is on speaking? One reason is that you will spend much more of your time in the audience than you will on the podium. Another reason is that you are studying *communication,* and that is a process dependent on the message being received. But there is yet a third reason: Anyone who does a lot of speaking to groups will tell you how important it is to get feedback from listeners. I know this is true for me, because I am personally energized by listeners who overtly react in a positive fashion. I like to see students looking at me while I lecture and taking notes when I make a significant point. I especially like to hear them laugh in the right places and see them nod in approval when they like something that I have said. I also believe that my lecturing improves when I observe positive feedback. Now, I'm not going to suggest that students do these things in order to stroke the ego of the professor, but I do want to call attention to the effect that the audience can have in the communication process. When students are the speakers, I want them to know that they are being heard. So, for the first round of speeches I sometimes assign a few members of the audience to give affirming nods from time to time while their classmate is making a presentation.

### Nonverbal Messages

When you are the listener in the presence of someone who is speaking, it is impossible not to send messages of your own. *Nonverbal feedback*—the way you sit or stand, the movement of your body, the expression on your face, the direction in which you cast your eyes—is an external indication of your internal reaction. It can be either positive or negative, and it can be an intentional or unintentional expression of your level of interest. An example of unintentional feedback would be a yawn. That kind of overt behavior on your part can have a demoralizing effect on a speaker, even though the yawn may have been an involuntary action having nothing to do with anything the speaker had been saying.

As listeners, we need to be aware of the way our feedback affects the speaker. And, as speakers, we need to recognize that the external reactions of audience members may make us feel good or bad, but they are not necessarily an indication of how well they are paying attention or whether they approve or disapprove of what we are saying.

---

[4]Michael Purdy, "The Listener Wins," http://featuredreports.monster.com/listen/overview/ (retrieved Feb. 21, 2004).

## Verbal Responses

The way people reply verbally to our message is a more reliable instrument for measuring reception than nonverbal feedback is. When listeners ask good questions or contribute relevant comments, we make the assumption that they were paying attention. But sometimes a speaker can be fooled. In social situations we learn how to make generic responses that fit all occasions even when we have no idea of what the other person has said. We can allow our thoughts to drift away, completely lose track of a story that is being told, and sound perfectly sincere by saying, "Oh, really, that must have been quite an experience." But this kind of "nonlistening" can also cause embarrassment, as illustrated by the following dialogue:

> Professor to a student in class: "You look like someone I've seen before. Do you have a brother who might have taken my class last year?"
> Student to professor: "No, it was me who took your class. I flunked it last year, and I have to repeat it."
> Professor: "That's strange, the resemblance is amazing."

That may be just an amusing story, but I was told that it really did happen. It's quite possible for us to look completely attentive without having the meaning of the message penetrate our consciousness. Let's analyze why this may occur.

- *We hear only part of the message and construct the rest of it ourselves.* In the example above, the professor heard the word *no* but didn't listen to the full explanation.

- *We focus on our own response.* We know that after the person has finished what he or she is saying, we are going to have to make some comment in reply. Instead of listening, we are framing in our minds what we are going to say when it's our turn.

- *Our thoughts go off on tangents.* Something that was said triggers an idea that launches us mentally in a direction that is not related to what the sender of the message is saying. It may be a very important direction for us to pursue, but it does not take us to the place where the speaker is going.

- *We want to disengage.* We stop listening when we really don't want to be in the conversation in the first place. Instead of trying to follow the road the speaker is taking, we are looking for an off-ramp.

## *Listening Passively*

The next step up from nonlistening is *passive listening*. Receivers may hear what is being said, but they are not focused on the subject matter. In the passive mode, their attitude toward the message is neutral, and they have no intention of making an effort to remember what the speaker says. Any response they might make is noncommittal.

Early studies in listening behavior attempted to quantify the amount of time the average person spends listening to speech. A more important study for you, however, would be to keep track of the time you yourself spend listening to other people. As an exercise some evening, try to recall as much as you can from the things that were said to you during the day. You may remember having a conversation with the passenger sitting next to you on the bus or exchanging jokes with fellow employees at the water cooler, but you may have forgotten what was actually said. Don't judge yourself harshly for doing that, because sometimes the personal contact is more important than the message itself. What should concern you more is your ability to focus attention on the content of verbal messages that are important and to retain information that you need.

## Listening Actively

Communication takes place only when the message of a sender is received. The professor who delivers an absolutely stirring lecture conveys no information at all unless someone in the room is awake. So, as an example, the student of communication would respond to the classic philosopher's conundrum by saying that if a tree falls in the forest, and there is no one there to hear, it does not make a noise. Ergo, the professor's lecture makes no impact if the minds of the students are elsewhere.

To be a good listener of speech, you must consider listening to be active behavior. You must be engaged in the process of communicating and regard your role as being equal to that of the message sender. Active listening means that you are focused on the present rather than the past or future, and are making a conscious effort to understand the sender's message at both levels of meaning, the cognitive and the emotional.

### The Cognitive Level

First and foremost, you want to understand the meaning of the message on the basis of the words that are being spoken. Even with all of its limitations, language is the best means people have of expressing what they know and what they want. The listener must be attentive to the words used if he or she is to comprehend the denotative meaning.

### The Emotional Level

To get the full impact of the message, the listener must be able to perceive the depth of the speaker's feelings. We are able to hear passion in the words of a poet, but we may have a more difficult time empathizing with an average person who has suffered a loss or experienced great joy. We must allow for the fact that emotion is often communicated by the *sound of the voice* rather than by the meaning of the words.

The emotional dimension of the message is often recognized by what we see rather than by what we hear. To be really good listeners, we must also use our eyes. Posture, gesture, and facial expressions are all part of what is being said. At the nonverbal level of communication, we monitor emphasis that is placed on words and that can affect the cognitive as well as the emotional aspect of the message.

## COMPREHENSIVE LISTENING

There are many different kinds of skills that can be learned in a course on listening, but we will cover just a few of them in this text. In this section we will discuss *comprehensive listening,* which means listening to understand and retain the substance of the message. It does not imply that we accept whatever is said; it suggests only that we comprehend the meaning. Later we will discuss *critical listening,* which adds the dimension of evaluating what we hear. There are two other kinds of listening that are important, but not closely related, to skills pertaining to public address: One is *appreciative listening,* which is behavior that enhances one's pleasure at a musical concert or poetry reading. The other is *empathetic listening,* which is something we do when we are relating to friends who are expressing their personal feelings. Comprehensive listening is pragmatic and objective and addresses our ability to absorb and retain the content of the message.

### Obstacles to Listening

There is an old saying that it is better to light a single candle than curse the darkness. We know that obstacles to listening exist, but there is no point in resenting the fact that they do. We have already spoken of the ways that speakers can compensate for the poor listening habits of the audience. Let's take another look at the list and see if we can give the same kind of help to people on the receiving end.

1. *Not listening from the beginning.* Speakers do not always tell you to start paying attention. They should do that, of course, but sometimes they don't. They assume you are listening, and they name the person, place, or thing that is the subject of their talk. They may do this too quickly; so be ready, and don't get caught napping. If you miss the antecedent, you will not know who, where, or what the speaker is talking about.

2. *Not getting the main idea.* The speaker may fail to express clearly the main idea of the speech. That is a serious omission on the part of the speaker, but nobody is perfect. If you miss the main idea, you are going to be confused until you get it. Try to construct in your own mind what you think the speaker wants to say. Let it be a tentative thesis until you are able to confirm that your interpretation is really what he or she meant.

3. *Listening only to what you already believe and not hearing new information.* Try to avoid falling into a pattern of not paying attention to facts that might

expand your thinking. Partial knowledge may not be enough for you to draw a conclusion. Examples of this kind of abbreviated listening are sometimes found in court trials. Jurors may hear the opening arguments of the attorneys and make up their minds on the basis of the claims that are made. Later, they may tune out when the evidence is being presented and not hear the proof that is needed to determine the validity of the claim. This happens because details are more difficult to comprehend than generalizations. To keep this kind of obstacle from getting in the way of your forming a reasoned conclusion, you must believe that the decision you are called upon to make is important and that hearing and weighing the evidence must precede your judgment.

4. *Not connecting important information to the main idea.* It's hard to know how many words are needed for an audience to relate information to the main idea. Sometimes the connection is not made by speakers when they think the receivers should be able to fill in the blanks. For example, a speaker may relate the details of tearing down the Berlin wall in 1990, and later comment that as a result, the United States has lost its national purpose. Would you, as a listener, be able to identify the national purpose as being the containment of communism if the speaker did not make the connection for you? If not, you would be missing an important part of the speaker's message. One of the most difficult aspects of effective communication is "listening between the lines" and discerning what the speaker means—even when the words are not explicitly spoken.

5. *Dividing your attention with other thoughts.* It's quite possible that while you are trying to listen to the instructor in your speech communication class explain the requirements of the next assignment, your mind keeps drifting off to other areas of your life that are competing for your attention. Perhaps your room rent is due and you don't have the money to pay it; your boss has said you have to work the morning shift next semester and that will interfere with the classes you want to take; and, worst of all, the weather forecast calls for rain on the day you were planning to go to the beach. Effective listening means that you have to set extraneous issues aside and focus your attention on the matter at hand. Certainly, peripheral concerns are important, but you must convince yourself that they just have to wait their turn.

6. *Allowing a speaker's mannerisms to interfere with your listening.* It's not always easy for a person inexperienced in public address to place emphasis on key points and speak in well-modulated tones. When you are listening to a speaker who talks in a monotone and perhaps has a rather drab personality, you need to turn up the intensity of your own receptors. Concentrate on the content of the message, not the speaker's mannerisms. Take responsibility yourself for recognizing what is important.

7. *Discounting a speaker's message because of age, race, sex, or ethnic origin.* Prejudiced thinking has no place in intelligent dialogue. Get rid of any antiquated

notions you might have that diminish the value of people who are not just like you. Stereotyping others on the basis of their being old, young, black, white, male, female, Muslim, Jew, Asian, or European is not only immoral and unethical, it is also ignorant.

8. *Not listening all the way through to the end of the message.* You might recognize this obstacle to listening if you have ever started to respond to a person in conversation before he or she had finished speaking. I must confess that I am guilty of doing this. I think I know how someone's sentence is going to end, and I react before I hear all of it. Often I'm wrong, and the person has to say, "No, that's not what I mean." In conversation this kind of listening error can be corrected right away, but in public address the speaker may not know that someone in the audience has jumped to a conclusion that distorts the intended message. Not listening through to the end may be something you do when a speaker is taking too much time to make a point. To be a good listener, you must be actively engaged in attending all the way through to the conclusion, even if your pacing is faster than that of the speaker.

## CRITICAL LISTENING

We can learn a lot when we listen, as long as we listen with a critical ear. It is not enough just to absorb information; we must also be prepared to analyze it and determine whether or not it makes sense. Are we willing to accept the whole message, or only part of it? What kind of response do we want to make? Should we affirm or refute what is said? Critical listening is especially important in a political setting. Our ability to process information given to us by a candidate for office is vital in order for a democracy to function. Year after year, public officials are returned to office by voters who may have heard the voices of the candidates but did not listen critically to their arguments and reasoning.

### Listening for Faulty Reasoning

Cleverness is not a substitute for substance. Catchy phrases and humorous anecdotes make a speech appealing to listen to and are certainly not to be condemned. But, as a discerning listener, you may want to ask yourself, "Is the speaker using clever rhetoric to cover up a lack of substance, or to avoid confronting the issue directly?" Look for the smoke screens that are designed to conceal rather than illuminate the speaker's meaning.

• Is the speaker trying to divert your attention away from the central issue? This tactic is sometimes called a *red herring.* In mystery stories it's the author's way of trying to make you think that one person is the culprit when actually it is someone else. In politics it may be that the speaker wants to direct your attention to a threat, such as terrorism, so you fail to recognize that new legislation will take away some of your civil liberties.

- Is the speaker making a show of attacking a weak argument of the opposition rather than the strong one? This is a rhetorical diversion that is sometimes called a *straw man*. Debaters who argue against capital punishment, for example, try to make it seem as though the main reason for executing criminals is to get revenge. The stronger arguments, however, and the ones that need to be addressed, are those that deal with protecting prison guards from inmates serving life sentences without parole, deterring thieves from carrying weapons during a robbery, and the possibility of criminals being released back into society where they can commit other crimes.

- Is the speaker appealing to the racial or ethnic prejudices of the audiences? For example, Adolf Hitler relied heavily on diatribes against the Jews and the Bolsheviks because he knew that fear and hatred of those groups already existed in the minds of his listeners. When speakers use prejudice as a means of gaining favor, they are exploiting the audience's weaknesses and are denying listeners exposure to rational arguments. Another word for this ploy is *demagoguery*.

- Is the speaker trying to influence you by *name-calling* or *mudslinging?* This is the strategy of making unsupported accusations to discredit an adversary's character rather than by confronting the person's real arguments. We hear this often during political campaigns. A speaker attacks the opposing candidate by saying he is unqualified to make decisions because he is a drunkard or a womanizer. By using this tactic the speaker says more about his or her own animosity than about the qualifications of the opponent.

- Is the speaker saying that one event is the cause of another simply because it preceded the first one? This is a fallacy that is sometimes called *post hoc ergo propter hoc*—after this therefore because of this. In actuality, the two events may just be coincidental. For example, people who live along the San Andreas fault in California try very hard to figure out when earthquakes will occur. Some projections are based on the weather, others on alignment of the planets. The reasoning is that because a certain condition existed just prior to the earthquake, there is a cause-and-effect relationship. In reality we cannot know whether one event is the cause of another unless we conduct a scientifically controlled study. Making a casual observation is generally not a reliable basis for forming a realistic belief. As listeners, we have a right to require more substantial evidence.

## Retention and Access

In a complex society such as ours, we are bombarded continually by a barrage of words that urge us to buy, sell, vote, and behave in a variety of ways. We are exposed to more information than we can possibly process—some of it valuable, much of it useless or counterproductive. If we accept that which is illogical and laden with fallacies, our own thought and discourse will become equally contaminated. We must learn to be selective in what we accept as truth and to base our conclusions on evidence rather than on unsupported assertions.

I've heard people say in jest, "I listen well; I just can't remember what I've heard." That's a fairly common dilemma. We hear a great deal more than we can retain. Much of it is stored in the cerebral cortex of our brain and would be available to us if we were able to retrieve it, but otherwise it's lost. It may be that retention and access are matters of experience. That is, we remember something better when we have a related thought or memory that we can connect it to. In other words, the more we know, the more we will be able to learn. Acquiring knowledge is much like putting together a jigsaw puzzle. The pieces have to fit somewhere. As you find where each piece goes, the picture begins to take shape, and it's easier to see where the new pieces belong. But unlike a jigsaw puzzle that comes in a box, we are exposed to more pieces than those that fit neatly into place. Some things we hear don't belong anywhere in our picture and need to be rejected. We have to learn to tell the difference between what fits and what doesn't, what is valid and what is nonsense.

## SEMANTICS OF LISTENING AND REACTING

The study of all the ways that meaning is conveyed and received is called *semantics*. Using words is the most explicit method for making ourselves understood, but words by themselves are often not adequate. Language is an invention that evolved from human thought, and, as such, it is far from perfect. At best it is a tool that can be used with varying degrees of skill for conveying meaning. We know that effective oral communication relies heavily on applications that are nonlinguistic. For example, volume and vocal inflection can alter meaning when we place emphasis on some words and not on others. From the visual perspective, we are aware that posture, gesture, and facial expression influence the way our message is received.

If you have ever had to ask a question of a person unfamiliar with your language, you know that it is difficult, but not impossible, to convey what you want to say without verbalizing. When you are in such a situation you probably rely on acting out the meaning, as you would do if you were playing charades. If your question pertains to a physical object that is close at hand, you can point to it; if there is an action verb in the message, you can go through the motions. You may even resort to drawing a picture for the person. One form of nonverbal communication that may be familiar to you is international signs that appear on highways and in public accommodations (Figure 4–1). Here we find an example of an important message that must be conveyed quickly and accurately, relying totally on the receiver's ability to interpret pictures. We call such symbols *icons*.

In the case of a "no smoking" sign, the message is clear even though no words have been used. However, if you are trying to get across an abstract idea, your task is more difficult. Imagine, for example, that you wanted to ask

**FIGURE 4–1**    One common form of nonverbal communication is the international sign, such as this icon for "no smoking."

the person who does not speak your language if the journey across the mountain would be *strenuous*. There is nothing you can point to that conveys the idea of *strenuous*. Neither the sound nor the letters in the word have any relationship to the concept of strenuousness. Pronunciation of the word conveys meaning only to those who have been taught to associate the word with the idea. This is why we say that *words are not containers of meaning;* they are simply *abstractions* to which we assign meaning.

## Levels of Abstraction

When I say words are abstractions, I simply mean that there is nothing about the sounds I make or the marks on the page that is inherently connected to the thing I am describing. All words are abstractions, but some are more concrete than others. For example, if I say that a man has "wealth," I am speaking on the *high level* of abstraction. You can't get a picture in your mind of what "wealth" looks like. To say that he owns real estate is moving down on the scale of abstraction, but only part way. To be concrete I would have to say specifically that he owns a colonial mansion on Long Island worth $8 million.

In the study of semantics we say that some word combinations have *operational meaning*—that means we are able to describe things in terms of size, weight, distance, volume, shape, number, or observable action. But when we get into the realm of aesthetic qualities, feelings, beliefs, values, categories, and concepts, we move higher up on the scale of abstraction.

## Semantic Reactions

Communication is complex because we know that much of what we say does not have concrete meaning. In many cases, the best we can do is to create *semantic reactions*—generating either a favorable or an unfavorable response. If I have good communication skills I should be able to get the kind of reaction from you that I want. If my intent is to have you to think favorably about a person,

I might say, "He is firmly committed to his beliefs." To create an unfavorable response I would probably say, "He is stubborn in his opinions." Although the two statements may appear to be similar, the *semantic reaction* in one case would be significantly different from that in the other. This is a principle we must be able to understand in order to communicate effectively.

## Euphemisms

Discussing subjects that arouse strong emotional feelings often makes us uncomfortable, and we have a tendency to try to soften the impact created by stark or abrasive words. This generally happens when we are talking about something that we fear, such as death, or something that embarrasses us, such as sex. When we use an inoffensive term to conceal our emotional anxiety or embarrassment, we are speaking in *euphemisms*. For example, we don't like to say that a person died, so we say he "passed away." If we are too embarrassed to say that two unmarried people were having sex, we say they were "having an affair." Euphemisms such as these are generally regarded as proper because they are more polite and less offensive to the senses than more coarsely worded terminology, but there are other euphemisms that are coined specifically to avoid confronting the real issue. A military action is sometimes called a "skirmish," and when bombs hit residential areas and civilians are killed, the news releases say that there has been "collateral damage." The press and the military defend language of this kind on the grounds that it communicates the message in a diplomatic way, but others criticize it, saying it insulates the listener and the reader from understanding the harsh reality of the events.

## Shortcuts

People who know each other well, have similar interests, or work in the same professional or vocational fields are able to communicate effectively without having to be explicitly detailed in their conversation. If you are connected to show business, for example, you might refer to "the house" rather than to "the number of people who attended the theater." Acronyms such as *FBI, FCC,* and *FDA* are all listed in the *American Heritage Dictionary* as though they were words. Many shortcuts are common enough for anyone to understand, but a speaker needs to be sensitive to the audience's background and not use jargon or initials that are not likely to be understood. For example, people in education may know that an "AP teacher" is one who has students in advanced placement classes, but the general public probably does not.

## Legal Language

In legal matters it is often necessary to clarify vague terminology in order to translate abstract concepts into principles of law. This is particularly well illustrated in decisions the Supreme Court has made pertaining to the word *speech* as it appears in the First Amendment to the Constitution. Is the meaning of *speech* confined to verbal expression? No, says the Supreme Court. Speech can include certain forms of nonverbal communication; therefore, wearing a black armband as a protest gesture is protected under the First Amendment and is referred to as *symbolic speech.* That term was used again in 1989, when the Supreme Court handed down a decision that said the burning of the U.S. flag was also regarded as symbolic speech. If it had been deemed an "act of violence," it could have been prohibited. However, because it was construed as a political statement, a legal statute could not forbid it. Each court decision contributes to the legal definition of words, and, because law is based on precedence, the terminology from one ruling can provide the basis of understanding in subsequent cases.

A significant part of being an effective communicator is to understand the conventional meaning that society attaches to abstract words. Certainly there is a difference between art that is called "erotic" and that which is labeled "pornographic." *Erotic art* depicts sexual love, whereas *pornography* is intended to incite lascivious feelings. You might be inclined to say that the difference is only in the mind of the beholder, but that's not good enough when it comes to establishing public policy. Your community may want to place restrictions on one but not on the other. Therefore, the outcome of the language used in verbal descriptions that become codified into law makes a big difference to merchants and to patrons of the arts.

## Shaping Perception

The power of words to shape perception has been proven by researchers in controlled experiments. The words you choose in the questions you ask can, in a very real sense, affect the way witnesses will recall a given event. This was demonstrated in a study conducted by psychologists Elizabeth Loftus and John Palmer. The researchers showed subjects a film of two cars colliding. They then asked their questions in several different ways: "How fast were the cars going when they *bumped* into each other?" Others were asked, "How fast were the cars going when they *smashed* into each other?" Those who heard the question using the word "smashed" estimated the cars were going faster than those who heard the question using the word "bumped."[5]

## Intentional Choice of Words

Choosing words in order to create a desired impression is in itself an art, and no one knows this better than people in the world of merchandising. Advertising copywriters are paid big salaries for thinking of words that trigger positive responses. Exhaustive studies are conducted to discover what kind of effect certain words have on the public. Terms such as *all new* and *patented formula* are catch phrases specifically designed to make us want to buy the product, and a

---

[5]Deborah Tannen, *The Argument Culture* (New York: Random House, 1998), p. 14.

"pre-owned car" is more attractive to buyers than a "used car" is. Is this practice limited to advertising agencies? By no means—we all do it to one degree or another. If we are *intentional* in our communication, we choose words that generate the kind of feeling we want to evoke in the mind of the receiver of our message.

We say *the word is not the thing,* but we know that people react to a notion on the basis of the term used to describe it. For example, if we are able to change the name of a band of mercenaries to *freedom fighters,* we are more likely to get financial support from Congress. And if a nuclear missile is unpopular because it is viewed as an offensive weapon, we may be able to create a more favorable impression by giving it a name such as the *Peacekeeper.*

Certainly, the question of ethics is one that serious students of public address must consider. Speakers must know that when they are standing on the podium they have a responsibility to their audience. They are there because they believe they have something to say that will contribute to truth and justice. If they use words deceptively to create a false impression, they are engaging in sophistry. But, at the same time, there is a responsibility on the part of those of us who are the receivers. We can defend our integrity by learning to become intelligent, perceptive, and discerning listeners.

## EXERCISE

Here is an exercise for testing comprehensive listening. Read the following paragraph out loud to someone who has not read it or heard it before. See if the listener can grasp the main idea and retain the information. This can also be regarded as an exercise in giving an oral explanation. Be as helpful as you can in making it possible for the listener to comprehend the message; speak slowly and emphasize the specifics that you think are important:

There are $365\frac{1}{4}$ days in a year. That means every fourth year is designated as a "leap year" and we have to add an extra day. But each year of $365\frac{1}{4}$ days is actually 11 minutes and 14 seconds too long. That adds up to 3 excess days every 400 years. In other words, we have to skip 3 leap year days out of every 400 years. So, to even things out, we did not have a leap year in 1700, 1800, or 1900. However, we were all caught up by the year 2000 and we did have a leap year. We will not need to skip a leap year again until the year 2100.

## QUESTIONS FOR DISCUSSION AND REVIEW

1. If a student can read a textbook faster than a professor can speak, why is it still a good idea for the student to hear the lecture?
2. How can the audience improve the delivery of a speaker's lecture?
3. What kind of nonverbal feedback might a listener give to a speaker? How reliable is that feedback?
4. What are some of the reasons "nonlistening" may occur?
5. What is meant by *listening passively?* What are the levels of listening actively?

6.  What are eight obstacles to comprehensive listening, and how are they overcome?
7.  How does *critical listening* differ from *comprehensive listening?*
8.  What is a red herring?
9.  What is a straw man?
10. What is meant by *demagoguery?*
11. What is meant by *mudslinging?*
12. What is meant by *levels of abstraction?*
13. What does *post hoc ergo propter hoc* mean?
14. What is meant by *operational meaning?*
15. What is meant by *semantic reaction?*
16. What is a euphemism?
17. What is symbolic speech?

## PROGRESS MANAGEMENT CHECKLIST

### *How can you tell if you are making progress?*

____ 1.  You will learn the comfortable rate at which you speak, read, and listen.
____ 2.  You will understand that *listening* is not the same thing as *hearing.*
____ 3.  You will recognize that listening is intentional and that you can choose to tune in or tune out when something is being said.
____ 4.  You will learn to listen for *strings* of words that *prime* you for the message the speaker wants you to receive.
____ 5.  You will begin to form good listening habits.
____ 6.  You will start giving verbal and nonverbal feedback to speakers.
____ 7.  You will begin to remember more of what you hear.
____ 8.  You will find yourself becoming more empathetic to the feelings of the speaker.
____ 9.  You will become aware of the obstacles to listening and learn to avoid them.
____10.  You will recognize and be able to name fallacies of logic.
____11.  You will listen for words that have concrete meanings and shun euphemisms.

 *Visit the book's Web site at* **www.mhhe.com/hasling8** *for study tools such as practice quizzes, activities, and Web links.*

P A R T  **II**

# *The Message*

# CHAPTER 5

# The Topic, Purpose, and Content of the Speech

---

**AFTER READING THIS CHAPTER, YOU SHOULD BE ABLE TO DO THE FOLLOWING:**

- Begin planning your speech by considering the appropriateness, complexity, significance, and scope of the topic.

- Know the distinguishing characteristics of speeches to inform, to persuade, to motivate, and to entertain.

- Know how to find information on the Internet; use a computer terminal or indexes in bound volumes to access material in periodicals.

- Recognize various forms of supporting information that add substance to the main assertions you make in your speech; know how to use "interest grabbers" to hold the attention of your audience.

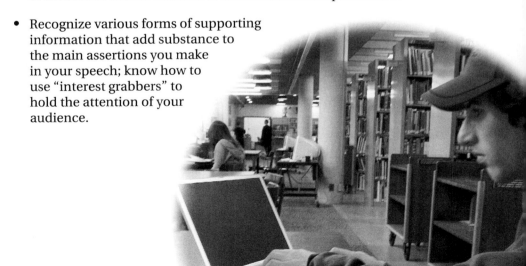

*A*bout now you might be asking yourself, "Even if I decide I am willing to make a presentation, why would anyone want to come to hear me?" That's a good question to use as a starting point. Public speaking is a *rhetorical* art, not a *performing* art. People are not going to come to hear how well you *deliver* a speech; they come because they are interested in the subject matter. You do, of course, want your delivery to be as good as you can make it, but, more important, you want the *substance* of your message to be worth the time that the audience is investing. People who make a lot of speeches know that it's not easy to attract an audience. If you are able to get 20 or 30 people together who are willing to listen to you for a half hour, you can regard yourself as quite fortunate. They have made an effort for you, so it's your responsibility to make an effort for them.

## THE TOPIC

Topic and purpose are interrelated, and it's hard to know which of those two should be your first consideration. The chances are that your instructor will be clear in assigning you either a speech intended to inform the listeners or a speech intended to persuade them. Or, if you are invited to speak to a community organization, the program chairperson will probably let you know whether or not the audience expects you to take a position on a controversial topic. Always observe the guidelines that have been prescribed. If your intent is to give a speech to inform, be cautious about selecting controversial topics that would reveal your bias.

If public speaking is a new experience for you, selecting the topic may seem at first to be difficult. Begin by thinking of things with which you have had direct experience—hobbies you pursue, trips you have taken, jobs you have held, organizations you belong to, computer applications you use, and so on. Consider also topics that you have studied or read about in books and magazines. As you begin listing possibilities, you may be surprised at how many subjects there are that you can talk knowledgeably about. Here are a few suggested topics for a speech that is intended to inform.

- The endangered polar bear
- The bicycle—a two-wheeled wonder
- The miracle of the Moringa tree
- DTV: It's a digital world
- Print on demand: Anyone can be an author
- Hydrogen: A clean alternative to fossil fuel
- Single-stream recycling
- Conserving water with drip irrigation
- Getting rid of stuff for fun and profit

- The cell phone revolution
- Solar panels in the desert
- Job hunting on the Internet
- New evidence of life on Mars
- The wealth of redwood trees
- A better diet for better living
- The joy of exercise
- Surfing in a kayak
- Fair trade coffee
- Opportunities in the helping professions
- Those amazing stem cells
- Serving in the Peace Corps
- The garages of Silicon Valley
- The Rock and Roll Hall of Fame
- Hiking the Appalachian Trail

It may be that you are given wide latitude in selecting your topic. Having lots of choices could make the task easier, but it could also make it harder. To be sure you are meeting the criteria assigned, make a checklist for yourself.

## Appropriateness

Be sure to consider the way the audience is likely to perceive your information. You may intend to give an informative speech on human fossils that were found to be a million years old; however, your claims could be regarded as controversial if you happen to be speaking to a religious organization that believes literally in the biblical story of creation.

## Complexity

Consider the complexity of the subject matter. You may know a great deal about a theoretical concept in physics or mathematics, but if the audience does not have the background that you do, your explanations might be too difficult for them to understand. Subjects that are extremely complex often lend themselves more to individual instruction than to public address. Giving a speech that is way over the heads of the listeners will lead them to believe that you are trying to make an impression by showing off your knowledge.

## Significance

Select a topic that has some significance. Don't waste your time or the time of the audience on trivialities. You don't want to go beyond the listeners' capabilities for comprehension, but you don't want to insult their intelligence either. Remember that you are making a serious presentation, not performing a comedy act in a coffeehouse.

## Scope

Don't overestimate the amount of material you can cover in the time you are allowed. If the subject area you are considering is too broad, you may find yourself under too much pressure to include everything you want to say. Bring your topic into focus. That means you must narrow the scope so that you have enough time to elaborate on the points you want to make.

## THE GENERAL PURPOSE

When planning your speech, consider your general purpose. You can *inform, persuade, motivate,* or *entertain.* These areas may overlap, but they should not be interchanged. If you are asked to give a speech to inform, it should not be a stand-up comedy routine. Certainly you can include humor, but mainly you want to provide your audience with useful information. There have been times when students in my class have given speeches that were absolutely hilarious, and all of us were thoroughly amused; nevertheless, the talks did not meet the requirements of the assignment, and would not have been appreciated in real-life situations.

The general purpose of the speech does not need to be stated directly. It's not a good idea to say to your audience, "My purpose is to persuade you . . .," because you may set up resistance to what you want to accomplish. Often, your general purpose will be suggested by the nature of the occasion. The person who invites you to speak will give you some indication by asking you to explain a procedure, support a recommendation, get a program moving, or lighten the mood of the audience. Try to accommodate your listeners by giving them what they want and what they expect.

We'll be discussing speech to inform and speech to persuade in detail in later chapters, but let's take a brief look at all four general purposes.

## The Speech to Inform

Almost all speeches contain some information, but the *speech to inform* has that characteristic as its primary function. Your speech falls into this category if you are making an effort to present your material objectively, without trying to persuade your audience to accept your solution to a problem. The subject matter might deal with controversial material, but when you are giving a speech to inform, you are not trying to influence the decision of the audience one way or another. You are simply giving them the information they need to make up their own minds. Sometimes you hear this type of presentation referred to as an *expository* speech.

## The Speech to Persuade

If you were making a speech in a courtroom or legislative hearing room you would probably be giving a *speech to persuade*. Your purpose would be to try to get your audience to think favorably about your cause and to believe as you believe. You would still be giving information to your listeners, but you would also be adding an interpretation that would lead them to a particular conclusion. In this type of speech you would anticipate opposition, and you would be prepared to refute it. You would probably be using both emotional and logical appeals.

## The Speech to Motivate

The kind of speech that is designed to inspire people is called the *speech to motivate*. When it is delivered from a pulpit it is called a *sermon* or a *homily*. It might also be a presentation made by a marketing manager who is introducing a new promotional campaign or trying to generate enthusiasm among the sales staff. It may contain some factual evidence, but the most successful speeches of this kind rely heavily on appeals to universal values, metaphorical language, and illustrations that reach people at the emotional level. The audience would probably be made up of people who already agree with the basic premise of the speaker but who are looking for inspiration. The purpose here is to move people to action: to live a better life, to work for a cause, to contribute their money, to join an organization, or to vote for a candidate.

## The Speech to Entertain

If you were an actor or a comedian and liked to perform on the stage, you might be asked to give a *speech to entertain*. Such a presentation is often referred to as an *after-dinner speech* and is designed primarily for the sake of amusement. You would not expect the audience to learn anything of significance or to be persuaded to a point of view; you would simply want the listeners to enjoy the experience. This kind of speech generally consists of humorous references, anecdotes, and narrations worked around a central theme. It is appropriate when an audience is in a relaxed or perhaps frivolous mood.

## Combinations

There are times when general purposes overlap. Some of the best speeches you hear will contain information and humor delivered in a motivational style. Perhaps the most notable examples are the occasions when Steve Jobs gives a speech to introduce a new product. Jobs has a way of wowing his audience by offering information in motivating language. *BusinessWeek* says that "Jobs unveils Apple's latest products as if he were a particularly hip and plugged-in friend showing off inventions in your living room."[1] To emulate his ability, however, plan on having a depth of knowledge, an exceptional product, and spending many hours in preparation and practice.

## THE CONTENT

Now that you have selected your topic and established your purpose, you need to gather information to make up the substance of your speech. Probably you already have a few ideas in your head, but those must be augmented by material found in published sources.

Start by recalling what you already know. Think of what you might have learned by working at an interesting job, traveling, talking to others who are informed on the topic, watching a TV documentary, or reading books and periodicals. Then make a visit to your library. Be sure you start your research early; you may find that the topic is more complex than you had thought. You might also discover that what you thought was true, actually is not. When that happens, you may have to change your thesis altogether. Begin your research with an open mind, and allow the information you gather to lead you to your conclusion. You will want the most reliable data, and also the most current.

### Computer Access

An easy way to begin finding information on your topic is to use the Internet. For all of the topics listed at the start of this chapter you can go to search engines such as Google.com, Ask.com, or Yahoo.com, type in the key words, and you will find a Web page that will give you enough information to get started. But don't restrict your research to the Internet only. Plan on using other sources in books and printed periodicals.

Let's say you want to give a speech on ways to deal with the water shortage on farms in arid regions of the state. Going to Google.com and typing in the word *irrigation* does not give the search engine enough information. Better to put in *drip irrigation California agriculture.* You will get a number of choices. Many of them will be commercial and will be trying to sell you a product, so employ discretion when you use them as sources. Whenever you can, select Web sites that end in .gov, .org, or .edu. They will generally be more reliable than the ones ending in .com. Most of the time .edu will give you a college or university. For example, you can access the library at the University of California by going to the Web site www.lib.berkeley.edu.

---

[1]Peter Burrows and Ronald Grover, "Steve Jobs' Magic Kingdom," *BusinessWeek* Feb. 6, 2006, p. 66.

Official government Web sites would include the following:

| | |
|---|---|
| Environmental issues | www.epa.gov |
| World oil reserves | www.eia.doe.gov |
| Endangered species | www.endangered.fws.gov |
| Homeland security | www.dhs.gov |

If you want to know what the president or Congress is doing about issues that concern you, you can go directly to their Web sites. You can even send them an e-mail to request specific information:

www.whitehouse.gov

www.senate.gov

www.house.gov

In addition to official government Web sites, many organizations can provide reliable information for speech topics:

| | |
|---|---|
| Disaster relief | www.redcross.org |
| Forest conservation | www.forests.org |

*The Internet will give you current information, but you must be able to recognize what is useful and reliable.*

| | |
|---|---|
| Globalization | www.ifg.org |
| Health care reform | www.allhealth.org |

Commercial Web sites can also be good sources if you choose them carefully. Some have a point of view that you may or may not be able to recognize. Avoid those that blatantly try to sell you something or abusively attack opposing opinions. Here are three examples of reliable Web sites that provide useful information:

| | |
|---|---|
| Economic issues | www.commerce.com |
| Water management | www.uswaternews.com |
| Mars exploration | www.space.com |

Web sites can be valuable tools for browsing. It may be that you are having trouble thinking of a topic and don't know where to start. A good plan would be to do some preliminary reading to see what information is available in a general subject area of interest. You don't have to do original research as you would in graduate school. Work with information that is obtainable. Find a few key facts or examples that will become the foundation for the body of your speech; then build on those by looking into additional sources. You can use your computer because most major newspapers and magazines post a great deal of information on the Internet:

| | |
|---|---|
| *New York Times* | www.nytimes.com |
| *Chicago Tribune* | www.chicagotribune.com |
| *U.S. News & World Report* | www.usnews.com |
| *The Atlantic* | www.theatlantic.com |
| *Newsweek* | www.newsweek.com |
| *Time* Magazine | www.time.com |

The World Wide Web has made, and will continue to make, a remarkable difference in the way we send and receive information. The quantity of words and pictures out there in cyberspace is immense, and that is a problem as well as an opportunity.

## Retrieval

The sheer volume of data available to us makes the task of retrieving information a bit overwhelming. First of all, we need to have the technical expertise necessary to operate the computer software; we need to be analytical enough to know what questions to ask and what key words to use in our search; we must be able to recognize useful information and separate it from the mounds of garbage; we need to evaluate the content and the source of the material; and we must know what to do with it after it has been downloaded. But there is yet another frustrating characteristic that you will discover when you begin doing research on the Internet: When you try to go back to the same site you used a few days before, you often find that the information you want is no longer there. A Web site does not have the same permanence as a magazine article. There are not thousands of copies of it in libraries and bookstores, and the words can be changed or completely deleted with a few clicks on a keyboard. So, once you find something of value, be sure you save it. If it is print rather than graphics, you can download it to your hard drive; that way you can return to it easily. You can also print a hard copy of it, or simply take good notes.

## Quality of the Source

The fact that the World Wide Web is so expansive means that we must be extremely alert when we use it. Think about the implications: Individuals or groups who have a product or a cause to sell, a little money, and a personal computer can set up a Web site. If they have some skills in graphic design, they can make up a really attractive Web page. It's like having their own magazine or newspaper. They can write whatever they want and make it available to thousands of people. What's more, they don't have to go through the evaluation or editing process that writers must when they submit work to professional journals. Then, you come along doing your research, and the Web site of someone with an ax to grind pops up, along with all the others. Therefore, when you gather information from the Web, you must read very critically; otherwise, you might find yourself quoting radical and one-sided assertions.

## Databases

While you may be able to do some of your research on your home computer, you will probably have to go to a library to find specific articles on the subject you have chosen. Your home computer is limited to Web sites, whereas a library gives you access to databases. The difference is that a database can give you the full text of articles from thousands of publications while a Web site generally gives you only a few selected excerpts. Databases are generally too expensive for individual subscribers and are only affordable for libraries and business corporations.

The biggest advantage, however, is that a library database provides references from reliable sources such as encyclopedias and professional journals. All the material has gone through a thorough editing process. By contrast, a source found on the Internet could come from someone whose qualifications might be questionable. The ease of creating Web pages and blogs (Web logs) makes it possible for people who advocate causes to post their thoughts and opinions for all the world to see. Many Web sites, such as Wikipedia, can be useful for finding information that may not be available elsewhere. But remember that the screening process is limited. Almost anyone can post material that may or may not be accurate.

## Magazine Indexes

The system the library uses to access articles in periodicals might be called Magazine Index or InfoTrac. Information on these systems goes back as far as 1980 and is kept current. (For earlier publications ask the librarian to help you check the archives.) Digital indexes have the capacity to locate many more sources than the average library could stock. In some cases you will be able to read or download an article from the computer screen, but in other cases you will have to find the hard copy of the magazine in the library stacks. Proceed in the same way you do on your home computer. Type in key words and you will get a list of articles pertaining to your subject. The list will include the date, the title, and the author and will start with the most recent.

The home page of InfoTrac has several categories:

- *General Reference Center:* Magazines, newspapers, and reference books on arts, science, sports, hobbies, etc.
- *Health Reference Center Academic:* Fitness, pregnancy, prescription drugs.
- *Academic ASAP:* Current events, economics, education, political science, psychology, religion.
- *Contemporary Authors:* Literature, biography, critical essays.

When you are typing in your key words, be sure you select the option of *text* rather than *title*. You want the computer to scan for key words in the body of the text that might not appear in the title of the article.

## Indexes in Bound Volumes

Yes, bound volumes are still available in many libraries: The *Readers' Guide to Periodical Literature* may be handy if you are looking for material that is more than 25 years old. Other good sources, also in bound volumes, are the *Social Sciences Index,* the *Business Index,* and the *Education Index.* These references are cross-indexed by title, author, and subject headings, similar to the *Readers' Guide.* They will direct you to the more scholarly articles and recent studies that appear in professional journals. The *New York Times Index* is an extremely useful library reference that can be used when you know the approximate time of an event and want specific information about the details. The volumes are arranged according to subject and in a chronological sequence. You will find a brief summary of the event itself and also a reference to the *New York Times* edition that carried the story in detail. For in-depth research you could go into the archives of the newspaper and retrieve the original article.

## Reference Books

You can use a great many other sources for specific information: the *World Almanac, Facts on File, Statistical Abstract of the United States,* and the *Congressional Quarterly Researcher,* to name just a few. For background material you can get caught up on past events by looking at the *Encyclopedia of Popular Culture.* As you progress in your college work, learn to use a variety of research tools. And, by all means, don't hesitate to ask the librarian for assistance.

## Taking Notes

Library research can be time-consuming and still not be productive if you fail to keep track of what you read. The beginning speech student may spend many hours in the library poring over books and periodicals, yet fail to include any concrete information in the speech. Don't rely on your memory alone; take notes as you read. Record names of people, places, and things; professional titles and positions; dates and times; costs and quantities; court cases and scientific studies; and any details you might need to put into your outline to help you develop and substantiate the explanations or historical accounts that you plan to include in the speech. Be sure you make note of your sources. On some occasions, the audience may be skeptical about what you say, and being able to cite the source will help validate the data.

If you find that your research takes a good deal of time and effort, you are probably going about it in the right way. Most preachers will tell you that it takes about an hour of study to prepare for every minute of a sermon.

## FORMS OF SUPPORT

A speech that is well balanced is one that has variety in its development. You would not want to give or hear a speech that is composed entirely of quotations or statistics, although those are both substantial forms of elaboration. Let's examine the kinds of supporting material that you can look for when you are gathering information and taking notes on what you want to include in the speech.

## Definition of Terms

Formal debates often begin with a definition of terms so that there is no misunderstanding of the issue. Normally, you don't need to start a speech that way, but there may be words and phrases used in specific ways that are outside the listener's frame of reference and must be explained at some point. While you are in the process of gathering your information, make note of what you think may need to be defined.

**Technical Words.**    A speech dealing with electronic equipment will be difficult for members of an audience to understand if they do not have a technical background. Listeners may give up trying to follow you if the terminology is not clear. You might need to explain to novices, for example, that *peripherals* refer to hardware such as scanners, printers, and Web cams that are attached to a computer.

**Legal Terms.**   If you were giving a speech dealing with legal issues, there might be specific terms you would have to define, such as *reasonable doubt* or *probable cause.* Ordinary reference books would not be much help to you; you would have to consult a source such as *Black's Law Dictionary.*

**Words in Other Languages.**   We are used to people borrowing words from other languages when the English word is not adequate to convey the idea. We are all conversant with the Hawaiian word *aloha* or the Hebrew expression *shalom.* But if a foreign word is not well-known, it requires a definition. For example, if you say that it's important for students to have *ganas* in order to learn, you might have to explain that *ganas* is the Spanish word meaning "desire" or "willingness."

**Common Words with Specialized Meanings.**   We may think we know the meaning of a word, but if it is used in a specialized way we may not understand it at all. In education, for example, the word *articulation* does not mean the ability to speak clearly. In that context, it refers to the arrangements two schools make to coordinate their programs.

**Words Defined by Quantitative Measure.**   If you were to make a speech in favor of giving federal aid to people living in poverty, you would have to define quantitatively what you meant by the term *poverty.* In this case, the definition is continually changing as the cost of living changes. In January or February of each year the federal government releases a directive called the *Federal Poverty Income Guidelines.* Benefits for many low-income assistance programs are based on those figures. On January 23, 2008, the official poverty level for the year was set at $21,200 for a family of four. You can see how the number of people living in poverty could be modified by raising or lowering those guidelines.

## Specific Instances

As you read, look for specific instances that are interesting and related to the point you want to make. Include details of the illustration in order to add credibility to your statement. You may wish to cite a number of such examples or take just one and elaborate on it. If your topic is controversial, you will have to point out how the incident you have selected leads to the conclusion you want to draw. This kind of rhetorical support is sometimes called *anecdotal,* and it is an excellent device for gaining and holding the attention of the audience. People like to listen to stories, particularly those that have unusual or mysterious characteristics.

Sometimes theories are based on anecdotal support: For example, the mystery of the Bermuda Triangle was created by an Associated Press reporter named E. V. W. Jones. He noted an incident that occurred on December 5, 1945, when five navy torpedo bombers took off from a base in Fort Lauderdale, Florida, and were never seen or heard of again. That incident, by itself, might not have attracted attention, but Jones discovered that a number of other mysterious disappearances had also occurred in the same triangle marked by Bermuda, Puerto Rico, and Fort Lauderdale. The story captured the imagination of people all over the world.

Anecdotes are fun and interesting for the storyteller as well as for the audience, but let's make sure we put their value and significance in perspective. By themselves, they cannot *prove* a generalization; they are simply indicators that a condition may exist. Too frequently people jump to conclusions based on anecdotal support, without asking for more substantial evidence. Medical theories, for example, may cite instances when people were cured of a disease by a particular herb or vitamin. The theory may begin to develop credibility if there are a great many reports of circumstances that produce the same result, but unless there are controlled studies to verify the theory, the scientific world is generally skeptical.

## Controlled Studies

When we conduct a controlled study, we are using what is called the *scientific method*. We start with a hypothesis or a theory. Then we proceed to test it by setting up a series of experiments in which we control all of the variables. By modifying one variable at a time and observing the results, we begin to learn what the outcome will be when a particular adjustment is made. To find out what causes cancer in rats, for example, we control the conditions of their environment and then proceed to make one change at a time in their diet or exposure to chemical substances. If we get to a point where we can repeat the experiment and are able to predict what result will be produced by a particular change, we say that the study has *reliability.*

As an undergraduate college student you will probably not be called on to conduct original research; you can simply examine the studies that have already been made. But you want to know how such studies are conducted so that you are able to tell if your information is really substantial. Studies conducted in physics and chemistry, of course, are going to be more reliable than those conducted in the behavioral sciences; however, the same methodology is used. Studies frequently have to be qualified by language that acknowledges that there are exceptions to the generalizations being made. You can cite studies, for example, that show that smoking cigarettes causes lung cancer, but you would have to acknowledge that there are people who smoke who do not get lung cancer and that there are people who get lung cancer who do not smoke. But even though there are exceptions to the findings, scientific studies are more reliable than the casual observations we make.

## Statistical Data

By *statistical data,* we mean any kind of information that can be expressed in numbers. It is sometimes called *quantitative information*—that is, evidence that can be counted or measured. It may be in the form of totals, percentages, averages, rates, or other numerical values. It can be obtained by actual count or from random samples. Statistics may be important in order to establish the validity of a claim. If you try to persuade without using quantitative evidence, your listeners may begin to believe that you are simply trying to sell them "blue sky" notions that have no substantive meaning. Consider the following claims that a speaker might make:

1. "There is a great deal of oil that can still be drilled off the coast of California."
2. "Most people are in favor of capital punishment."
3. "Students who go to parochial schools score higher on achievement tests than do those who go to public schools."

All of these claims require quantitative support; specific instances or anecdotal evidence alone would not be sufficient. In the first example, you might report on the barrels of oil that have already been pumped from one well. But, in order to make the claim that a lot is still available you will need an estimate from an expert in the field who has conducted reliable studies. Even if you had that figure, listeners might also want to know how much that is in comparison to other oil fields and how long it would last at the present rate of consumption.

The second statement would also have to be supported by statistical information. It would not be enough to ask eight or ten people whether they favored capital punishment. You would have to present figures gathered from a recent survey that was conducted using a random or representative sample of a given population. And then you would have to restrict your generalization so that it applied to people in the particular area that was surveyed.

In order for the third statement to be an acceptable claim, you would have to compare the scores of the parochial school students with those of students in public schools. The comparison would have to be based on the same test given to a significant sample of students under identical conditions.

Use statistics to support a generalization when it is necessary, but use them in such a way as to provide clarification and credibility for what you are saying. Here are some suggestions:

- Don't inundate your listeners with more statistics than they can retain. If you have a long list, put the figures on a chart for them to see, write them on a whiteboard, or distribute copies of a handout sheet. Doing this will help them remember and will also impress on them that the numbers are important.

- Round off large numbers when it's possible to do so without distorting the information. For example, an expenditure of $1,468,216.00 can be expressed in a speech more easily as "almost one and a half million dollars."

- Don't use figures deceptively. Avoid the habit of substituting percentages for adjectives. Although you may have reason to believe that a large portion of the staff favors a four-day workweek, don't say, ". . . and 90 percent of the people on the staff like the idea," unless you have actually taken a survey.
- Don't compare absolute numbers with percentages. It is not very useful to say "a neighboring district cut its expenses by $200,000, whereas our reduction was only 6 percent."

## Accuracy

Statistics can be misleading if you are not careful. For example, figures that show a rising crime rate may not necessarily indicate an increase in crime; they may merely reflect an increase in arrests. As a similar example, records show that more automobile accidents are caused by men than by women. However, this doesn't mean that women are better drivers; it just means that men do more driving. Recognizing such fallacies in the use of statistics is not just the responsibility of the audience, it is also the responsibility of the ethical speaker.

The advantage of employing statistics is that they give the listener the "big picture" and add significance to your assertions. The danger is that statistics can be carelessly used. Numbers can be manipulated by words, as illustrated in the following example:

> Three men decided to share a hotel room that cost $30. They each paid the clerk $10 and went up to the room. Later, the clerk remembered that the room had been reduced in price to $25, so he told the bellhop to take $5 back to the three men. On the way up to the room the bellhop decided to keep $2 for a tip. He gave the men $3, so they each got a dollar back. The room then cost each man $9 instead of $10. Three times nine is twenty-seven; the bellhop kept $2. What happened to the other dollar?

In this example, the arithmetic is accurate, but the conclusion is false, because the words used to relate the story are deceptive. (The men paid more than nine dollars for the room, because they each gave a third of a dollar tip to the bellhop.) The point is that *figures do not speak for themselves.* The speaker has an obligation to interpret statistical evidence in a responsible way so that the numbers clarify an issue rather than obscure it.

## Emphasis

The emphasis you place on the statistical data and the way you state the evidence will have a lot to do with the impact the numbers have on the listeners. For example, it may be true that a corporation's profit increased 100 percent. But it could also be true that its net profits went from 2 to 4 percent. Both of those statements might be perfectly accurate; the speaker has the prerogative of selecting which one to use.

There are certain extrapolations you can make from statistical data. For example, if a survey indicates that 54 percent of the eligible voters cast a ballot, you can assume that 46 percent did not. But there are precautions you must take in making assumptions. A speaker might claim that in the past decade the number of marriages per 1,000 population remained the same, but that the number of divorces doubled. The ratio of marriages to divorces in this country is now about 2 to 1. That evidence does not mean, however, that 1 of 2 marriages will end in divorce, because many people get married and divorced more than once. What's more, it is not a reasonable extrapolation to say that any particular couple has a 50 percent chance of getting a divorce. Statistics, no matter how accurate they may be, are not able to predict individual behavior.

### Interest

Another thing we can say about statistics is that they tend to be dull. You can make them more interesting if you can provide an illustration that listeners are able to visualize. If you wanted to support the claim that a modern bicycle is one of the most efficient machines for propelling human beings under their own power, you could use verbal comparisons rather than numerical ratios. For example, pound for pound a person riding a bike can go farther on a calorie of food than a gazelle can running, a salmon swimming, or an eagle flying.

## Testimonial Evidence

Much of the evidence you will want to include in your speech will not be quantitative and will need to be expressed in words rather than numbers. Again, you will want to go beyond your own experience and relate observations that have been made by other people. This type of support is called *testimonial evidence,* and it can be divided into two categories:

### Eyewitness Accounts

Suppose an issue under consideration at your college is whether or not security officers should carry guns on campus. Because it is a topic of local interest, you will need to have the perspective of people who have had direct experience with the situation in your particular area. Probably the best person to talk to would be a campus security guard. He or she might tell you that there is no reason for an officer to carry a gun, because there have been very few instances of physical attacks. In the cases when an officer has had to intervene, the perpetrator was unarmed, and either ran off or submitted without resistance. A different impression, however, could be given by a guard who has been on night patrol. "It may seem like a safe campus in the daytime," the guard might report, "but at night it becomes a meeting place for drug dealers. They carry guns, and they know that we do not." Which of these two eyewitness accounts would you use? If you were giving a persuasive speech and advocating a position, you would have to pick one or the other.

Court trials rely heavily on eyewitness testimony. Witnesses will often be called upon to describe in detail precisely what they saw or heard. They must testify only to that which they actually experienced—what other people told them is called *hearsay evidence* and is not admissible. Although judges and juries give eyewitness accounts great weight, such testimony is not infallible. Many experiments have been conducted showing that wide discrepancies can appear in the accounts of different witnesses to the same event. When there are several eyewitnesses who all testify to having seen the same thing, the evidence is very strong. But if one person saw something that no one else did, the evidence may be open to some question.

### Expert Testimony

Often, courts will call to the stand people who are referred to as *expert witnesses*. These are people who have expertise in a particular field and are able to verify the results of a study, experiment, or observation. They are able to understand technical data and relate scientific findings that are pertinent to the case. A ballistics expert, for example, can testify that two bullets were fired from the same gun. The jurors do not need to witness the actual test; they only need to hear the testimony of the expert.

For a speech you are preparing on the cost of education, for example, you might want to gather information from the bookstore manager. Rather than relying on your own observations about the cost of books, you can add credibility to your speech by quoting someone who is directly involved in pricing policies. That person becomes your "expert" and might be able to give an explanation that is better informed than your own could be. It may be that the cost of a large volume containing highly specialized material with many color illustrations would be priced even higher than it is, if the expense were not balanced by increasing the markup on smaller books that are sold in larger quantities. That's a policy that could be modified, perhaps, but any change would need to be based on the testimony of an expert.

## Explanation

In both the speech to inform and the speech to persuade you may need to provide explanations. As the speaker, you must be sure you understand the material thoroughly yourself. Explanations can be regarded in a number of different ways.

### Analysis

When we analyze an event, we try to discover what happened, what worked, and what didn't work. Football coaches do this all the time when they watch the playback of a game. They observe what each player did on every down, and from this analysis they can develop strategies for future games. Conducting an in-depth analysis on a complex issue is probably not something you would do as an individual; instead, you might report on an analysis made by an institution or an expert in the field. The National Academy of Sciences, for example, is conducting a study of the greenhouse effect—a global condition that traps harmful gases within our atmosphere. The conclusion of the academy's analysis is that the danger of the greenhouse effect is real, that it could adversely affect the weather patterns of the entire world, and that carbon dioxide produced by the burning of fossil fuels is the most serious offender. The value of an analysis of this kind is that it tells you what questions need to be asked in order to find a solution: How can we generate electricity in the quantity we need without jeopardizing the global environment? Do we have to stop relying on the burning of fossil fuels? What other energy sources are available to us? Questions of this kind are extremely important in the process that leads to workable solutions.

## Historical Background

At the time you are doing your research, try to think of what historical background your audience will need in order to understand the point you are trying to make. For example, you might refer to the Supreme Court decision of *Brown v. the Topeka Board of Education* in 1954. Some audiences would understand that reference; others would not. You might have to elaborate by explaining that ever since the end of the Civil War, the South had claimed that it was the right of the states to determine if they wanted to maintain separate facilities for blacks and whites. Until 1954, federal law allowed the southern states to do that. But, in the *Brown* decision, the Court said that the constitutional rights of black children were violated when state law required that they attend separate schools from white children, even if the facilities provided were equal.

Providing this kind of background information might be necessary if your audience is composed of people who are new to this country or perhaps are young and have not studied the social conditions of earlier generations.

## Description

Another form of explanation is *description*. If you have the ability to paint word pictures, you can create images in the minds of your listeners. You may want to tell what it is like to live in an urban slum; or you might wish to describe the beauty of Yellowstone National Park. This form of rhetorical development can be extremely effective if you are skillful in selecting relevant details and using vivid language. Description can be a powerful persuasive device if employed for that purpose.

## Narration

Examples can be conveyed to an audience simply by presenting the bare facts, but you can generate more interest and create a stronger impact by relating the information in narrative form. Instead of making a declarative statement that the library was an important influence in your life, convey the message in the form of a story:

> My favorite uncle took me to the library when I was eight years old. He helped me browse through the stacks and look at a lot of books, but he knew exactly the one we were going to check out. It was the child's version of *Treasure Island.* We took it home, and he read me the story. At the end his eyes got very wide and he said, "Look, there's a piece of paper here—it looks like a map!" Sure enough, it was a treasure map that he had surreptitiously slipped in between the pages. Ever since then I have been going back to the library looking for treasure maps. And I have found much wealth.

For a narration to be effective, it needs to have a "punch line" at the end, so that your audience will get the point.

### Analogy

An effective aid to explanation is *analogy.* Most people can learn better when new information is compared to something they already understand. For example, if you wanted to explain the flow of electricity through a wire, you might compare the concept to the flow of water through a pipe. In a speech on this subject, you could say that the water's motion is called the *current,* the pressure that pushes the water is the *voltage,* the valve that controls the flow is the *resistance,* and the work done by the water is the *power.* With this picture in mind, the listener might better be able to understand your explanation.

In addition to simplifying complex material, analogies can also be used to add color and vividness to your language. In doing this, the points you make and the ideas you advance are more likely to be remembered. In a speech on career planning, for example, you may want to say that sometimes it is necessary to move on to a new occupation, even though there may be some risk in doing so. Your analogy could be that of a circus aerialist who must let go of one trapeze and spend an agonizing few seconds in midair without any support before grabbing on to the next bar. Having established the analogy, you can reinforce the point by making reference to the trapeze artist again later in the speech.

Analogies can be used in comparing any two concepts that have similar characteristics. Suppose you wanted to recommend that the United States extend free or low-cost health insurance to all citizens. You could say that good health is just as important to the citizens in a democracy as a good education is, and that because we provide free public schools, we should also see that every citizen has access to affordable medical care.

## *Interest Grabbers*

In either the speech to inform or the speech to persuade, it is necessary for the speaker to hold the listeners' attention. In doing your research and gathering your thoughts, look for *interest grabbers*—examples or references that are not only informative but will make the audience want to listen. Here are a few ideas along those lines.

## Humor

One of the most effective means of establishing rapport with the audience is humor. When you get people to laugh, they are actively participating in the communication process. You don't need to be funny all the way through the speech, and your jokes don't need to be sidesplitters. But work your humorous remarks into the theme of the speech so that they're relevant to what you are saying. *Example:* "One of my colleagues recently asked me if I believed in free speech. I told him that I certainly did. 'That's good,' he said, 'because I'd like to have you give one to my class next week."

## Suspense

The reason adventure stories are popular is that they keep us in suspense. We read or listen through to the end to find out what is going to happen. In the *Tales of the Arabian Nights,* Scheherazade was such a good storyteller that the king let her live as long as she continued to keep him in suspense. Take a lesson from this ancient tale and learn to hold the attention of your audience by not revealing the ending of your story until you build it to a climax. The same principle applies to telling jokes. Don't give away the punch line until you have sparked the curiosity of the listener.

## Unusual Examples

Not all examples have to be unusual ones, but if you are able to add a few that have really interesting features, you can change an ordinary speech into one that people will remember. Some topics lend themselves to unusual examples more than do others. For example, new products in the high-tech industry provide us with a wealth of material. One of my students described in his speech a new electronic device that would help keep people from losing their credit cards. It was designed in such a way that it started playing a tune after it had been exposed to light for several minutes. It continued to play until it was programmed to stop. An added feature was that you could pick from among a hundred tunes one that you wanted it to play. Presumably, you could program it to cry out for help if it were stolen.

## Familiar References

Have you ever been daydreaming during a lecture and then snapped back to attention when the speaker mentioned the name of a friend, or a place you had visited, or an incident you were involved in? This is a phenomenon that good speakers recognize and use as an effective attention grabber. It's not always possible for you to know what will be familiar to your audience, but you can make some good guesses. To start with, you can use references to other speeches that have been made in class, personality traits of your instructor or other students, or names of local places and events. Mentioning the names of popular entertainers, musical groups, or sports figures is another way to get the attention of the audience, or you might tie your information to an item that has just recently appeared in the news.

**Personalized Connections**

People generally pay attention to things that are going to affect them directly. This is why newspapers try to find a "local angle" when reporting the news. If U.S. military troops are being sent on a mission, people want to know if the reserve unit near their city will be called. And if a large corporation announces that it will be downsizing, workers want to know if their local plant will be affected. When you are planning your speech, try to think of how you can respond to the question that you know will be in everyone's mind, "How is this event going to affect me and my family?"

## Selecting Your Material

At this point in the preparation stage you should have the material for your speech spread out in front of you. You have now come to what may be the hardest part of the process. The next thing you need to do is to become as familiar as you can with your information. You may find that you have more than you can use. In that case, you will have to select the best and leave the rest for another occasion. Resist the temptation to squeeze it all in if you have too much; you don't want to run the risk of going over your time limit or talking so long that the audience loses interest.

On the other hand, you may discover that you don't have as much information as you thought you did, and you don't have time to gather more. In that case, go with what you have, and keep the speech short. Don't try to pad your material just to fill up the time. The quality of the speech is not determined by its length.

Your next step is going to be to arrange the information in a logical and coherent sequence. This will help you make sure that the ideas you want to include are clear in your mind.

## EXERCISE

Find five Web sites or five sources from the computer access terminal for periodical literature in your college library. Prepare a bibliography of five sources of information pertaining to one of the speech topics suggested in this chapter. In addition, find an example from one or more magazines to illustrate the five forms of support: (1) definition, (2) controlled studies, (3) statistical data, (4) testimonial evidence, and (5) explanation.

## QUESTIONS FOR DISCUSSION AND REVIEW

1. Why do we say that public speaking is a *rhetorical* art rather than a *performing* art?
2. What are the four general speech purposes?

3. What is meant by a *homily?* Where would you expect to hear such an address?
4. What is meant by *expository speech?*
5. What kind of speech might draw on universal values and metaphorical language?
6. Why would you probably not want to say to your audience, "My purpose is to persuade you . . ."?
7. What are the reasons you might want to be cautious about doing your research on the Internet?
8. Why is a database more reliable than a Web page or a blog?
9. What are the indexes that will direct you to articles in professional journals?
10. What is meant by *anecdotal* information?
11. What is meant by *quantitative* information?
12. Why do we say that figures do not speak for themselves?
13. How can you make statistical data more meaningful to the audience?
14. In a court trial, what is meant by *expert testimony?*
15. What is the value of using analogy as a means of support?
16. What are interest grabbers, and what value do they have in a speech?

## PROGRESS MANAGEMENT CHECKLIST

### *How can you tell if you are making progress?*

_____ 1. You will begin thinking of subjects of interest that could be developed into speeches.

_____ 2. You will begin to critique speeches you hear for appropriateness, complexity, significance, and scope.

_____ 3. You will recognize the differences between a speech to inform and one designed to persuade.

_____ 4. You may find yourself being more motivated by inspiring speakers.

_____ 5. You will get bigger laughs at parties when you tell a joke or a funny story.

_____ 6. You will be able to think of key words when you are trying to find information on the Internet.

_____ 7. You will spend more time in the library.

_____ 8. You will learn to recognize when information you find in sources is slanted or distorted.

_____ 9. You will recognize the difference between controlled studies and anecdotal information.

_____ 10. You will begin observing details and become better at relating them verbally.

*Visit the book's Web site at **www.mhhe.com/hasling8** for study tools such as practice quizzes, activities, and Web links.*

# *Organizing and Outlining*

**AFTER READING THIS CHAPTER, YOU SHOULD BE ABLE TO DO THE FOLLOWING:**

- Recognize the importance of making an outline when you prepare a speech; understand the basic structure of a speech outline.

- Prepare an introduction that includes an attention statement, a purpose statement, and a presummary.

- Write main headings for the body of the speech; find a place under each of the main headings for supporting information; know how to include transitions in your speech.

- Plan a conclusion to your speech consisting of a brief summary, a statement that reinforces the thesis, or a relevant quotation.

- Write your outline in finished form; prepare note cards.

*I*nformation has become the principal economic commodity of our social structure. The year that began to happen was 1956, when white-collar workers in technical, managerial, and clerical positions for the first time outnumbered blue-collar workers. Today, most of us in the workforce occupy our time gathering, creating, and distributing information rather than producing goods. Consider the huge quantity of data that is available to us on the World Wide Web, plus all the print material from the time of Johann Gutenberg. Add to that the fact that Americans spend as much money on computers as they do on television sets. There is so much data available to us that the problem becomes one of selecting and sorting material to make it useful.

## THE NEED TO BE ORGANIZED

Don't ever think that people who are well-organized lead boring lives. Actually, the contrary is more likely to be true. They are better able to expand their breadth of knowledge, fill their lives with enriching experiences, and communicate in greater depth than those who move through life at random. The same is true in public address: When you are a well-organized speaker, you are able to gather and assemble interesting examples, hold the attention of the audience, and convey a great deal of information in a short period of time. You also raise your confidence level when you have the sequence of your ideas clearly in mind, because you have less fear of forgetting what you planned to say. The advantage to listeners is that they can easily follow a logically constructed speech and are more inclined to assimilate and retain the information.

### The Value of an Outline

Writing an outline is the most effective means of organizing your material, because you can see the *structure* of what you want to say. Plan on making a rough draft first; you can't expect to get all your ideas down on paper in a neat, well-organized fashion the first time. When you do make your final copy, you may decide it is something you want to keep and use on more than just one occasion.

### The Basic Structure

The outline you develop will be composed of several divisions. Think of them as boxes that you are going to use for the sake of sorting out your material (Figure 6–1). Each box has its own purpose: Use the one labeled "Introduction" for words that will gain the attention of the audience and launch the main purpose of the speech. In each of the boxes labeled "Body," provide a main heading, supporting information, and a transition statement that leads to the next thought. In the box labeled "Conclusion," put material that will summarize or

INTRODUCTION

A Attention statement
B Purpose statement

BODY

I Main heading

A Supporting information
B Supporting information
(Transition)

II Main heading

A Supporting information
B Supporting information
(Transition)

CONCLUSION

A Summary statement
B Reinforcement of thesis

**FIGURE 6–1**   The basic structure of an outline.

reinforce what you want your listeners to remember. Let's look at each of those elements separately.

# THE INTRODUCTION

Think back to what we said earlier about the obstacles to communication. People do not always listen well. One reason they don't is that they often tune in late. They may not hear what the speaker says in the beginning, and they may therefore fail to grasp the central purpose of the message.

## The Attention Statement

You don't want to run the risk of having your listeners think about something else when you are stating your thesis. Therefore, plan something to say that will get their attention. There are several ways you can do this:

**The Humorous Anecdote.**   The *humorous anecdote* is a fairly standard method of getting listeners' attention, because laughter helps to relax both the audience and the speaker. When you get a response from your listeners early in the presentation, you will feel more confident, knowing that you are off to a good start. Make sure, however, that your funny story has a point to it that is related to the purpose of the speech. It's quite possible that your anecdote will not get a laugh. If that happens, you are still all right as long as you can relate the punch line to something you want to say in the speech. It does not need to be a joke like the ones you find on the Internet. As a matter of fact, it's better to use something original if you can. To make the story your own, think of a punch line and then build the situation around it. For example, if I'm giving a speech on cultural differences, I might tell about the Irish cab driver in Belfast who was always getting lost but wouldn't use a GPS because the voice on it had an English accent.

It's not a good idea to make the opening remark too long, because you risk losing the audience's attention. And if the joke is not funny, you have wasted a lot of time. Be cautious about off-color jokes; they may backfire if the audience does not appreciate that kind of humor. And don't tell ethnic or sexist jokes; they could do a great deal of damage to your integrity.

**An Illustrative Anecdote.**    One type of introduction that can be used if you don't want to begin by setting a mood of levity is an *illustrative anecdote*. In all cases, when you relate a story of any kind, plan the way you are going to tell it; think especially of how it should start and how it will end. The impact of all anecdotes, humorous or serious, depends on the phrasing of the punch line or climactic statement. Here's an example, again on the topic of education:

> A young man came into my office recently who had been in my class several years earlier. He had been just an average student when I had him, but he must have improved a lot. He had managed to get his BA degree and was planning to enter graduate school. Of course, he wanted me to know that. We talked philosophically for a while, and at one point he said, "You know, if truth were self-evident, there would be no need for persuasion." I recognized the line because it is my paraphrase of what Aristotle said, and I have used it often. But the student had forgotten that he had learned it in my class. I was pleased, however, because he had made the idea his own.

**A Surprising Fact or Claim.**    Beginning a speech with a *surprising fact* or *claim* is a device that works well, because it creates what might be called the "gee whiz" effect. For example, you might begin a speech on education by saying, "According to the California Department of Education, 60 percent of the students enrolled in public schools in this state are listed as minorities." That fact could also be used as supporting evidence for the claim that the public school curriculum must be adjusted to the needs of a changing student population, and you certainly would want to reaffirm the point later in the speech. But because of its surprising nature, the fact can serve effectively as an attention statement.

**A Rhetorical Question.**   An opening line that you can use when you want to gain the audience's attention before you advance an argument or an assertion is called a *rhetorical question.* For example, you might begin by saying, "Why does the United States—a nation that spends more money on education than any other nation in the world—have such a high rate of illiteracy?" When you pose a rhetorical question you are not asking for a response from the audience, you are leading into what you want to say. Such a question serves as a transition as well as a method of gaining attention.

**A Response Question.**   When you want answers from the audience, you might begin by asking a *response question,* such as "How many of you have lived in this community for more than 10 years?" When you say this, raise your own hand to indicate what it is that you want the people to do. This method is quite effective because the audience members become actively involved, and those who respond help you gain the attention of the others. What's more, you can tell by the show of hands if they are really listening.

**A Reference to the Occasion.**   An easy way to get started is by making a *reference to the occasion.* You can begin by thanking the person who introduced you and letting the audience members know that you are happy to have the opportunity to address them. If the day is a special occasion—an anniversary or the beginning of an event—let people know you are aware of that. If you can make a connection, tie the occasion into the topic of your speech, as in the following example:

> I'm pleased to be here on the occasion of this school's 40th anniversary. It might be interesting to note that some of the students who attended this school when it first opened are now heading up corporations that are making products that weren't even invented when the foundation of this building was poured.

Any of these methods can be used as an attention-getting device. The important thing is for you to give the audience the opportunity to get ready to listen.

## The Purpose Statement

Once you have gained the audience's attention, you can move on to the second phase of the introduction—the *purpose statement.* It is at this point that you provide the audience with orientation to your topic. You let your listeners know where you are going and how you are going to get there. To do that, you should try to phrase your statement so that it is brief, clear, and well qualified.

> *Brief.* You don't want to go into detail right at the outset, because people will think you are beginning your speech in the middle. The body of the speech is the time for you to elaborate on your purpose statement.

> *Clear.* Don't use sentence structure that is too long and complicated. The audience must be able to understand your intent. If the listeners don't understand it, they will lose interest right at the start.

*Well Qualified.* A well-qualified purpose statement means that you tell your listeners how you have limited the subject matter and what you are going to emphasize. Sometimes this is referred to as setting the *parameters* of the topic. Because the purpose statement is so important, let's start at the very beginning, when you are deciding on what the substance of your speech will be.

## Giving Focus to the Subject

Your interest and involvement in a particular activity may be the reason for your being invited to speak. Suppose you have been asked to make a presentation because of the work you have been doing in the public library. It may be that you have training in library science and know a lot about the subject. You have to be careful that you don't go into so much detail that you lose the attention of your audience. On the other hand, you have to be specific enough so that the information you present is fresh, useful, and thought-provoking. Your own experience may be your primary source of information, but you might need to gather more material from published sources. Always use more than just one source, and arrange the material in a way that makes the presentation distinctly your own. As you begin to read and take notes, you may discover that there is a particular aspect of the issue that is especially important; that's when you start to narrow your topic down to a central idea. At this point, you can phrase your purpose statement.

## Phrasing the Purpose Statement

The purpose statement is the keystone of the speech; it lets your audience know what it is that you are going to talk about. If the topic is controversial, it is called a *thesis statement,* and it serves to prepare the listeners for the point of view you want to express. The statement brings the subject area into focus and lets the audience know what limitations you have placed on the topic. Give a lot of consideration to the way you phrase the purpose statement; it is important to the listeners, but it is also important to you. It will help you get a good firm handle on what it is that you intend to say. I suggest that you write the purpose statement on your outline pretty much the way you plan to say it and *keep it in the back of your mind the whole time you are delivering the speech. Everything you say should be related to that purpose statement.* If you follow this guideline, you will be less likely to go off on tangents—that is, into areas that are not related to the central idea of the speech. Here are several ways you can phrase the purpose statement. Notice that each has a different emphasis and suggests a slightly different focus.

- The people of our county are fortunate to have one of the finest library systems in the nation.

- Library services in our county have been severely cut in recent years, and residents of this community must find a way to restore the services that were once provided.
- In the past 10 years we have seen tremendous growth and development in our county, and it's essential that we expand our library facilities in order to keep up with the times.
- Some areas in our county have excellent library facilities, but others need a great deal more help than they are getting.
- Let me explain some of the new services that are now being provided by our local library.

## The Presummary

The purpose statement conveys to the audience the particular aspect of the topic you plan to cover, but you also may need to tell your listeners how the speech is organized and what sequence you will follow as you progress from one point to another. To do that, you add what is called a *presummary*. This is a list of the main ideas that will be contained in the body of the speech:

- Well-used services
- Modern technical facilities
- Friends of the Library

In order for the audience members to listen well, they must be able to recognize the speaker's organizational pattern. The presummary will help them do this. Be sure that the items listed in your presummary follow the same sequence as your main headings. The main headings form the basic skeletal structure of the speech and need to be arranged in a pattern that accomplishes the intent of the purpose statement.

## THE BODY OF THE SPEECH

The body of the speech is the substantive portion of the presentation. It needs to contain main headings and supporting information. Each *main heading* is a generalization that leads the listener into the portion of the speech you want to discuss. The purpose of the main heading is to introduce one section of the speech at a time and lay the groundwork for the more detailed material that follows. The *supporting information* consists of the evidence or examples used by the speaker to elaborate on the thought expressed in the main heading. There is a third element, and that consists of the *transitions* in the speech. These are the phrases that connect one item to another. They are extremely important; however, they do not necessarily need to be written into the outline.

## Main Headings

Writing the main headings is the first step in working out the organizational structure of the speech. There are several things you should note:

- Make sure the main headings are phrased so that they are easily recognized when you deliver the speech. I suggest that you designate them with Roman numerals in the outline.
- Limit the number of main headings to five or six. If you have too many, your speech will become fragmented.
- Remember that the main headings must be directly related to what is said in the thesis or purpose statement of the speech.
- Make the main headings broad enough to cover what you want to say, but not so vague as to be meaningless. Saying "Let me give you some statistics" doesn't tell the audience what you are thinking.
- Don't make your main headings statements of fact; make them generalizations. The factual information comes after you tell the audience your main idea.
- The main headings must follow some sort of logical organizational structure. Using the library topic as an example, here are a few possible patterns.

### The Topical Pattern

Often your material will break down into clearly divided subject areas that form a natural organizational pattern. The subject areas might be the main reasons that support your thesis. The example below could be used when you are giving an informational speech to the people who use the libraries and to the taxpayers who provide the funding.

- The people of our county are fortunate to have one of the finest library systems in the nation.

    I   Its services are well used.
    II  It has modern technical facilities.
    III Friends of the Library has given strong support.

### The Problem–Solution Pattern

It might be that the libraries in your county need help. In this case, the first heading should make the claim that there is a significant problem; the second heading should tell why the problem is there; the third heading should suggest alternatives and possible solutions. This organizational method is called the *problem–solution* pattern.

- Library facilities in our county have been severely cut in recent years and residents of this community must find a way to restore the services that were once provided.

I   Our libraries are not being used.
II  Budget cuts have forced us to reduce our services.
III We need to take measures to restore our facilities.

## The Chronological Pattern

The *chronological* organizational pattern follows a historical progression. Start with the earliest incidents, and proceed to those that are the most current.

- In the past 10 years we have seen tremendous growth and development in our county, and it's essential that we expand our library facilities in order to keep up with the times.

  I   Ten years ago our county launched a campaign to improve our library system.
  II  Five years ago we won a state award for having a high-quality program.
  III Since then we have fallen behind, and today our facilities need a great deal of improvement.

If the focus of your speech is on the solution, you might use the chronological pattern so that it progresses from the first step to the second step to the third step.

I   First, we must set goals for improvement.
II  Next, we must raise the money we need.
III Finally, we must recruit a well-qualified staff.

## The Spatial Pattern

The problem you are describing might differ from one locale to another, in which case you could use the *spatial* pattern for organizing your material. Notice that the example below could also be one that moves from most severe to least severe.

- Some areas in our county have excellent facilities, but others need a great deal more help than they are getting.

  I   Our county libraries are best equipped in the northern area.
  II  Facilities in the western part of the county are average.
  III We need to give more help to the southern section.

When you have settled on the wording of your main headings and the order in which they are to be arranged, you can look at the information you have gathered and see where it fits.

## Supporting Information

Main headings cannot stand alone; they must be supported by items of information. The kind of material you need to elaborate on in your main headings is that which was described in the previous chapter: *Definition of terms, specific instances, statistical data, testimonial evidence,* and *explanation.* Look over the rough notes you have made from the books, periodicals, and other documents that you have used. Your job now is to figure out where each piece fits into your outline. Be sure to write down *all the details that you don't want to commit to memory.* This is an important point, because you are not going to deliver a memorized speech and you are not going to read it word for word. You are going to explain what you want to say in your own words as you do in conversation, but you are going to include more specific details than you usually carry around in your head.

The important thing is that you have your information arranged in a clearly organized sequence so that it makes sense to your audience. Your speech would be a disaster if you were to recite the specifics at random, as they appear in your initial notes. Here is how the items might look in your notes before you begin to sort them out:

- Over 250,000 books.
- 8,000 CD-ROMs, DVDs, audiotapes, and videos.
- Friends of the Library gives strong support.
- Continuous operation since 1902.
- Online computer terminals and printers.
- Enough copies of best-selling novels / Wait less than a month.
- Hosts regular author events.
- 35 percent of residents use library more than 15 times per year.
- Provides homework help programs.
- Visits have risen 20 percent.
- Latest books and most modern technical facilities.
- Open 68 hours per week.
- 33,000 people attended 517 events.
- Foreign-language learning materials.
- Access to ProQuest database.
- Regular storytelling sessions for children.
- Over 900,000 visits last year.
- Residents in some areas wait five months for a best-selling novel from the library.

As you can see, it would make no sense to relate the information in this sequence. Each item must be connected to an appropriate main heading. We'll see how that is done in the sample outline at the end of this chapter.

## Transitions

The organizational structure of your speech is going to be clear to you, because you are the one who planned it, and you can see what it looks like on the outline in front of you. You know that there are divisions in the speech and that each division has a main idea; you also know the point at which you complete one main idea and begin to develop another one. However, this may not be as clear to the audience as it is to you.

In order for the listeners to be able to follow the flow of your organizational structure, you have to provide for them signposts that we call *transitions*. A transition is a phrase that leads the audience to your next idea. For example, you might use a statement such as one of the following:

- "But there are other problems to consider. . . ."
- "Now, in order for us to understand, we need to look at . . . "

As you begin to get more experience in public speaking, you will develop a sense for where transitions need to go. Transitions do not have to be written down in your outline; they are easy enough to extemporize. The main point is to be aware of their importance.

## THE CONCLUSION

When you reach the end of the presentation, you will have to let the audience know you have finished. If you conclude with a piece of specific information such as "in some libraries, residents wait five months for a best-selling novel," the audience is going to look at you with the expectation that you say something more. You can't end a speech that way; you need to pull your ideas together either by summarizing what you have said or by reinforcing your purpose statement. The conclusion is important because it may be the thing that the audience is most likely to remember. As evidence for that claim, let me ask you what you recall from the famous speech of Patrick Henry. I'm sure you are able to remember "Give me liberty or give me death," even if you have forgotten all the rest.

When it comes to the speech you are preparing, remember that you have to *plan* what you are going to say in the conclusion. Don't expect that the right words will come to you in a moment of inspiration. Think about how you are going to end the speech, and write it on the outline pretty much the way you plan to say it.

### The Summary

If your speech is fairly long and contains detailed and complex material, you might want to end with a summary of the general ideas. This is a good practice when it is important that the audience be able to remember what you have said. Be careful, however, that your conclusion does not recapitulate too much of the speech itself.

### Reinforcement of the Thesis

When you have a short speech, it might be a better idea to simply paraphrase your thesis as a means of reinforcing your main idea. Be sure that your conclusion is *consistent* with the thesis. I have heard speakers who have negated the effectiveness of their presentation by using words in the conclusion that seemed to contradict what they said in the body of the speech. It's very important that you have a clear understanding yourself of what it is that you want to reinforce.

## Quotation

An effective way to conclude a speech is to use a quotation. This works well for two reasons: first, because the quote you selected will probably be one that is pithy or clever, or has emotional impact; second, because you are bolstering your own credibility with the words of someone else who supports the point you want to make. As David H. Comins said, "people will accept your ideas more readily if you tell them Benjamin Franklin said it first."

# THE FINISHED OUTLINE

We have examined all the elements of an outline; now let's put it together. This sample outline in the box entitled "A Speech Outline" contains everything that has been described: the attention statement, the purpose statement, the pre-summary, the main headings, the supporting information, and the conclusion.

## The Outline on Note Cards

If there are a lot of facts and figures in your speech—names of people and places, dates, numbers, percentages, amounts, and so on—you probably will want to use note cards. What you put on your note cards will be arranged the same as your outline. However, you might not need to use as many words as you do on your outline, because you will be able to extemporize around the basic information. But you probably want to include each main heading so that you don't take a chance on forgetting any of the important generalizations you want to make. You could, of course, deliver the speech directly from the outline, but sometimes a full sheet of paper is cumbersome and keeps you from having good audience contact. Using 3 by 5 or 6 by 8 note cards works better.

## The Framework of the Speech

It's important that the outline say what you want it to say and that you be familiar with the material. Read all the way through the outline. Then, go over it again and practice extemporizing around the main ideas. Remember that the outline is just a framework, not a complete manuscript. When you deliver the speech, you are going to elaborate on the specific information and use verbal transitions to make it all fit together. As you practice the speech out loud, listen to how the ideas are expressed, and make your own critical evaluation of the organizational structure. If changes are needed, make them in the preparation stage; don't expect to do it spontaneously at the time of delivery. *Plan the speech you want to give, and give the speech you plan.*

# A Speech Outline

### THE PUBLIC LIBRARY: A CONNECTION TO THE WORLD

**Attention statement:** Public libraries are still alive and well. They have not been replaced by café bookstores, the Internet, or cable TV.

**Purpose statement:** We are fortunate to have one of the finest library systems in the state.

- Its services are well used.
- It has modern technical facilities.
- It's strongly supported by Friends of the Library.

I. Tax money was wisely invested because library services are well used.
   A. Continuous operation since 1902.
   B. Open 68 hours per week.
   C. 35 percent of residents use library more than 15 times per year.
   D. Visits have risen by 20 percent.
      1. Over 900,000 last year.
      2. 33,000 people attended 517 events.
II. The library has the latest books and the most modern technical facilities.
   A. Over 250,000 books.
      1. Enough copies of the best-selling novels.
      2. Wait less than a month.
      3. Residents in other towns wait five months.
   B. 8,000 CD-ROMs, DVDs, audiotapes, and videos.
   C. Online computer terminals and printers.
   D. Foreign-language learning materials.
   E. Access to ProQuest database.
III. Friends of the Library has given strong support.
   A. Raises money for new equipment.
   B. Contributes to basic collection and reference materials.
   C. Provides homework help programs.
   D. Sponsors regular storytelling sessions for children.
   E. Hosts author events.

*Conclusion:* Library Director Paula Simpson reminded us in her recent speech that libraries open the door to books and learning for all. They connect their communities with the knowledge and culture of the world.

## EXERCISE

Select any speech from the periodical *Vital Speeches* and analyze its organizational structure by answering the following questions:

- What did the speaker say to gain the audience's attention?
- What did the speaker say to establish the main purpose of the speech?

- What are three main ideas developed in the body of the speech?
- What is the most significant piece of evidence presented by the speaker?
- What did the speaker say in order to bring the speech to a conclusion?

## QUESTIONS FOR DISCUSSION AND REVIEW

1.  What was the significant change in U.S. industry that occurred in 1956?
2.  What are three reasons that good organization is essential in public speaking?
3.  What are the three basic structural elements of a speech outline?
4.  What are the two important functions of the introduction?
5.  What are the attention-getting devices that can be used at the start of the speech?
6.  How does a rhetorical question differ from a response question?
7.  What is a presummary? What is its purpose?
8.  What are you doing when you qualify the purpose statement?
9.  What are you doing when you focus the topic?
10. Why should you keep the purpose statement in the back of your mind while you deliver the speech?
11. What is the function of the main heading in the outline?
12. Name four patterns for organizing the main headings in an outline.
13. What is the conclusion of the speech designed to do?
14. Why is a quotation often a good way to end a speech?

## PROGRESS MANAGEMENT CHECKLIST

### *How can you tell if you are making progress?*

____ 1.  You will find that you are able to accomplish more during the day and have more time to do the things you enjoy.
____ 2.  Letters you write to friends will be easier to start and to finish.
____ 3.  Memos you write at your workplace will be more comprehensible.
____ 4.  What you say in conversations will be more fully developed and articulate.
____ 5.  The stories you tell will have a beginning, a middle, and an end.
____ 6.  Examples you use in writing and speaking will be more coherent.
____ 7.  The conclusions you draw will follow more closely from the observations you make.
____ 8.  You will feel better prepared and more relaxed on the day you are to give your speech.

 *Visit the book's Web site at www.mhhe.com/hasling8 for study tools such as practice quizzes, activities, and Web links.*

# The Speech to Inform

**AFTER READING THIS CHAPTER, YOU SHOULD BE ABLE TO DO THE FOLLOWING:**

- Know how to focus the topic and subject matter of a speech to inform so that it is distinctly your own; understand that a speech to inform is defined by the way it is presented, rather than by the topic.

- Know how to give a speech to inform on a topic that has controversial aspects; to hold the audience's interest while giving information; to give unbiased information on political issues to voters before an election.

- Outline and deliver a short announcement.

- Be aware of the speaking opportunities in business; know how to prepare for a job as a training specialist; be able to participate effectively in a group discussion; know what you have to do to make an informative presentation to a decision-making group.

*A*s members of the audience we have certain expectations when we go to hear someone speak. If we visit a courtroom and listen to lawyers pleading their case, we expect to hear persuasive speaking; when we go to church and see the preacher in the pulpit, we expect that he or she will be delivering a motivating sermon to inspire us to become better people; when we are at a dinner show, we expect to be entertained by a comedian. We don't want to hear a sermon at a comedy club or a string of jokes in the closing arguments of a court trial. Expectations also apply when we attend a lecture on an academic topic. We are not there to be persuaded, inspired, or amused—we are there to be informed. It's true that the speech may contain brief expressions of each of those three elements, but none of them should dominate over the primary purpose of conveying information. If the audience comes to hear a speech to inform, that's the kind of speech you should give. It may be more fun to do a comedy routine, and more exciting to debate a controversial issue, but you are not in front of an audience to meet your own needs; you are there to meet the needs and the expectations of the listeners.

## THE QUALITIES OF EXPOSITION

As we noted in Chapter 5, a speech to inform is sometimes referred to as an *expository* speech, because it deals with the *exposition* of information rather than the *interpretation* of it. The essential qualities are fairness and objectivity—speakers must not favor one side over another, and they must not be subjective in their evaluation. A speech to inform can be given on a controversial topic, but it must be done with thoughtful consideration to questions that are disputable. If you select such a topic, be sure to examine your own motives. Are you willing to take a neutral position and trust the listeners to make their own decisions on the basis of the information that you provide? You will have to bring into the speech evidence that supports each side of the issue and present all of it with equal emphasis. You must not indicate with your words or with the tone of your voice that one contention carries more weight than another.

### The Focus Makes It Your Own

You don't have to feel that you must be an expert in a given field or have scholarly knowledge in order to deliver a speech to inform. If you know enough about the subject matter to converse intelligently and if you understand the vocabulary and terminology, you should be able to make a respectable and competent presentation. What's more, it's not necessary for you to have all the information committed to memory; your statistics and specific examples can be written on note cards. It's quite possible that some people in the audience may know more about your subject than you do. Don't let that shake your confidence. This is your speech, not theirs. The focus you give to the material is what makes it distinctly your own. People who are truly experts might be able

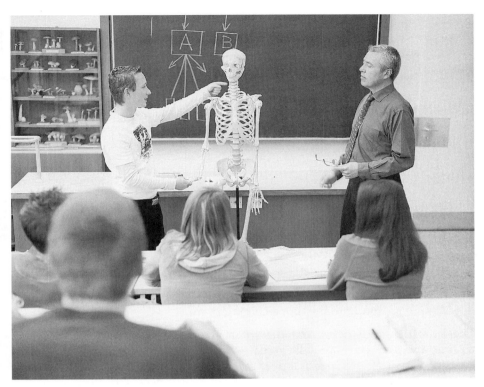

*If you can explain something in a way that others are able to understand, you can perform a valuable service.*

to present more facts, but that doesn't mean that their speeches would be better than yours. If you can explain something in a way that others are able to understand, you can perform a service that may be more valuable than that of a genius who can't communicate.

## Being Familiar with Your Subject

Speaking to a group can be intimidating, especially when you know there are high-status people in the audience. You may never be as smart as they are, but what you can do is tell them something they don't know. One of the first public speaking experiences I can remember occurred when I was 13 years old and a member of a Boy Scout troop in Berkeley, California. The occasion was our annual dinner, and I was scheduled to do a slide show presentation. I learned, to my dismay, that in the audience was the man who designed and built the first cyclotron and nuclear reactor—Dr. Ernest Lawrence. Fortunately, my topic had nothing to do with atomic science; I was talking about our summer camp in the Sierra. Even though Dr. Lawrence was perhaps one of the smartest people in the country, I like to think that I was the one who taught him how to pack a donkey and tie a diamond hitch. My point is that you can be an expert even to the best-informed people if you pick a subject that is familiar to you but new to your audience.

## Speaking Opportunities

In real-life situations (as opposed to classroom settings), there probably will be more opportunities for you to give a speech to inform than there will be for you to give a speech to persuade, entertain, or inspire an audience. Let's look at a few examples:

- Explaining the features of a new product to a company's sales representatives.
- Reporting to members of an organization what happened on a field trip.
- Giving information to a board of directors that has to make a decision.
- Outlining a new policy or procedure to fellow workers.
- Presenting the findings of a special committee or task force.
- Teaching new employees how to operate equipment they will need to use.
- Making an announcement of a coming event.

These are the kinds of presentations that you are very likely to be called on to give, and a speech class will prepare you for the experience. Notice that, in most of the situations listed above, the information could probably be communicated by a written directive or memo. Why is it necessary to make an oral presentation?

For one thing, you can see the faces of the people who are being exposed to your message. You may not know for sure that they are listening, but you know that the information was expressed in their presence. A written memo, on the other hand, might be ignored.

Another reason is that the oral presentation allows listeners to ask questions—something that is not easily done when the message is written.

Finally, the oral message can be more emphatic. The speaker can place emphasis on key points, and the writer has less chance to do that.

## Topics for a Speech to Inform

The topic you pick for a speech to inform might pertain to something that you have experienced directly, or it could be one that requires some research. Look at a few example titles:

- Cross-Country Travel on a Mountain Bike
- The Potential of Electric Automobiles
- Making Movies with a Digital Camera

- Animal Life in Our Local Nature Areas
- The Culture of the Navajos

These are all good subject areas—as long as you can be objective about them. That means you have to set aside your personal biases and opinions and just stick to the facts. If you identify a controversy within the topic and begin interpreting your information to support a point of view, you are treading into the area of persuasion. This leads us to an important observation: *A speech to inform is defined more by the way it is presented than by the topic itself.*

Any subject can be made into a speech to persuade or a speech to inform, depending on the way the information is presented. A speech with the title "Cross-Country Travel on a Mountain Bike" certainly seems to be noncontroversial, and it is—unless the speaker suggests that bikers should be given the right-of-way over hikers. "The Potential of Electric Automobiles" appears to be safe enough—unless the speaker begins to criticize federal standards and quotas imposed on car manufacturers. What about "The Culture of the Navajos"? That sounds all right, too, so long as the speaker does not dwell on unflattering characteristics of the tribe. It probably is impossible for the speaker not to have a bias, but the speech can still be regarded as informative in nature if the subject matter is treated fairly and objectively.

## TAKING A NEUTRAL POSITION

Consider issues such as capital punishment, welfare, birth control, national health care, assault weapons, or drug testing. It would be hard not to have an opinion on these questions, and they would all make good topics for persuasive speeches. But if you are able to remain neutral, you could make any of them into a speech to inform. The variable that makes the most difference is the way you phrase your purpose statement. You would not begin an informative speech by making the claim that the death penalty has a history of preventing violent crime. However, you might say in your purpose statement that you want to clarify the federal and state court rulings made in the past two decades that pertain to capital punishment.

In addition to the phrasing of the purpose statement, there are other factors that will determine whether the speech is to be classified as informative or as persuasive.

- *The balance of evidence.* You are being persuasive if you have more evidence or stronger evidence on one side than you do on the other.
- *The objectivity of sources.* You are tilting the scales in favor of one side if you get most of your information from sources that have an intentional bias.
- *The language you use.* Your speech will not be regarded as truly expository if you treat one side of the issue with sarcasm or contempt.

## Priming the Audience's Interest

To say that you must take a neutral position when delivering a speech to inform is not to say that enthusiasm is unimportant. You must prime the audience's interest in what you are saying, and to do that you need to project excitement and commitment. For the speech to be successful, the audience must believe that you regard the subject matter as worth an investment of time and effort. If you really believe your material is important, you will want your listeners to pay attention and try to retain the information you are giving them. Don't imitate the boring lecturer who drones on and on as though there were no one else in the room. And, conversely, don't be in such a hurry to get through your speech that you leave the audience behind. To be really effective, you must be aware of how the audience is receiving the message. Pace your speech so that you hold the listeners' attention, and give them a chance to digest what you say. Be pleased if audience members ask questions afterward because it means they are interested in your subject.

## Helping to Inform the Voter

Every time there is an election, our mailboxes fill up with literature advising us how to vote. There is so much information in newspapers and magazines that we can't absorb it all. Sometimes we don't read as thoroughly as we should in order to be well-informed; then, a few days before the election, we quickly try to catch up on the background of the candidates and issues. What we discover is that almost everything we read or hear has a point of view. The flyers in the mail, the radio and television announcements, the columns and editorials in the newspaper—all try to give an interpretation of events that will lead us to the conclusions that the advocates want us to draw.

Speakers who can uncover information on candidates and ballot measures, and then make clear and unbiased presentations at election time, perform a valuable service for electorates. One group that is noted for its efforts to do this is the League of Women Voters (LWV). The LWV sponsored the first presidential debates on television, and, over the years, it has acquired a well-earned reputation for fairness. The LWV has local chapters in many communities. Organizations that wish to have speakers talk to small groups can contact these chapters. Their mission is to see that voters make informed choices when they go to the polls.

## Instant Speech

Organizing and outlining a short speech to inform is something you can learn to do quickly in your head. It might be referred to as "Instant Speech." It's something you may be called upon to do when you attend a meeting for the first time, and it could happen quite unexpectedly. The chairperson starts the procedure by asking the new members to introduce themselves. She might say, "Please stand and tell us who you are, where you're from, what you do, and how you happened to come to this meeting." Notice she has given you your organizational structure and even your main headings—Who, Where, What, How. All you have to do is fill in the details.

On other occasions your opportunity to speak at a meeting might require that you instantly create your own organizational structure. Suppose you are attending a meeting of the World Affairs Council discussing the Middle East issue. You have an opportunity to announce an important speaker coming to your church. Follow the same pattern but arrange the headings to your specific purpose:

**Attention statement:** I'd like to make an announcement.

1. Who:     Father Ilias Chacour, a Palestinian Catholic Priest who has been nominated three times for the Nobel Peace Prize . . .

2. What:     . . . is going to be speaking about his efforts in northern Israel to build schools attended by Christians, Muslims, and Jews.

3. When:     The program starts at 7 p.m. on Sunday, April 18 . . .

4. Where:     . . . in the sanctuary of the Presbyterian church.

Conclusion: I hope you can all come.

A message like this can be delivered without notes and without any advance preparation, as long as you have the information clearly in mind. But you do have to think about the way you are going to organize what you want to say. Many times I've heard announcements of this sort given when essential information was left out, or too much unnecessary verbiage confused the issue.

Delivering a short speech to inform is a good way to begin practicing your public speaking skills. After you develop more confidence, you might want to take the procedure to the next level. Sometime before the meeting, ask the chairperson if you can be on the agenda and be called upon to make a longer presentation—maybe five minutes or so. You'll probably need to prepare a few notes or an outline so you can elaborate in more detail. Good organization helps listeners fit the information into their thinking and retain what you have told them. It also contributes to gaining their favor, because it lets them know you put some effort into the presentation.

A speech to inform could be a full 50-minute lecture that you might hear in a college classroom, or it could be a 3-minute announcement made at a business meeting. The length is not what determines the purpose. Sometimes students will gather too much information and try to squeeze it all into one speech. A better idea is to be selective, so that the points you make have greater impact.

## Speaking in the Business World

Sometimes students ask me, "How am I going to use the skills I learn in this class? Is it likely that I will ever be asked to give a speech?" My answer is that there are indeed opportunities for those who are willing. You don't have to be in one of the "high-profile" professions—there are many people who prepare and deliver speeches every day as part of their work. Classroom teachers do this, of course, but there are also an increasing number of business and professional people who are regularly called on to make presentations.

### Training Specialist

In this age of technology, companies that sell computer software and highly specialized electronic equipment must do more than simply provide their customers with a user's manual. If the equipment is extremely complex and highly specialized, companies often need to hire professional people to give lectures and demonstrations to the users as part of the sales package. When a library purchases and installs a new retrieval system, for example, all of the personnel who use the equipment and teach others to do so would need a training program to learn about its operation and capabilities. The supplier of the product would send someone who can speak well to do this kind of instruction. Such a person can be called a *training specialist* and may work full-time at developing course material and making presentations. This may be one of the best examples of a practical application of the speech to inform. The specialist would prepare for a lecture in the same way that you do for a class assignment. He or she would consider the following questions:

- What do the customers already know, and what new information do they need?
- How much information can I give in the time that is available?
- What is the best way I can organize the material?
- How can I help them understand and retain the information?
- What handouts will I need to give them?
- What sort of graphics and visual aids should I prepare?
- What questions will they ask, and what are the best answers I can give?

If it is a high-tech item you are going to be explaining, you will need to have some technical background in addition to teaching skills. That doesn't necessarily mean that you have to start out being an expert on a particular product, but you must have enough education in the field so that you can learn what you need to know. Large companies or consortiums hold workshops and seminars to teach training specialists how to conduct classes and make presentations.

## Speaking to a Committee

Learning how to function effectively as a member of a discussion or decision-making group is an area of speech communication that is different from public speaking; however, there are certain elements of similarity. Normally, you do not need to make the same kind of preparation for a committee meeting as you do when you are going to be a principal speaker, but there might be occasions when you have very specific ideas you want to contribute. Rather than relying on your ability to speak in an impromptu fashion, make a few notes beforehand. By doing that, you will be sure to include all the details that you want the other members to know. There are some differences, of course, between group discussion and public speaking. One is that in the former situation, you will do your speaking sitting down rather than standing up. That has both advantages and disadvantages. The advantage is that you may feel less nervous; the disadvantage is that other members of the committee will probably interrupt you from time to time with their own comments, and that may throw you off stride. There's an observation that we can make here about nonverbal communication: If you stand when you speak, you are saying nonverbally, "I have the floor and I expect to be heard all the way through before you respond." Sitting down says, "We are communicating on an equal basis, and I invite you to speak if you want to comment on what I am saying."

There is another important difference between public speaking and group discussion: Public speaking is an individual endeavor in which you arrive at a conclusion that is based on your own thought and research; you then defend the position you have taken with the best evidence and reasoning you can produce. Group discussion is thought in process. That means you come to the meeting with a tentative idea, but you know that your conclusion is subject to change on the basis of the input you receive from other members of the committee. You may prepare your presentation in the same way you prepare for a public speech, but you may have to modify your position after you hear what others suggest.

## The Informative Presentation

The complexity of our society places a heavy burden on committees and individuals who have authority in a broad area of responsibility and who need to make policy decisions based on specific information. When neither the chairperson nor the members of the committee feel that they have the expertise to make such a decision, a specialist may be called in to provide the information that is needed. You may be the person chosen to make a presentation that serves this purpose, not necessarily because of your skill in public speaking, but because of your knowledge of the subject matter.

Although your presentation may be essentially informative, you might be asked to make a recommendation. Be prepared to do so, but remember that ultimately it is the committee's decision and not your own. Your job is to tell your listeners what they need to know to make an informed choice; therefore, give them a complete picture, and don't gloss over the obstacles.

Let's say, for example, that you are employed by a company that has been contracting out its printing jobs and now it is considering producing its own brochures and flyers using an in-house operation. Assume that you have had some experience in this field and have been asked to describe the feasibility of purchasing printing equipment and hiring personnel to operate a shop to do this work. You would have to take into consideration the capital investment, office space that would be needed, and the impact that hiring new employees would have on the company's budget. You would need to know what volume of work there would be and the quality that the company expects. Let's further assume that you have been given a limited amount of time to make your presentation and that you will be talking to a group of busy and high-paid executives.

*Plan your strategy.* Talk with people beforehand who understand the goals of the company and the standards of quality that are expected. Learn as much as you can about the equipment you would need to buy, the cost of its operation and maintenance, and its dependability. Also be prepared to explain what operating skills the personnel would need and what the hourly wage would be for people who do this kind of work.

*Find out the group's level of understanding.* Determine how much members of the committee already know and how much they need to know. It is necessary for them to have a clear comprehension of cost and quality, but they do not need to know the details of operation.

*Put together a set of visual aids.* The impact of your presentation will be enhanced if you use visual aids. Let the audience see samples of the quality of work that could be produced. If there is going to be an additional cost in order to obtain better quality, the members of the committee will have to weigh that differential. They must be able to see what the finished product will look like in order to make a judgment.

*Have your specific data available in printed form.* You can display the figures on a computer screen, a flip chart, or an overhead projector, or you can give each person a handout sheet. The members of the committee may need to have time to think about what you will tell them, and quantitative information is difficult to retain if it is presented only by the spoken word. Before the meeting adjourns, be sure you know what further service is expected of you.

# The Hundredth Monkey

Sometimes you may feel as though there is nothing you can say that will have any effect on what people do or what they believe. If you have a concern for social issues, you may get discouraged when you read about government policies that seem to ignore human needs, business ventures that perpetuate greed and corruption, or industrial practices that pollute the environment. But before you become resigned to accepting what appears to be the inevitable, consider the notion that Ken Keyes Jr. advanced in a book called *The Hundredth Monkey*. He describes a study made of a Japanese monkey that had been observed in the wild on the island of Koshima for a period of 30 years. The study began in 1952, when scientists began dropping sweet potatoes into the sand on the island to add to the monkeys' diet. The monkeys liked the potatoes, but didn't like the taste of the dirt on them. One monkey solved the problem by learning to wash the potato in a stream. A few other monkeys picked up this practice, but after several years the scientists observed that there were still a great many monkeys who had not learned the trick. Keyes relates:

> Then something took place. In the autumn of 1958, a certain number of Koshima monkeys were washing sweet potatoes—the exact number is not known. Let us suppose that when the sun rose one morning, there were 99 monkeys on Koshima Island who had learned to wash their sweet potatoes. Let's further assume that later that morning the hundredth monkey learned to wash sweet potatoes. Then it happened. By that evening almost everyone in the tribe was washing sweet potatoes before eating them. That added energy of this hundredth monkey somehow created an ideological breakthrough.*

You never know when you might be the person who provides insight to the "hundredth monkey" by saying the right thing at the right time. If there is validity to the theory that Ken Keyes proposes, and if it does indeed apply to human behavior, your efforts to make constructive social changes by sharing your thoughts and ideas can make an important difference.

*Ken Keyes Jr., *The Hundredth Monkey* (Coos Bay, OR: Vision Books, 1982), pp. 11–15.

## EXERCISE

Select a topic similar to one that is mentioned in this chapter and develop an instant speech to inform. Check to see that it discusses only one point by examining the evidence you have gathered and by seeing that it all fits logically under one main heading. Even though the body of the speech is short, there should still be an introduction, a purpose statement, and a conclusion. Deliver the speech in three minutes or less.

## QUESTIONS FOR DISCUSSION AND REVIEW

1. How does a speech to inform differ in purpose from other types of speeches?
2. Why is presenting information orally more effective than writing a directive or a memo?
3. Why is a speech to inform sometimes called an *expository speech?*
4. How can a speech to inform be defined other than by the topic?
5. Can a speech to inform be given on a controversial topic?
6. What function is performed by the League of Women Voters?
7. What opportunities are there for giving speeches in the business world?
8. What questions should a training specialist consider in preparing for a presentation?
9. Under what circumstances might you prepare notes for yourself before participating in a committee meeting?
10. How does speaking at a committee meeting differ from making a regular, "stand-up" presentation?

## PROGRESS MANAGEMENT CHECKLIST

*How can you tell if you are making progress?*

____ 1. You will develop an appreciation for people who are able to present information without giving it an argumentative slant.
____ 2. You will be able to avoid an antagonistic response when you give information on a controversial topic to someone whose opinion is different from yours.
____ 3. You will be willing to modify your position if someone has information that causes you to reevaluate your thinking.
____ 4. You will not hesitate to speak up at a committee meeting and will be able to organize your thoughts on the spur of the moment if necessary.
____ 5. You will take the time to prepare if you're on the agenda for an extended talk.
____ 6. You will find yourself being called on to make announcements and give explanations.
____ 7. You will begin developing and projecting enthusiasm for subjects that interest you.
____ 8. You will be able to stay focused even when someone asks you a hard question.

 *Visit the book's Web site at www.mhhe.com/hasling8 for study tools such as practice quizzes, activities, and Web links.*

# CHAPTER 8

# *Thinking and Reasoning*

**AFTER READING THIS CHAPTER, YOU SHOULD BE ABLE TO DO THE FOLLOWING:**

- Give serious thought to social issues, and examine what you believe to be true; test for accuracy what you read and hear; be aware of what you need to know in order to draw rational conclusions.

- Tell if a piece of evidence is a *sign* of something or a *cause;* be able to reach a conclusion through the *inductive* process.

- Reach a conclusion through the *deductive* process by using a syllogism; understand how syllogisms can be used in rules of law; construct a *prima facie* case.

- Develop a framework for problem solving by defining and analyzing a problem, establishing criteria, considering alternatives, and selecting the best solution.

*P*resentations that are of real value to an audience are not the clever platitudes of a glib stage personality, but the intelligent deliberations of a person who is well-informed and has a sincere commitment to the topic and to the interests of the listeners. Becoming an effective speaker requires that you develop your ability to recognize the significance of the information you hear and read, interpret its meaning, file it away in your mind, and retrieve it when you need it. The most effective speakers are those who have a good grasp of their own beliefs. They are well-informed and are able to organize their thoughts when the occasion demands. As you acquire the skills of public address, you will also be training your mind to *think critically.* You will learn to approach problems in a logical fashion, evaluate your data, correct for error, and avoid jumping to irrational conclusions. These are important capabilities for you to refine because ideas must make sense to you before you are able to express them persuasively to anyone else.

## CRITICAL THINKING

The term *critical thinking* refers to our ability to go beyond mere rote learning. Formal education is often faulted for teaching facts without regard for developing the student's capacity to analyze, interpret, challenge, and see the implications and consequences of the data. If we are going to be able to write and speak intelligently, we must be able to think critically. Richard Paul sees this as being an essential part of our education:

> What we say or write . . . is only a small portion of the thinking process—the proverbial tip of the iceberg. Surrounding any line of thought is a large substructure of *background thought,* logical connections not lying on the surface of reasoning, but prior to it, underlying it, or implied by it. In the background of all thinking are foundational concepts, assumptions, values, purposes, experiences, implications, and consequences—all embedded in lines of thought radiating outward in every direction.[1]

What this theory implies is that the roots of public speaking go deep into the cerebral processes, and in order to make substantive changes in your rhetorical skills you must learn more than methods and techniques.

### Selective Learning

First of all, we must understand that we apply a selection process to the substance of our learning. Because we cannot possibly assimilate all the information that we are exposed to, we must open our minds to that which seems to be useful to us and filter out what we don't need. Even data we have mentally processed are not always retrievable, so we are limited to what we can recall or

---

[1]Richard Paul, *Critical Thinking* (Rohnert Park, CA: Center for Critical Thinking and Moral Critique, Sonoma State University, 1990), p. 70.

rediscover through experience or research. We can expect that our information is always going to be incomplete; what we would like to know may be unavailable to us, or it may not yet be discovered by science. No matter how hard we try, we will never know it all. Nevertheless, we must make evaluations and judgments based on the best information that we have.

## Examining Beliefs

By the time you become an adult, your brain contains an abundance of information; some of it is accurate, and some is inaccurate. That which you believe to be true is what you call "reality," but it may be simply a belief pattern and not resemble the real world at all. For example, the "reality" of a man who believes that women biologically are not capable of understanding principles of finance is quite different from the "reality" of a woman who knows she has a talent for such work. Even though facts and evidence do not support his conclusion, the man will be inclined to act on what he believes to be true. Because reality forms the basis of our behavior, such a man would probably not hire a woman to be his budget director, regardless of what qualifications she may have. Thinking critically means we can learn to avoid making these kinds of irrational mistakes that adversely affect our lives and the lives of those around us.

### Direct Experience

Some of our information comes to us by direct experience. We perceive it through one or more of our five senses—hearing, seeing, touching, tasting, and smelling. Knowledge that we acquire through personal experience has more impact on us than does what we learn indirectly. It is also more apt to affect our thinking and will be retained for a longer period of time. For example, being in an automobile accident would surely have a profound effect on the way you think about traffic safety. Being witness to an accident also makes a strong impression. Other forms of learning, such as seeing a film, hearing a lecture, or reading an account, may to some degree influence your thinking, but not nearly as much as the direct experience will.

### Influence of Other People

Although direct experience may be the most powerful form of learning, it is not always possible, necessary, or even desirable to acquire knowledge firsthand. A great deal of what we believe to be true comes about as a result of information we receive from other people. As small children, we learn from parents, siblings, other relatives—even eccentric relatives—and peers; later in life we also learn from books, from teachers, and from the mass media. Because our information comes to us from such a variety of sources, we can assume that a certain portion of it will be inaccurate, biased, or misleading. The quality we call *wisdom* depends to a large extent on our ability to perceive the difference between information that is valid and that which is faulty.

## Testing What You Hear and Read

Some reports you hear and read in the mass media are more reliable than others, and if you are to base your beliefs on what appears in newspapers, on television, and online, you must have some way of knowing whether or not you can trust the source. The validity of material that is printed, broadcast, or published electronically can be tested by asking the following questions:

1. Is the source reputable? Has other information from the same source been found to be accurate?
2. Does the source have any obvious bias? Is it financed by an organization in support of one side or another of an issue?
3. Has the source provided complete information, or have important data been left out? Have quotations been taken out of context? Would the rest of the context change the meaning?
4. Has the source given the most current information? Have later events changed the circumstances?
5. Does the information meet the test of reason, or are there internal inconsistencies? Does the information contradict something else you know to be true?
6. Do other sources corroborate the information? If so, are those other sources reliable? Are there reasons that one source would possess facts others do not have?
7. Is the language of the source objective? Does the information contain emotionally loaded terminology designed solely for the purpose of arousing fear or hatred? Is the source attempting to discredit a person or a cause with diatribe rather than reason?

Be suspicious of sources that do not meet these criteria. If you are not sure that the information is accurate, seek verification. If you find that you have been misinformed and have arrived at conclusions based on erroneous data, don't hesitate to make corrections in your thinking.

## Learning What You Need to Know

By itself, memorizing words, theories, and facts is not a path that leads to critical thought. However, you cannot test data and draw conclusions unless you have a foundation of knowledge to use as a starting point. You can argue that there is no need to learn a lot of big words and commit facts to memory, as long as you know where to find the information when you need it. That's true to a certain extent; however, unless you have some fundamental background, you will be unable to determine which specific words, theories, or evidence you need to investigate or uncover.

### Vocabulary

Words and their definitions are important, not just for the sake of expressing ideas, but for thinking about them. For example, the word *xenophobic* means "fearful of strangers," but the implications of the word go beyond its literal translation. The term does not make reference to people who run away from someone they don't know; it refers to those who feel threatened by people of different cultures who move into their neighborhood. Knowing the terminology not only helps us to understand the concept, but also opens up possibilities for talking about things such as cultural diversity and immigration. Memorizing words and definitions out of a dictionary certainly does not contribute to our capacity for critical thought, but reflecting on their meaning and implications will expand the horizons of our thinking. Words have limited value unless they are used in context. We must learn to recognize the significance of their meaning in relationship to other words.

### Literary and Historical References

Communicating effectively requires more than just having a broad vocabulary and knowing the meaning of a lot of words. It is also incumbent upon a speaker to be familiar with the historical and literary references that are common to the culture. Words, including names of people, places, and things, take on new meaning when they are used symbolically rather than literally. By the same token, historical references often convey a broader meaning than the actual event when they are applied as a metaphor. For example, reference to someone's "Achilles' heel" means that the person has a vulnerable spot, as did the Greek hero. When people meet their "Waterloo" they have been defeated, as Napoleon was in his famous battle. Richard Lederer quotes Max Müller as saying, "Language is the Rubicon that divides man from beast."[2]

## Interpreting Information and Drawing Conclusions

Educators continually strive to find the most effective mix of pedagogical methods that will stimulate the critical thinking process. Do students need to learn facts? Certainly they do; otherwise, they will believe that everything is simply a matter of opinion. Do they need to learn how to interpret information and draw conclusions? Absolutely. If our schools rely totally on rote learning, they are engaged in a conditioning process rather than education.

Thinking critically is difficult and is frequently rejected in favor of easier and less taxing methods of reaching conclusions. All too often people rely on platitudes or simplistic slogans—a thought process that might be called "bumper sticker mentality." This is a term that refers to applying some cleverly phrased statement to a situation without analyzing the meaning of the words or their validity in a given application. The man in the earlier example who had a fixed belief about women and the principles of finance may have drawn his conclusion

[2]Richard Lederer, *Word Wizard* (New York: St. Martin's Griffin, 2006), p. 39.

*"Bumper sticker mentality" leads to simplistic conclusions.*

from the saying "A woman's place is in the home." Such a statement is not based on evidence or reason but on mindless repetition. The problem is that we tend to listen to people without making a critical evaluation of what we hear.

## THE INDUCTIVE PROCESS

One way we can arrive at a reasoned conclusion is by using a method called the *inductive process.* This method is similar to the *scientific method,* in that conclusions are deferred until the evidence has been gathered. The process starts with the formation of a *hypothesis.* That means you make a guess about what the conclusion might be, but you do not rely on it until you have examined the data. For example, the man who believed that women were not capable of comprehending principles of finance might have reached a different conclusion if he had first considered the facts:

1. Standardized tests indicate that women score just as high as men on instruments that measure quantitative reasoning.
2. Colleges and universities report no difference in grade point averages between men and women in classes dealing with financial matters.
3. Women who have pursued careers in finance have proved to be equal to men in every respect.

All these facts conflict with the hypothesis; consequently, the man mentioned earlier would have had to alter his conclusion and acknowledge that a woman could be just as good a budget director as a man could be. When you follow this procedure, you are using the inductive method of reasoning—allowing the evidence to lead you to a conclusion rather than accepting a notion because of previous beliefs.

The scientific method works in the same way. When a study is conducted, researchers set up a series of experiments, being careful to control the variable factors. Let's say the research involves the effects of the omission of a particular nutrient in the diet of laboratory rats. The researchers will then make alterations in the conditions by varying the diet of the rats. After observing the results, they will form a hypothesis and conduct the study again. If the same results occur each time the experiment is performed, and if the researchers are able to predict each time what the outcome will be, they are able to say that the study has *reliability*. If the results are consistent with the results of other studies of the same nature, a conclusion can be drawn that there is a cause-and-effect relationship between the variable and the result.

## Signs and Causes

All too frequently we draw conclusions on the basis of insufficient evidence. If several of our friends were to lose their jobs, for example, we might be tempted to say that the country is in a recession. Certainly, the loss of a few jobs is not sufficient reason to form a generalization. If we were to look at nationwide statistics, however, we might get a more valid indication. When unemployment figures climb to 6 or 7 percent, we might be able to say, with greater confidence, that a recession is occurring, but still we would be basing our conclusion on just one index. There is other evidence we need to support a declaration concerning the economic health of the nation. We would look at the gross domestic product, the balance of trade, and perhaps the number of new housing construction starts. If all the evidence were consistent with our hypothesis, we might be able to see a pattern. Even then, we would need to recognize that in a subject area as complex as the economic condition of the nation, the claims we make are going to be based on subjective values as well as quantitative evidence.

Data we use to form a belief that a problem exists are called *signs*. We must be careful not to confuse signs with *causes*. Sometimes the language we use distorts the logical progression of our thoughts. For example, we might say, "The nation is in a recession, because the unemployment rate has risen to 7 percent." We don't mean that the high unemployment rate has *caused* the recession; we mean that the 7 percent rate is a *sign* that a recession exists. It is for this reason that we need to study the use of language simultaneously with examining the processes we use in interpreting data and forming conclusions. We must be able to speak clearly and logically to ourselves as well as to others.

# THE DEDUCTIVE PROCESS

When we are reasoning through the inductive process, we don't begin with a premise or a generalization; we begin with specific evidence and then follow it to see where it leads. This is why we say that inductive reasoning proceeds from specific information to a general conclusion. When we reason *deductively,* we start with a general principle that we believe to be true and apply it to a particular situation. You may read, for example, a story in which Sherlock Holmes notices a bit of red mud on the boot of a suspect and concludes that the person has been walking through the moors. That's when Dr. Watson says, "Brilliant deduction, Holmes." The master detective is using what we call *syllogistic* reasoning, which is constructed in the following manner:

Red mud can only be picked up on a boot by walking through the moors.

That man has red mud on his boot.

That man has been walking through the moors.

Holmes would probably reply, "Elementary, my dear Watson." Indeed, it does appear to be elementary; however, it is the *method* of reasoning that we want to examine.

A *syllogism* is a rhetorical device that can be used to analyze the validity of a conclusion. We won't go too deeply into the rules for syllogisms, because they can get very complex; all we need at this time is to have a basic understanding of the theory behind them. A *categorical* syllogism has three parts:

1. A major premise that must be accepted as an unqualified truth.
2. A minor premise that is a specific case governed by the major premise.
3. A conclusion.

The classic example is as follows:

1. All men are mortal. (Major premise)
2. John is a man. (Minor premise)
3. John is mortal. (Conclusion)

If the major premise is true, and if the minor premise is governed by it, the conclusion must *necessarily* be accepted as true. Be sure to note, however, that both the major premise and the minor premise are subject to refutation. If you wanted to reject a conclusion drawn from syllogistic reasoning, you would have to demonstrate either that the major premise was not true or that the minor premise was not governed by it. To challenge Sherlock Holmes's reasoning, for example, you might argue that red mud could be picked up somewhere other than on the moors or that the boots had been worn by some other person.

It's not just in detective work that we find applications for syllogistic reasoning. The syllogism is a rhetorical tool that can be used whenever you want to argue that a specific example is or should be included in the category of a major premise. It can become a way of making the social system work for you, as shown below:

1. All children are entitled to an education.

2. Jane is a child.

3. Jane is entitled to an education.

As long as there are no exceptions to the major premise that all children are entitled to an education, and as long as Jane is included in the category of all children (minor premise), the conclusion must logically be accepted.

The *rule of law* provides for us another example of where syllogistic reasoning can be applied. In this country we say that all people are "equal under the law." That means that everyone is entitled to *due process* of the law; it also means that the *penalties* for violation of the law must be applied equally. The law, then, can be used as the major premise in a syllogism:

1. All persons using a gun in committing a crime must go to jail.

2. The defendant used a gun in holding up a liquor store.

3. The defendant must go to jail.

This example leads us to an important principle of our social structure. If we are to have a fair system of justice, the rules of law must be based on reason rather than on the inclination of judges. In this country we say that a person is innocent until proven guilty and that the burden of proof is on the prosecutor rather than on the defendant. Even before a case is allowed to come to trial, the district attorney must be able to satisfy a judge that there is evidence against the person charged. Then, the prosecutor must be able to present a prima facie case in order to get a conviction.

A *prima facie case* is one that is inherently complete at its face value. It is constructed in such a way that the conclusion must necessarily be accepted unless one or more of the major contentions is rejected. Normally, the prosecuting attorney would begin the trial by presenting to the jury an outline of the case that the state has against the defendant. If the charge were armed robbery, for example, the following claims would have to be proved:

- That a robbery was committed.

- That the defendant was the one who committed the robbery.

- That the defendant carried a weapon at the time of the robbery.

The next step would be for the prosecutor to support all three of those claims with evidence. If the jury members believed all of them to be true, they would have to return a verdict of guilty. And if the law were to be upheld, the defendant would have to go to jail. In order to discredit the case, the defense attorney would have to successfully refute the evidence that supports one or more of the main contentions.

As you can see, there is a similarity between the prima facie case and the syllogism. In both circumstances the conclusion must necessarily be accepted unless the opposition is successful in demonstrating that one or more of the main contentions is not true.

# Framework for Problem Solving

Every time we pick up the newspaper we read about problems that need solutions. The word *problem* should not be regarded as a synonym for *trouble*. We are imperfect people living in an imperfect society, and problems are part of our everyday life. We can look at problems in several different ways: We can ignore them and pretend they don't exist, we can worry about them and do nothing, or we can confront them and find solutions. The last choice seems to be the most sensible, as long as we use effective methods in dealing with them. Sometimes our gut-level response works all right, but complex issues call for a more rational approach.

The philosopher and educator John Dewey has given us a method called the *reflective thinking process*.[*] It has been adapted in a number of ways to a variety of situations, but here is the basic framework:

- *Define the problem.*  State the problem in a way that clearly identifies it. If you can't put it into words, you probably don't really understand what it is.
- *Limit the problem.*  Bring the problem into focus so that it is distinguished from other issues. The better you are able to pinpoint the problem, the better chance you will have to find a solution.
- *Analyze the data.*  Gather and examine information that is related to the problem. Your data may suggest how the problem developed, how serious it is, and what effect it is having.
- *Establish criteria for solutions.*  Before you decide on a solution, you need to have some idea of what you want the solution to achieve.
- *Consider possible solutions.*  Here you have a chance to think creatively. Don't get locked into believing that there is only one answer to a problem; open your mind to more possibilities.
- *Select the best solution by checking each possibility against your criteria.*  Consider all the alternatives in light of what you said you wanted your solution to accomplish; then pick the one that fits best.

This framework can be a useful tool in dealing with complex problems. But, remember that you have to be realistic. There is no such thing as a perfect solution.

## THINKING THROUGH A PROBLEM

To illustrate the problem-solving framework, let's look at the issue of street drugs. Everybody has an opinion on how to deal with this problem, but often the conclusion people reach is based on oversimplified thinking that doesn't take into consideration the complexities of the issue. Don't make the mistake of making a speech on a topic such as this before you have pursued in your mind a logical progression of thought.

---

[*]John Dewey, *How We Think*, (Boston: Heath, 1933), pp. 106–115.

# Framework for Problem Solving

### Define the Problem

Begin by identifying in a general sense what you perceive the problem to be. Do you want to address the debilitating effects that drugs have on the individual, or are you more concerned about the damaging consequences to the society? A broad definition of the topic might be something such as this: "The sale and use of street drugs in the United States continues to be a serious social problem."

### Limit the Problem

Once you have the general idea, you can begin thinking about how to limit the problem, or topic. The scope of the problem as stated is too extensive for you to handle in one study, so that you will have to be more specific in order to make an effective report. The limitations you put on the topic might be to evaluate it in terms of the particular drugs and the specific segments of the society that are affected. For example, you might sharpen the focus of the topic by posing the question in the following way: "How extensive is the sale and use of crack cocaine in the public schools, and what methods work best to deal with the problem?"

### Analyze the Data

Begin by doing some reading on the subject, and talk to people who are informed on the topic. You may also want to structure your research by posing a list of questions:

- What effect does crack cocaine have on the people who use it?
- How much does it cost, and how do students get the money to buy it?
- How many students use the drug, and how old are they when they start?
- What motivates students to begin using crack cocaine?
- How much crime is related to drug trafficking?
- What role do students play in the gangs that supply the drug?
- Where does the drug come from? How does it get into the country and into the schools?
- What effect does the drug problem have on the quality of education?
- What are school officials doing to curtail the use of drugs?
- What happens to a student who is caught using or selling drugs?
- What are the courts and law enforcement officials doing about the problem?

You may not be able to find answers to all these questions, but at least the list will help you to think about what you need to know and what the audience might ask.

# Framework for Problem Solving

### Establish Criteria for the Solution

Establishing the criteria for the solution is an important step and one that is too often left out. It is a hard step to take because it requires insight, judgment, and objective thinking. What frequently happens is that solutions come to mind while you are analyzing the data. Those solutions may appear to be very attractive, and you might be tempted to start right away to build a case in their support. Before you do this, however, consider what goals you want your solution to accomplish. Here are six possible criteria:

1. Significantly reduce the sale and distribution of crack cocaine in public schools.
2. Modify the attitude of students so that they are not motivated to use drugs.
3. Improve the learning environment for students.
4. Provide rehabilitation for those addicted to drugs.
5. Punish the offenders and prevent them from repeating their crime.
6. Provide a means for students to earn money without having to sell drugs.

Some of these criteria may be more important than others, and you will have to decide which ones you want to focus on in this particular study.

### Consider Possible Solutions

Now you are ready to start thinking about possible ways to solve the problem. This step in the process calls for *creative thinking* as well as *critical thinking.* You very likely will find that complex social problems are much easier to *describe* than they are to solve. Open your mind to possibilities, and get them down on paper. Your list might look something like this:

1. Develop support programs and rehabilitation centers for students who want to quit the drug habit.
2. Give special privileges to students who stay off drugs.
3. Provide job opportunities for students who would otherwise be tempted to sell drugs.
4. Close the campus so that no one is allowed in or out until school is over.
5. Require that students who are caught using drugs attend school in separate facilities.
6. Prosecute students in adult courts when they are caught selling drugs.

### Select the Best Solution

The way to select the best solution is to measure each one of them against your criteria and see which one comes the closest to accomplishing your goal. In addition to producing the most effective solution, this method also gives you one that is *defensible*—that is, you will be able to explain why you selected that solution over the other possibilities. This is an important feature of the method, because it is quite likely that you will be called on to do precisely that.

# DISCOVERING WHAT YOU BELIEVE

The process of discovering what you believe is sometimes referred to as *dialectical thinking*. Richard Paul says,

> Whenever we consider concepts or issues deeply, we naturally explore their connections to other ideas and issues within different domains or points of view. Court trials and debates are dialectical in form and intention. They pit idea against idea, reasoning against counterreasoning in order to get at the truth of a matter. As soon as we begin to explore ideas, we find that some clash or are inconsistent with others. If we are to integrate our thinking, we need to assess which of the conflicting ideas we will accept. . . .[3]

There is some risk involved in this practice because the evidence and the logical thought process may lead you to a conclusion that you don't really want to accept. Oliver Wendell Holmes said, "What is true is what I can't help believing." Being in that position may make you uncomfortable at first, but it will also make you a better and a more reasonable public speaker.

Do not expect to receive unanimous approval when you make specific declarations on a controversial issue; you may gain the favor of some, but you are bound to lose the support of others. You can urge your listeners to protect the environment or fight to preserve their freedom, for example, but such assertions have no functional application. It isn't hard to get people to see the value of some abstract virtue; disagreement occurs when you begin to talk about details. For example, you can easily say in your speech that unnecessary expenses must be cut, and every person in the audience will thoroughly agree. But if you are forced to be specific about where those cuts should come, you are likely to confront opposition.

Learning to think critically helps us to appreciate those who have the responsibility for inventing and implementing solutions to social problems. Lawmakers, administrators, and people in positions of authority have more difficult jobs than we sometimes believe: After they win the office or appointment and receive the cheers of the crowd, they must translate their political rhetoric into operational procedures that deal with real problems in a real world.

# EXERCISE

Review the steps in the section "Framework for Problem Solving" and the issue of the sale and use of street drugs in public schools. Note that there are six choices under the subheading of "Establish Criteria for the Solution." There are also six choices under the subheading "Consider Possible Solutions." For each criterion, there is a corresponding solution, and your task is to match the ones that go together. Remember that when you develop a speech on an issue of this kind, the solution you advocate must correspond to the problem you have described.

---

[3]Richard Paul, op. cit., p. 254.

# QUESTIONS FOR DISCUSSION AND REVIEW

1. What do we mean by *critical thinking?*
2. What do we mean by *selective learning?*
3. Which has more impact on us, direct experience or reports we read? Why?
4. What questions should we ask to test the validity of sources?
5. Why is vocabulary important in both the thinking and speaking processes?
6. Why is the Rubicon used to mean a dividing point?
7. To become educated people, what do we have to do in addition to learning facts?
8. What is another term for *inductive reasoning?* Describe how the process works.
9. What is the difference between a *sign* and a *cause?*
10. What are we doing when we reason deductively?
11. What are the three parts of a categorical syllogism?
12. What do you have to do before you can logically reject the conclusion of a syllogism?
13. How can a syllogism be applied to the rule of law?
14. In what way is a syllogism similar to a prima facie case?
15. What are the steps in the problem-solving framework?

# PROGRESS MANAGEMENT CHECKLIST

### *How can you tell if you are making progress?*

_____ 1. You will become more critical of what you read and hear.
_____ 2. You will begin to let go of opinions you hold that lack valid evidence.
_____ 3. You will apply the test of reason to what you believe.
_____ 4. You will begin to see the significance of historical and literary references and how they expand your ability to understand what you read and hear.
_____ 5. You will avoid relying on simplistic "bumper sticker" conclusions.
_____ 6. You will make it a practice to gather evidence before you draw a conclusion.
_____ 7. You will recognize the difference between a sign and a cause.
_____ 8. You will begin to approach problems with a method that helps you find better solutions.

 *Visit the book's Web site at www.mhhe.com/hasling8 for study tools such as practice quizzes, activities, and Web links.*

# CHAPTER 9

# The Speech to Persuade

AFTER READING THIS CHAPTER, YOU SHOULD BE ABLE TO DO THE FOLLOWING:

- Know how persuasion differs from coercion, manipulation, bribery, and deception; understand what Aristotle meant by the *modes of proof*—logos, pathos, and ethos.

- Construct an argument that defends or opposes the status quo; identify evidence that creates the condition of *cognitive dissonance* in the minds of people you are attempting to persuade; phrase information in a way that contributes to the support of your argument.

- Know how to construct an argumentative case by advancing a claim, using evidence, providing a warrant to reinforce the evidence, forming and qualifying a thesis.

- Present a speech on a controversial topic to an audience that opposes your point of view without creating antagonism or hostility.

- Apply emotional appeals to a persuasive speech by calling attention to shared values that you have with the audience and establishing your own personal integrity; know how to talk about your feelings and experiences using emotional language that contributes to your sincerity.

You might say that every speech you prepare is designed to persuade in one respect or another. Even in a speech to inform, you try to persuade your audience that you are a credible person, that your information is accurate, and that your message has significant value. In terms of rhetorical categories, however, the speech to persuade is classified as a message that favors one side of a controversial issue. When you prepare for this kind of speech, you must assume that there will be people in the audience who will be opposed to your thesis; your intent is to persuade them to reevaluate their thinking and accept what you want them to believe.

## THE PERSUASIVE MESSAGE

Before going any deeper into this subject, reflect a bit on how you feel about the term *persuasion*. You may be one of those people who believe that persuading others is the same as trying to get them to do something they really don't want to do. "After all," you might ask, "what right do I have to tell people what they should believe or how they ought to behave?" You may personally resent having someone try to persuade you to do something—particularly if you have had bad experiences with high-pressure salespeople. Even if the persuaders have your best interests at heart, you may object to their insistence on your doing things their way. And it probably doesn't reduce your irritation much when they tell you they are doing it "for your own good."

### The Inherent Qualities of Persuasion

In order to discuss the art of persuasion intelligently, we must understand that, in its pure classical or academic sense, it is neither coercive nor deceptive. If it were, its methods would certainly not find a proper place in a college textbook. The reason the term sometimes evokes a negative reaction is that it frequently is associated with practices that *are* designed to threaten or deceive. What we need to do is to qualify the definition of *persuasion* and show how it differs in nature from terms that appear to be similar.

> *Coercion* is one way to get people to do what you want them to do. Here you are using force or the threat of force to get them to comply. It is different from persuasion in terms of the end result. People who are coerced may do what they are told to do as long as the pressure is applied, but they will usually return to their former behavior when the threat is removed. They conform to your wishes, not because you have offered persuasive evidence, but because they fear the consequences if they do not. Coercion is not persuasion; it is the exercise of power.
>
> *Manipulation* is a devious way of getting what you want. It plays on emotional insecurities such as guilt, shame, fear, or a sense of obligation. It is difficult to detect because it is very subtle. People who comply with a tactic

of manipulation may not realize that the sender of the message is taking advantage of them. Manipulators are generally people who are perceptive enough to recognize human weaknesses and know what buttons to push to get the reaction they want. Fear is perhaps the most common example. It certainly is legitimate for a speaker to urge caution regarding threats of terrorism or communism, but it's another matter to generate an irrational fear of unlikely events for the sake of gaining political control.

*Bribery* is offering gifts with a view to gaining a favor. It is probably the easiest way to influence people, but the person who bribes is employing an underhanded, rather than a persuasive, method. The person who accepts a bribe is making a choice based on personal gain rather than on the merits of the proposal itself.

*Deception* is another practice that can be used to change a person's belief or behavior, but deliberate falsehoods certainly have no place in the legitimate art of persuasion. Deception means distorting the facts or exaggerating the claims when you know that a true statement would not be effective. This does not meet the definition of persuasion because it denies recipients the ability to make a choice based on accurate information. When people realize they have been deceived, they will reject not only what you have told them, but also any further efforts you may make to try to influence them.

When we practice the art of persuasion, we are expressing what we honestly believe to be true. We are not trying to take advantage of our listeners—we want them to be the *beneficiaries* of our message, not the *victims*. We share with the audience the evidence, the reasons, and the logic that we, ourselves, have used in arriving at a conclusion. And we recognize that our listeners have *free choice* to accept or reject what we are saying. If we do anything that deprives them of that choice, we are using devious, rather than persuasive, methods.

## Modes of Proof

Aristotle analyzed persuasion in terms of the elements that affect the people to whom the message is directed. He contended that those elements or modes were the *logos*, the *pathos*, and the *ethos*. These terms correspond roughly to the *argumentation*, the *emotional appeals*, and the *ethical qualities* that the speaker brings to the speech.

### Logos

The term *logos* refers to the efforts the speaker makes to prove a case argumentatively by offering facts and reason. If the controversial aspect of a speech can be addressed at the cognitive or rational level, a speaker might be successful in changing the minds of the listeners by offering evidence that refutes what they had previously believed. By Aristotle's definition, *persuasion* has a broader meaning than *argumentation*. This may seem to be a fine point of difference, but when you are sitting on a jury, for example, it is important for you to know whether the prosecutor is attempting to persuade you by appealing to your reason or by appealing to your emotions. Certainly, emotional appeals are legitimate as a means of persuasion, but rhetorically they are not the same as the proofs that Aristotle calls the *logos*.

## Pathos

An appeal to the emotions is what we call the *pathos*. A speaker may be able to influence an audience by arousing feelings of fear, anger, compassion, or a sense of justice. Here again, we can use the courtroom as an example. An attorney for a plaintiff in a personal injury suit has to prove through evidence (logos) that an act of violence was committed, but the extent of suffering that the victim endured can only be measured on an emotional scale. The jury might agree that the defendant was responsible for the act, but individual jurors might differ in terms of their compassion for the offended party. The difference here might be quite real when it comes to the amount of damages awarded to the plaintiff. The U.S. Supreme Court ruled that testimony pertaining to "victim impact" could be considered by juries in cases that involve the death penalty. This decision allows the punishment of a person convicted of a capital crime to be influenced by emotional appeals.

Although we certainly strive to be logical in what we say and do, a great many of the issues of our time are judged by emotion rather than by reason. We are called on to make decisions based on whatever evidence is available, but we frequently find that facts are not enough. One of the most powerful speeches of this century is the one Martin Luther King Jr. delivered on August 28, 1963, from the steps of the Lincoln Memorial. In that address he said:

> I have a dream that my four little children will one day live in a nation where they will not be judged by the color of their skin, but by the content of their character.

Consider the influence these words had upon civil rights legislation in this country. There is nothing here that could be called factual evidence; yet, people were profoundly moved by the power of the statement.

## Ethos

Neither of the first two modes of proof mentioned—the logos or the pathos— would influence an audience unless the speaker displayed a sense of ethos. To use Aristotle's words, "There is persuasion through character whenever the speech is spoken in such a way as to make the speaker worthy of credence; for we believe fair-minded people to a greater extent and more quickly than we do others . . ."[1] The evidence presented in a speech or the phrases used to create an

---

[1]Aristotle, *On Rhetoric*, trans. George A. Kennedy (New York: Oxford University Press, 1991) p. 38.

emotional impact have a much greater effect on listeners who have confidence in the integrity of the speaker. Certainly, words themselves have influence of their own. However, in order to explain why it is that Martin Luther King Jr. was able to achieve the success he did, we have to look beyond the words and give credit to the persona of the speaker. It is unlikely that the same words spoken by someone else on the occasion of the 1963 civil rights rally would have had the same effect.

## TAKING A POSITION

At an early stage in your preparation of a speech to persuade you must decide which side of the issue you are going to take. Are you going to attack the prevailing conditions, or defend them? To know that, you need to have a clear understanding of the status quo.

### Status Quo

The term we use to mean "the way things are" is *status quo*. That could refer to the laws that are in effect, the generally accepted standards of morality, or any other present state or condition. Your argumentative position will be either to support the status quo or to call for some modification of it.

Let's say, for example, that you are giving a speech on teenage pregnancy. You have examined the evidence and have found that a great many teenage girls are impregnated by men who are in their 20s or older. Often, the young girl is left with the baby, and the father is allowed to get away without taking any responsibility. Men are hardly ever prosecuted for doing this, but states do have laws on the books against statutory rape and child abuse. However, these laws are seldom, if ever, enforced. If you were to recommend in your speech that the state begin to bring charges against older men for having sex with teenage girls, you would be advocating a change in the status quo. But you have to be careful about which side you are on: If you are debating with someone who says that statutory rape laws should be abolished, you would be supporting the status quo in maintaining that the laws should remain in place and that they be enforced.

The status quo is also an important consideration when you are deciding whether to support or oppose a proposition that is on an election ballot. Sometimes, the wording of a proposition is misleading, and if you are not careful, you may wind up voting in favor of something that you actually oppose. Remember this: Any time you vote "yes" on a proposition, you are voting for a change in the status quo; when you vote "no," you are voting to retain the status quo. Therefore, it is necessary that you know what the status quo is. For example, the proposition may pertain to the construction of a new dam, and you may want to prevent it from being built. The status quo may be that previous legislation has granted rights to build the dam, and the proposition would be to repeal that action. Therefore, you would vote "yes" on the proposition because you are *opposed* to the dam.

Once you have established in your own mind what side of the issue you want to be on, you can begin to consider what information you need to include in your presentation that will have an effect on the way the people in your audience draw their conclusions.

## Conflicting Beliefs

When people establish for themselves a belief structure pertaining to issues they regard as important, they like to hear facts supporting their concept of truth. They also want to feel assured that they are acting in accordance with what they are convinced is the truth. For example, if they are making contributions to a television evangelist, they want to believe that their money is going for a good cause. To reinforce their convictions they likely will associate with other people who have similar beliefs and tune in to media presentations that say what they want to hear. When they are confronted with information that conflicts with their beliefs, they will probably try to find a way to reject it or refute it. If the evangelist is accused of having an illicit love affair or is charged with misusing funds, supporters may have a difficult time reconciling the new information with what they want to believe to be true. Some of them might attempt to discredit the source of the critical information and claim that the charges are false; others might try to minimize the importance of the accusations, maintaining that the evangelist was doing such good work that a few minor infractions and indulgences should not be cause for criticism. On the other hand, there may be people who allow the new evidence to change their minds.

The painful experience of being confronted with irrefutable evidence that conflicts with a deep-seated belief structure is what sociologists call *cognitive dissonance*. It is sometimes referred to as "buyer's remorse," because it is similar to the feeling you have when you are dissatisfied with a purchase you have made. The feeling is especially strong when the purchase was an expensive item and was something you thought you wanted for a long time. TV viewers who "buy into" an evangelistic movement may not give up easily, even when the evidence of a scandal is strong; in fact, many of them may continue to support the movement while all the time they know that the leaders are squandering their money. When people don't really want to change, they can always find a reason for not doing it.

The condition of cognitive dissonance does not necessarily bring about the alteration of a belief or commitment, but it frequently is the step that precedes such a change. This is why we say that cognitive dissonance is the first stage of persuasion.

What you need to recognize when you are delivering a speech to persuade is that some people in the audience may have an intense commitment to the point of view that you are about to attack. You are not going to be successful if you make unsupported accusations. For example, to claim simply that a charitable institution has been irresponsible with its money is not going to have any effect on those who fervently believe in what it is doing. You will have to provide documented evidence that significantly challenges the credibility of the institution. The information must be damaging enough so that opponents are required to refute the charges in order to logically maintain the allegiance that they previously held. Even when you are able to produce this kind of evidence, the people you are trying to persuade may still not be sufficiently persuaded to change their minds. If, however, you create in them the condition of cognitive dissonance, you can consider your efforts to be successful. Persuasion generally does not occur immediately after a single speech, so be patient.

## Persuasive Information

In its raw state, information is rhetorically neutral. That is, it can be employed to develop any kind of a speech, whether the purpose is to inform, to persuade, to entertain, or to motivate. The significance of the material you gather is not always self-evident—it can enlighten, convince, amuse, or inspire, depending on the way it is used.

Information that is intended to be persuasive must be presented in a persuasive framework. The listener must be able to perceive two things: (1) that the new evidence is valid and (2) that it conflicts with previous beliefs. It is up to the speaker to facilitate both of these conditions for the first step of persuasion to take place. The perceived validity of the information will depend on the confidence the listener has in the speaker, as well as in the source of the speaker's information. The extent to which the information conflicts with previous beliefs depends on the way the speaker integrates the information into his or her claim.

The information used to support a speech to persuade is called *evidence*. Evidence could, of course, be physical as well as rhetorical, but right now we are primarily concerned with the latter. Rhetorical evidence can be in the form of statistics, testimony, specific instances, case histories, or any of the other forms mentioned earlier. When your purpose is to lead audience members to a conclusion you want them to accept, your evidence must be presented in a way that will accomplish that end. Extraneous information should be deleted from the speech, and contrary material should be justified in some way. What do you do when you come across evidence in your research that seems to contradict your postulate? You could leave it out, of course, but then someone might ask you about it during the question period. A better plan would be to include it in the speech, but refute it. If you can't refute it, explain to your audience how you are still able to take the position you do in the light of what seems to be conflicting evidence.

Part of the strategy of developing a speech to persuade is to phrase your information in a way that supports your claim. It's important to remember that facts do not speak for themselves; the interpretation you give to the facts is what will influence the audience. For example, you might be giving a speech in support of government-funded health insurance. While researching the topic, you discover that 86 percent of the people in the United States are already covered by some sort of medical plan. If you simply present the evidence and let it stand without comment, you are suggesting that there is not much reason for your proposal. But you don't have to phrase it that way. You can say that 14 percent of Americans—41 million people—have no coverage at all. With such wording, the same information communicates a much different message.

## CONSTRUCTING AN ARGUMENTATIVE CASE

The speaker who addresses an audience that is listening critically must know how to construct an effective argumentative case. To persuade an audience through reason rather than through emotion requires that we have an understanding of the theory behind argumentation. An argument is more than just a statement of fact or the expression of an opinion. It is a combination of parts, each with a specific function, and all of them have to work together. Let's begin our analysis by defining some of the commonly used terminology.

### Advancing a Claim

A *claim* is a sentence or phrase that expresses a belief that you have arrived at through reason. By itself, it does not constitute a statement of fact, but it does imply that there is factual evidence that supports it. It could also be called an *assertion* or a *contention*. In your outline, it might be one of the main headings. For example, a claim would be as follows: "Coffee is an important product on the world market." Note that a claim is different from an opinion. You can express an opinion anytime you want—with or without evidence. When you say, "I don't think many people would be willing to give up their morning coffee," you are not constructing an argument, you are simply stating your opinion. It's all right to do that whether you have evidence or not. But when you advance a claim, you are required to provide factual support.

### Using Evidence to Support a Claim

Evidence is the factual support behind the claim, and it must be linked to the claim before we can say that an argument has been advanced. In other words, evidence does not speak for itself. The reason it does not is that it can often be interpreted in a number of different ways. It is your job as a speaker to provide that interpretation for the audience to know what you mean. Here is an example of a piece of evidence: "Coffee is grown in more than 50 countries." If the statement were allowed to stand by itself, we would not know what significance the speaker might be attaching to it. The evidence needs to be *linked* to the claim in order to form an argument:

> Coffee is an important product on the world market since it is grown in more than 50 countries.

## Providing a Warrant to Reinforce the Evidence

For an argument to be firmly established, the significance of the evidence may need to be reinforced. In other words, the audience members might be saying to themselves, "Why is that evidence so important?" Remember, we observed in an earlier chapter that listeners may not be able to see how a piece of information is linked to the idea that you want them to accept. Therefore, it might be necessary to explain how the evidence contributes to the support of the claim. In the theory of argumentation, a linking statement of this kind is called a *warrant*. To establish that the evidence in the coffee argument is really important, the speaker might add, " . . . and provides income for small farmers."

## Forming a Thesis

When you develop a series of arguments, they will begin to form a pattern, and you can start thinking about phrasing your *thesis*. The thesis is the main proposition of a persuasive speech and the one you want your audience to accept. It needs to be expressed in such a way that it embraces all the assertions you make and accounts for all of the evidence. On the subject of coffee, your thesis might be phrased this way:

> Small farmers in developing nations can barely make a living from growing coffee beans.

Note how the elements of an argumentative case come together in the sample outline "Fair Trade Coffee" on page 138.

## Facing Opposition

It's common for people to have friendly arguments. But there are times when the subject matter is so emotionally charged and feelings run so high that you may be tempted to avoid talking about the issue altogether. It's hard to face an audience, or even close friends and relatives, when you know that what you want to say will cause severe antagonism. It may be that you like them and agree with them most of the time, and you don't want to jeopardize the relationship by getting into a discussion that will cause hostility. But at the same time you want them to know what you believe and possibly win them over to your side. Here are some ways you can do that:

- **Start with a nonthreatening thesis.** Establish common ground by basing your claims on something upon which your audience can agree. You don't need to create unnecessary antagonism by launching an attack on other people's cherished beliefs. It may be that you think large corporations and retail outlets are exploiting small farmers in developing nations, but you can frame your thought in a different way by saying, *"Treating people fairly is good business."*

# A Persuasive Speech Outline

### FAIR TRADE COFFEE

**Attention statement:** Johann Sebastian Bach liked his morning coffee so much he wrote the "Coffee Cantata" in praise of the beverage he called "The most precious of joys."

**Thesis statement:** Few Americans would be willing to give up drinking coffee, yet small farmers in developing countries can barely make a living from growing the beans.

I. Coffee is an important product on the world market.
   A. Coffee beans are the world's most valuable agricultural commodity.
      a. Grown in more than 50 countries.
      b. 70 percent on small family farms.
   B. In the United States coffee is the second largest import next to oil.
      a. 2.8 billion pounds of coffee imported in 2003.
      b. United States consumes 20 percent of world production.
II. Low coffee prices have a devastating effect on small farmers.
   A. Prices are less than the cost of production.
      a. Subsidies force price down.
      b. As low as 40 cents per pound.
      c. 20 million coffee farmers in financial crisis.
   B. Slumping prices have increased poverty.
      a. Agricultural workers toil in sweatshop conditions.
      b. Loss to small producers is $4.5 billion a year.
   C. Central America and Africa hardest hit.
      a. Poverty rose 2.4 percent in Nicaragua.
      b. Growers turning to drug crops.
   D. Banks that loan money to farmers are also hit hard.
III. We can make a big difference by buying Fair Trade coffee.
   A. In 2002 Oxfam launched its "Coffee Rescue Plan."
      a. Called for major roasters to increase market for Fair Trade coffee.
      b. Promoted sustainable production and marketing practices.
   B. TransFair USA certifies buyers to use Fair Trade label.
      a. Must pay farmers minimum of $1.26 per pound.
      b. Provide credit and payment in advance.
      c. Give agricultural assistance for organic farming.
   C. Schools, churches, unions, business organizations can help.
      a. Procter and Gamble offers Fair Trade certified coffee.
      b. Demand can be created by large corporations selling Fair Trade.
      c. Price will be higher, but U.S. consumers can afford it.
      d. Ask for a cup of Fair Trade coffee at Starbucks.

**Conclusion:** Paying a fair price for coffee is good for the world economy. It eases the burden of poverty that oppresses us all. Valerie Orth, organizer of Fair Harvest, says there must be a structural change in global trade. She calls for "increased involvement of consumers at all levels."

- **Fill in information gaps.** Disagreement may be due to the audience not knowing what you know. Present your evidence in an objective way so that it cannot be denied. Never exaggerate your claims: *Most of the coffee we drink— approximately 70 percent—is grown by small farmers in developing countries.*

- **Stick with the issue.** Attacking the policy is more effective than criticizing the person who makes the policy. Don't let the audience believe that your position is based on your dislike for a particular person. Such a practice is called "bashing" and notifies the audience of your bias. Instead of forcing others to be defensive, make them consider your argument: *Agricultural subsidies paid by rich nations drive prices down and prevent small farmers from making a fair profit.*

- **Acknowledge valid opposing arguments.** If the issue is truly controversial, the side you support is not immaculate. Denying the obvious does not contribute to the strength of your position: *It's true that paying a higher price for coffee contributes slightly to inflation, but the benefit outweighs the disadvantage.*

- **Treat the opposition respectfully.** Avoid making flagrant accusations of misconduct and resorting to name-calling. Describing people or corporations as being greedy manipulators is not going to win them over to your side. A more effective strategy is to cite examples of fairness and decency: *Companies such as Starbucks and Procter and Gamble offer Fair Trade certified coffee—others can do the same if customers request it.*

- **Keep your cool.** Don't let overzealousness jeopardize your credibility. Leave the impression that your opinion is based on clear thinking. Let go of the notion that you have to win the argument. Even if your audience disagrees, you accomplish a lot by getting them to hear you and consider what you have said.

Remember we are talking about persuasion, not demagoguery. You will hear speakers on television, particularly in an election year, violating all of these guidelines. Generally that strategy is designed more for the sake of puffing up the speaker's ego and firing up the emotions of supporters than for changing the minds of opponents. As an ethical speaker, your aim should be to win the hearts and minds of people through reason and sincere emotional expression rather than calculated manipulation. If you believe that what you say is true, you must learn to say it effectively.

## EMOTIONAL APPEALS

The best approach for developing a speech to persuade is to present strong supporting evidence whenever it's available, but there are occasions when it may be more effective to base your appeals on values you hold that you know are shared by members of the audience. Attorney Clarence Darrow said that when the defense of a person on trial is a matter of justice, you do not have to give the jury reasons to acquit the client; you make them want to vote for acquittal and they'll find their own reasons.

## Shared Values

There are times when our convictions are founded upon emotions rather than on fact, and the message that we want our audience to accept may not be one that can be supported by evidence and clinical studies. For example, we all share a belief in justice and the protection of human rights, and we don't require that documented proof of their value be provided. People in the audience are going to be moved by a speaker whose appeal is founded on the same principles to which they subscribe themselves and who conveys a sincere and dedicated commitment to the moral tenets that are basic to their belief structure.

Shared values can be focused on a small group or can be broadened to include a larger population. A football coach, for example, might give an emotional pep talk to urge his team to go out and fight for the old alma mater. On the other hand, a presidential candidate has a national constituency and must reach out to a much larger audience to bring everyone together. It was in this spirit of inclusiveness that Barack Obama called for unity within the political system by claiming "We cannot solve the challenges of our time unless we solve them together."

Speeches at solemn occasions such as the dedication of a battlefield do not require strong evidence and documentation. Abraham Lincoln's Gettysburg Address would not have worked well as a PowerPoint presentation. And Franklin D. Roosevelt did not need to site statistical information from the Wall Street Journal to bolster the courage of the American people during the Great Depression. He was far more effective by making an emotional appeal and saying "The only thing we have to fear is fear itself."

In order to be successful in making emotional appeals work for you, it is necessary that you identify the values you share with the audience and project them with a sense of conviction. Probably the most important quality you need is sincerity. If you attempt to apply lofty values to trivial issues, the phoniness will become immediately apparent to your listeners. To make the claim that you are fighting for freedom against totalitarian aggressors who are raising the parking meter fees, for example, will not inspire confidence in your sincerity.

Shared values are much easier to establish at a high level of abstraction. For example, we might all be able to agree with the generalization that the lives of innocent people should be protected. It's when we begin to apply those values to specific cases and define what we mean by "innocent lives" that we find ourselves confronted by differing opinions. Those who oppose the legal status of abortion would include an unborn fetus in the definition of "innocent lives." People who support a woman's right to have an abortion would argue that life does not begin until after birth. This issue is a particularly difficult one because the underlying principle that forms the basis of what people believe is not a matter that can be established with factual evidence.

*Barack Obama called for national unity and bi-partisan agreement to solve the nation's problems. Here he is giving his "A More Perfect Union" speech at the National Constitution Center, Philadelphia, March 18, 2008.*

## Personal Integrity

The use of emotional appeals in a speech is, in itself, a controversial issue. There are some critics who contend that decisions ought to be based on reason alone and that attempts to arouse emotional feelings are rhetorically unscrupulous. That may be true if the speaker is feigning emotions as a means of manipulating an audience into accepting a claim that would not stand up to the test of reason. But there *are* other types of emotional approaches that you might find useful to consider that are generally regarded as being within the parameters of ethical behavior.

### Feelings and Experiences

If the feelings you have about an issue are genuinely strong, you are not deceiving an audience by expressing them. In fact, if you fail to communicate sincere concern for the plight of people who deserve compassion, the audience might regard you as being cold and uncaring. To engage the emotions of the audience, you must begin with your own emotional involvement. You can't expect the audience to be moved unless you are willing to speak from the heart and convey the depth of your own feelings.

Selecting a topic in which you have had personal experience is an excellent way to help establish for yourself the credibility that you want the audience to perceive. If you are able to say, "I know because I was there . . . ," your listeners are more likely to pay attention than they would be if you were making a secondhand report. There are a few caveats, however, to this approach. First of all, you don't want to come across as a braggart. If the listeners get the idea that you are telling about your experiences in order to extoll your own virtues, they may reject your claim, regardless of the merit it may have. Second, make sure you are able to keep your emotions from getting out of control. If your topic is child abuse, for example, and you yourself were an abused child, you may be able to make your point in a very powerful way. But if you can't talk about the subject without breaking down, you might find that the public speaking mode of communication makes the experience too painful for you to handle.

### Language of Emotion

Effective arguments may influence the way people think, but it's the emotional appeals that are built into a speech that inspire listeners to act. As a speaker, you can move people to action if your timing is good and conditions are right. Listeners must have a concern for the cause that is being addressed, they must be willing to take personal responsibility, and they must believe that their efforts will make a difference. What the speaker can do is reinforce those beliefs with motivating language and provide an opportunity to direct and release the energies of the audience. During times of crisis, a key phrase can be a powerful force. In 1941, for example, tens of thousands of young men enlisted in the military forces after hearing the call "Remember Pearl Harbor."

There are many examples we could cite of times when the words of the speaker were clearly the inspiration for action. We know that people were profoundly affected by the language John F. Kennedy used in his inaugural address. He might have made a simple request for people to volunteer for government service; instead, he reached out in a much more dramatic way:

> The energy, the faith, the devotion which we bring to this endeavor will light our country and all who serve it—and the glow from that fire can truly light the world. And so, my fellow Americans, ask not what your country can do for you; ask what you can do for your country.

The thought, the phrasing, and the quality of the language make this a great speech, but even more important is that people were challenged and *acted* on the words. A follow-up to this speech was the formation of the Peace Corps, and thousands of young people from all over the country answered the call to serve their country in the cause of peace.

## Credibility of the Speaker

Having gone to all the trouble of gathering the information, organizing it, and practicing the delivery, can you be sure that the audience is going to believe what you say? If you are known in the community and have acquired a reputation for being honest and well-informed, your words will carry considerable weight. But what if people are hearing you for the first time? How will they know if your information is accurate and if you are telling the truth? The capacity to establish your credibility when you are unknown to the audience is one of the most important variables in determining success in public speaking.

If people are going to trust that you know what you are talking about, you have to speak as though you do. Make sure you are familiar with your own evidence. If you appear to be seeing it for the first time on your note cards, your credibility is going to take a nosedive. Cite your sources whenever you need to so that your listeners know that you are not making things up out of your own head. And, above all, make sure that you let them know that what you are saying is what you yourself believe.

Don't make the mistake of assuming that your sincerity will be self-evident. Even though there are people who proclaim they can tell whether or not someone is telling the truth, the evidence indicates the contrary. Those who declare they can perceive the sincerity of a speaker are just guessing and are wrong half the time. What people in the audience do is observe and evaluate characteristics of delivery—the posture, the gestures, the facial expressions, the eye contact, and the vocal inflection—all the features that appear to be the indicators of integrity. However, the effective application of these speaking techniques is available to any speaker—honest or not. It's clear that just *being* sincere isn't enough; you have to know how to *project* sincerity if you want people to believe what you say. Whether you like the notion or not, the audience members are going to apply subjective criteria in making their determination of whether or not they are going to believe you.

Truth is not self-evident. The only way it can prevail is if it is advocated by honest and just men and women who are effective in their communication. Sixteen hundred years ago St. Augustine wrote:

> Who would dare to say that truth should stand in the person of its defenders, unarmed against lying, so that they who wish to urge falsehoods may know how to make their listeners benevolent, or attentive, or docile in their presentation, while the defenders of truth are ignorant of that art? Should they speak briefly, clearly, and plausibly while the defenders of truth speak so that they tire their listeners, make themselves difficult to understand and what they have to say dubious? . . . Who is so foolish as to think this to be wisdom?[2]

## EXERCISE

Address the issue of gasoline consumption by writing a *thesis statement* supported by a *claim* and two or more pieces of *evidence* listed below. You can interpret the evidence any way you want. Be prepared to elaborate extemporaneously on what you have written.

- Federal gasoline tax is now 18.4 cents per gallon.
- Raising the gasoline tax to $1 per gallon would draw about $100 billon per year in revenue.

[2]Saint Augustine, *On Christian Doctrine*, book 4, trans. D. W. Robertson Jr. Copyright © 1958 by Macmillan Publishing Company. Reprinted by permission of the publisher.

- Imports account for 56 percent of all U.S. oil consumption and are projected to reach 70 percent over the next two decades.
- Of the world's recoverable oil reserves, 60 percent are in the Persian Gulf.
- Gasoline taxes in the United Kingdom exceed $3 per gallon.
- Auto industry marketing experts report that consumers care more about power, payload, comfort, and safety than about economy.
- Doubling the federal gasoline tax would reduce oil demand by about 500,000 barrels per day; the world market produces 85 million barrels per day.

## QUESTIONS FOR DISCUSSION AND REVIEW

1. How do you define *coercion, manipulation, bribery,* and *deception?* In what way do they all differ from persuasion? Why do we say that free choice is an important element of persuasion?
2. What did Aristotle mean by the "modes of proof"—the logos, the pathos, and the ethos?
3. What is meant by the term *status quo?* Which way do you vote on a ballot measure when you favor the status quo? Explain.
4. What is meant by the term *cognitive dissonance?* What do people tend to do in order to avoid experiencing cognitive dissonance?
5. Why do we say that information in its raw form is not persuasive? What do you have to add to the information to make it persuasive?
6. In the theory of argumentation, what is meant by a *claim?* What is meant by *evidence,* and how does evidence affect the claim?
7. What is the difference between physical and rhetorical evidence?
8. What is a warrant for a claim? Why is a warrant sometimes necessary for an argumentative statement to be clear?
9. What is a thesis statement? What role does it play in a speech to convince?
10. What is the most important personal quality needed to make the emotional appeals of a speaker effective? Why is it not a good idea to apply lofty values to trivial issues?
11. What are three approaches a speaker might use as a means of appealing to the emotions of an audience?
12. What is meant by the *credibility* of the speaker?
13. What did St. Augustine have to say about the defenders of truth learning effective methods of persuasion?

## PROGRESS MANAGEMENT CHECKLIST

### *How can you tell if you are making progress?*

\_\_\_\_\_ 1. You will recognize when someone is trying to manipulate or coerce you into doing something, and you will avoid doing the same thing to others.

\_\_\_\_\_ 2. You will know the importance of having reasons for the opinions you hold.

_____ 3. You will be able to identify your emotions and express what you really feel.

_____ 4. You will begin to apply an ethical philosophy to what you do and say.

_____ 5. You will be willing to change your mind when valid and indisputable evidence conflicts with what you previously believed.

_____ 6. You will be able to advance an argument by combining a claim with supporting evidence.

_____ 7. You will be able to expand on your opinions by formulating a thesis.

_____ 8. You will become willing to confront others with opposing viewpoints without being afraid of generating hostility.

*Visit the book's Web site at www.mhhe.com/hasling8 for study tools such as practice quizzes, activities, and Web links.*

# The Speaker

CHAPTER **10**

# *The Speaker's Frame of Mind*

**AFTER READING THIS CHAPTER, YOU SHOULD BE ABLE TO DO THE FOLLOWING:**

- Think to yourself that you really want to have people hear what you have to say; understand that preparing thoroughly before giving your speech is the best way to overcome anxiety.

- Create a self-image that serves you well by giving yourself positive messages; know how to set the self-adjusting mechanism in your brain to the point where you are able to achieve your highest potential; understand what is meant by *comfort zones;* know how you can expand your comfort zones by changing the picture you have in your mind of what is possible for you; make adjustments in your self-perception through a six-step process.

- Imprint the new image you have of yourself by writing down and reviewing the assets you have that make you an effective public speaker; convince yourself that you are a capable speaker by going through the process of desensitizing yourself to the anxieties of public speaking.

*I*f you can honestly say that you do not suffer from speech anxiety, you may not need to read this chapter. I certainly don't want to call your attention to something that is not a problem for you in the first place. But if you do feel the proverbial butterflies in your stomach when you have to speak in public, you can be assured that you have a great deal of company, and there are steps you can take to relieve the condition. It is quite understandable to have an aversion for giving a speech, and there is nothing unusual about wanting to shy away from it. Public speaking generally ranks close to the top of the list of experiences that people say they fear the most. The fact that you are nervous simply means that you regard the situation as being important and that you want to do your best. If your concern makes you put more effort into your preparation, speech anxiety can actually work in your favor. I have heard some excellent speeches given by people who were highly stressed but well prepared, and very poor ones given by those who were completely relaxed but had nothing to say. My conclusion is that anxiety itself need not be an inhibiting factor. However, if the fear disrupts your thought process while you are speaking, you need a plan to prevent that from happening. Taking a speech course will help, but there are also other things you can do.

## DESIRE TO BE HEARD

Sometimes I hear a student in my class say, "Let me give my speech first so that I can get it over with." If you have ever had this feeling, it probably means that you are not motivated to give the speech because you want the message to be heard; you are viewing the experience only as something to be endured. If you really want to overcome speech fright, direct your attention to the importance of what it is that you are going to say.

### Thorough Preparation

Almost all of the literature pertaining to stress reduction in oral communication emphasizes that making thorough preparation is the best way to deal with public speaking anxiety. This confirms my observation that it is generally the least prepared students who have the most anxiety. It seems that anxiety often begins not at the moment speakers step onto the podium, but at the very beginning stage when they are planning what they are going to say. Think about that and see if it applies to you. You might be going through the motions of preparation when you really don't want to give the speech at all. Sometimes students will manage to begin the speech, but their volume is so low they can't be heard. What's happening is that subconsciously they don't really *want* to be heard. The reason for this may be that they lack confidence in the quality of the message and fear that it may not be adequate. Often, speech anxiety is used as an excuse by people who really mean that they are not prepared. There is a certain logic to that thinking: If you don't prepare a speech, you can't be expected to give one. That rationale is called *creative avoidance.* It may get you out of having to give speeches, but it doesn't help you cope with the problem, and it tends to reinforce the anxieties. A better procedure is to confront the fears and deal with them.

## Techniques to Relieve Anxiety

Most of the evidence we have pertaining to techniques for overcoming speech anxiety is anecdotal. Some people have reported success by taking a walk just before speaking or doing breathing exercises. These methods can't hurt, and you should try anything that works. However, if you begin to feel anxiety even as you are preparing the speech, it is important that you take remedial measures early. Experts who teach public speaking in the business world list preparation, positive thinking, visualization, relaxation, and confidence in yourself as the key elements in reducing anxiety.[1] But the process begins with forming a positive attitude.

# CREATING A NEW SELF-IMAGE

A great deal of your anxiety is related to the attitude you have toward public speaking. The word *attitude* simply means "the way you lean." If you have a positive attitude, you lean *toward* something; if you have a negative attitude, you lean *away* from it. Attitudes develop over a long period of time, and we never know when they start. Your attitude toward public speaking may have begun when you were very young and your parents had you stand up to recite a poem for company. Later on, you probably had to do "show and tell" in school, and your attitude was reinforced. If those were good experiences for you, the attitude you have toward public speaking may be positive; if they were bad experiences, you probably have a negative attitude. The point is that you did not *choose* the attitude intentionally; it just happened.

Attitudes are formed out of your experiences—not the way they really happened, but the way you *perceived* they happened. If someone laughed when you were doing "show and tell," you may have thought the laughter was directed at you, and you probably became embarrassed by it. The laughter may actually have been totally unrelated to anything you did, but if you thought at the time that the other students were laughing at you, that's the way the experience was recorded in your subconscious mind. What's more, every time you recall the experience, the memory of it is reinforced, until it becomes a permanent part of your mental data bank.

It's that kind of data that makes us feel the way we do. In later life, when we are confronted by new situations, such as an opportunity to give a speech, we automatically search the memory banks in our subconscious mind to recall occasions that might be similar. If the previous experiences were unpleasant

---

[1]Robert Edward Burns, "Combating Speech Anxiety," *Public Relations Journal,* March 1991, p. 28.

ones, we might be inclined to say "No, thank you" and make up some excuse for not doing it, without ever giving our conscious mind a chance to review the decision.

## Self-Esteem

The attitudes we hold constitute a significant part of our self-concept—the image we have in our minds as to who we are and what is or is not appropriate behavior for us. Self-esteem is how we feel about that image.[2] A positive self-concept means we have high self-esteem. If we feel confident that we are able to deal with a wide variety of challenges that life hands to us, we will be willing to take risks and explore opportunities that lead us into new experiences. If our self-esteem is low, we might be reluctant to do anything that would jeopardize our security or expose us to criticism.

## Messages to Ourselves

Our self-concept is reinforced by the messages we give to ourselves in the form of thoughts or even words spoken out loud. Have you ever heard yourself saying, "Boy, am I dumb!" Listen sometime to what is being said by students when they come into the classroom on the day they are to give their speeches. You will hear a great deal of disparaging language that can result only in creating a negative self-concept. Some students will say, "I wish I didn't have to do this," or "I'm not ready," or "My topic is going to be really boring." This is called *self-talk*, and it has a profound effect on the way we think about ourselves. The negative self-talk affects our attitudes, and our attitudes in turn affect our self-talk. The result is a downward spiral of our self-esteem that often leads to poor performance. What we do is talk ourselves into falling below our true potential—not because of low ability, but because of the image we create of ourselves. The unfortunate thing is that it all happens without our even being aware of it.

But the spiral effect can work the other way, too. Positive messages can lead to successful performance, successful performance leads to high self-esteem, and high self-esteem means we give ourselves more positive messages. It all gets back to that self-concept, or self-image. How do we change the picture of ourselves from something we don't like and don't want, to an image that more accurately portrays what we can do and really want to do?

## Changing Our Self-Perception

If you find that any part of your self-image is not serving you well, you can change it. We call the process *cognitive restructuring*—that means you can redesign the way you think about yourself so that your self-image becomes more

---

[2]Em Griffin, *A First Look at Communication Theory* (New York: McGraw-Hill, 1991), p. 70.

like what you *want* it to be. This process serves as more than just a pill to calm your nerves; it is a "refined, systematic technique that alters the cognitive dimension of anxiety."[3] The idea is not a new one, nor does it always go by the same name. Maxwell Maltz calls it *psychocybernetics,* and he describes it in the following way:

> Whether we realize it or not, each of us carries about with us a mental blueprint or picture of ourselves. It may be vague and ill-defined to our conscious gaze. In fact, it may not be consciously recognizable at all. But it is there, complete down to the last detail. This self-image is our own conception of the "sort of person I am." It has been built up from our own beliefs about ourselves. But most of these beliefs have unconsciously been formed from our past experiences, our successes and failures, our humiliations, our triumphs, and the way other people have reacted to us, especially in early childhood. From all these we mentally construct a "self" (or a picture of a self). Once an idea or a belief about ourselves goes into this picture it becomes "true" as far as we personally are concerned. We do not question its validity, but proceed to act upon it just as if it were true.[4]

## Self-Regulating Mechanism

You may have all the potential in the world to give excellent speeches, but if you have somehow acquired the notion that you stumble over words and forget what you want to say when you are in front of an audience, that's probably what will happen. You have a self-regulating device that will go to work to see that the image you have of yourself becomes reality.

Your self-regulating device is what Maxwell Maltz calls a *psychocybernetic mechanism.* A good example of such a device is a *thermostat*—a mechanism that allows the temperature of the room to rise and fall within a limited margin. If the room gets too hot or too cold, the thermostat cuts in and makes an adjustment. You have a similar kind of mechanism in your mind that tends to confine your behavior to a range that your self-image has said is appropriate for you. If you begin to deviate too much from that central zone, you start to feel uncomfortable, and you adjust your behavior to bring yourself more in line with your picture. The interesting thing about the mechanism is that it regulates your behavior whether you're doing better or worse than you think you should be. You may have observed this phenomenon if you play sports—let's say, tennis. Maybe you are playing someone who always beats you, but in this set you are ahead 5 to 4; you are serving, and the score is 30 to 15. Suddenly you start thinking, "I'm playing a better game than I have ever played before!" What happens? Your psychocybernetic mechanism goes to work and tells you

---

[3]William J. Fremouw and Michael D. Scott, "Cognitive Restructuring: An Alternative Method for the Treatment of Communication Apprehension," *Communication Education,* May 1979, p. 130.

[4]Maxwell Maltz, *Psycho-Cybernetics,* copyright © 1974 by Dr. Maxwell Maltz. Reprinted by permission of Pocket Books, a division of Simon & Schuster, Inc.

to get back where you belong. So, you start blowing shots, you lose the next three games, and your opponent beats you 7 to 5.

Why does this not happen to champions? Because they have adjusted their psychocybernetic mechanisms to the high end of the scale, where they have to win in order to feel comfortable. That seems to be a good way to become a winner, and it is. However, be sure to heed a word of warning: When you do that, you place yourself under a great deal of stress, and the discomfort of losing can be quite severe.

## Comfort Zones

What our self-image does is to establish for us behavior patterns that make us feel comfortable. If we find ourselves forced to do something that is in conflict with our self-image, we become stressed and start resisting in any way we can. Attending a lecture may be well within your comfort zone, but *giving* a lecture perhaps is not. People who have rich and fulfilling lives are those who have a broad comfort zone—one that permits them to feel OK about themselves in a variety of situations. If you perceive that your comfort zone is too narrow and restrictive, can you change it? Yes, you can, by cognitive restructuring.

Sometimes people try to make changes in their behavior patterns by writing resolutions for themselves; often this is a ritual that takes place on New Year's Day. But generally people who sit down on January first and list all the things they intend to do in the coming year wind up forgetting what they wrote even before the ink is dry. Often they include on their list what they believe they *ought* to do rather than what they really want to do. What's more, change in their behavior fails to come about because the *picture* they have of themselves is still the same as it was before. When you try to do something that conflicts with your self-image, you make yourself uncomfortable. So, in order to bring about change in your *behavior,* you have to change your *picture.* The question is, Which one should you change first? If you have a strong resolve you might try changing the behavior first—that is, just grit your teeth and do it, regardless of how uncomfortable it makes you feel. Eventually, if you have successful experiences, your self-image might also change. But if the stress level is very high and you get no satisfaction from your efforts, you will ultimately abandon that behavior. That's why we may need to make a different approach.

## Making Adjustments

The key to changing behavior patterns is your internal self-adjusting mechanism—you need to know how to set it to a challenging, but realistic, point. If you decide you want to embark upon this program, what you will be doing is restructuring the way you picture your communication behavior and your attitude toward being a public speaker. But this time, instead of letting it all happen at random, you will be selecting intentionally the skill level that you want. To begin the process, you must decide that you really have the desire to be a person who is able and willing to speak to groups. The choice must be made freely—without pressure from your parents, teachers, or anyone else. This process is not going to work if you are merely trying to comply with goals that someone else has set for you. If you can honestly say that you want to make some changes, you are ready for the next phase of the process. Start by taking out a notebook and making the following entries:

1. *Goals.* First, decide specifically what you want to be able to do. You don't have to set a goal of having the ability to address large audiences on high-minded topics. You may want to begin by saying you would like to be able to talk to small groups of 15 or 20 people on subjects pertaining to your business or hobby. Or you may simply want to be able to speak up during class discussion. Whatever your goal is, get a picture of it in your mind as you write it down.

2. *Limitations.* Identify any real limitations that you will have to deal with in order to attain your goal. For example, if you are a recent immigrant from another country, you may be struggling with English as a second language, or you may have a speech impediment or a learning disability. These are real obstacles that will not go away just by reconstructing your self-image. You may have to enter into a specialized program to bring about the change you want. What your self-regulating mechanism can do, however, is to make it possible for you to confront those obstacles and not allow them to defeat you.

3. *Assets.* Your next entry will be a list of characteristics and abilities you have that will assist you in achieving your goals. You may say, for example, that you really enjoy relating to people, that you listen well and remember what you hear, that you read a lot and have a good vocabulary, that you are interested in a variety of topics, or that you have some expertise in a particular subject. Put down on your list anything you think will contribute to your ability to give a good speech.

4. *Previous experiences.* Even if you have never made a speech before, there are occasions in the past when you have communicated effectively to someone. Think back and recall times when you have been able to say something just the way you wanted to say it. It may have been in conversation with a small group of friends or in a class discussion; perhaps it was at a meeting or on a radio talk show. Try to remember what the subject was and what point you were making. Re-create the episode in your mind, and as you write it down, reinforce the good feeling you had about speaking on that occasion.

5. *Topics for speeches.* Make a list of topics that you would be able to address after you have had some time for preparation. You could list things you know about already, or you could include subjects you would be interested in researching. What this list will do is help you relieve the anxiety of feeling that you don't have anything to talk about. It will also help you to focus

*An affirmation is a positive statement you can make about yourself.*

on the subject matter of the speech rather than on your nervousness in delivering it.

6. *Affirmations.* Select three or four items from your list of assets and previous experiences, and write them on a separate piece of paper in the form of *affirmations*. An affirmation is a positive and realistic statement you can honestly make about yourself that will reinforce the best characteristics that you have at the present time. The statement should be phrased in such a way as to replace your negative self-talk with assertions that are designed to improve your self-concept and raise your self-esteem. They need to be fairly specific so that you can get a clear picture of what you do or have done that substantiates the positive messages you are giving to yourself. For example, a list of affirmations might look like this:

- I am well acquainted with environmental problems and have an appreciation for wilderness areas. I have given thought to conservation measures, and I can elaborate on my opinions with sound and concrete evidence.

- I have good conviction in my voice, and people take me seriously when I speak. In social conversations my ideas are heard and respected.

- The nervousness I sometimes feel when I am speaking to groups does not inhibit my ability to say what I want to say.

These are *suggested* affirmations. The ones you write for yourself must be your own. Be sure you don't exaggerate or make false claims. You have to believe with all sincerity that what you are saying is realistic and that you want these qualities to be the prominent features of your personality. It is important that you phrase them in the *first person, present tense* ("I am . . . ," not "I will be . . .") because the idea is to reinforce the positive characteristics that you have now, not vague speculation of what you think you could be in the future. People who continually say to themselves, "Someday I will become . . . ," usually put off indefinitely making any constructive changes.

## IMPRINTING THE NEW IMAGE

Once you have written your list of affirmations in this form, carry the paper around with you and read the statements to yourself several times a day for about two weeks. Soon you will find that when you change your self-talk, the image you have of yourself will also begin to change. And as your image changes, so will your feelings and your behavior.

Richard Weaver, professor of speech communication at Bowling Green State University, defines *imaging* as the process of creating mental pictures that substitute for the real thing.[5] In a speech delivered to the Golden Key National Honor Society at Ann Arbor, Michigan, he described how he got through college by creating in his mind an image of himself as a university student. You must understand, however, that it is not the image alone that does the trick. What makes this method work is your accepting responsibility for behaving in a way that is commensurate with the image you have created. Just picturing yourself as a student is not enough. You must be able to see yourself doing what a student does—going to class, spending time in the library, staying up late at night studying for an exam. If those pictures do not appeal to you, a little voice inside your head is going to say, "Whom do you think you're kidding?"

### Convincing Yourself

If you can really convince yourself that you are a person who fits the image of a public speaker, there are a number of ways to imprint your new self-concept. Take some time when you are alone to relax in a comfortable chair and create an image in your mind of yourself going through the process of preparing and delivering a speech. Picture yourself writing the outline and thinking about what you are going to say. Then get a picture of yourself as you come into the room on the day you are going to give your speech. Get the feeling of waiting until you are introduced; then going to the front of the room, stepping up to the podium, and turning to face your audience. As you create all these mental images, keep thinking to yourself that you are well-prepared, you have sound ideas, and your supporting evidence is interesting as well as factual. Now picture yourself as you deliver the speech. Try to get a clear image of what you are doing and how the audience is responding. See yourself making good eye contact, gesturing, and maintaining a relaxed and composed posture. Imagine

[5]Richard L. Weaver II, "Self-Fulfillment through Imaging," from the keynote address delivered at the induction ceremony, Golden Key National Honor Society, Ann Arbor, Mich., Nov. 8, 1990, *Vital Speeches,* Jan. 15, 1991, p. 217.

as much detail as you can—the way you are dressed, the pacing of your speech, the energy you are projecting, and the reaction of the audience. In other words, picture it just the way you want it to be.

The value of this exercise is that you desensitize yourself to the real experience. When the time comes to actually give the speech, you will already have been through it and will know what it is like.

## Rewards of Speaking

To become an effective speaker, it is essential to develop and maintain a positive attitude toward what you are doing. If you simply endure the experience with reluctance and distaste, you will not have a good feeling before, during, or after the presentation. Consequently, the next time you do it, you will suffer the same anxiety, and it may be even worse. On the other hand, if you project to the listeners that you like being there and believe that your message is important, they will respond in a positive way and reinforce your good feelings. Some of the rewards of speaking come in the form of applause and affirming statements that people make to you afterward. But you will find that the approval that makes the most difference is that which you give to yourself. Preparing and delivering public statements provides you with the opportunity to clarify your thoughts and values—and having the confidence of knowing that what you believe is clear in your mind contributes significantly to the upward spiral of your self-esteem. The method of cognitive restructuring makes it possible for you to communicate effectively with the most important person of all—yourself.

## EXERCISE

Make arrangements to have one of your speeches videotaped; then watch the playback with your instructor or with someone who is able to give you constructive feedback. First, write down on a sheet of paper all the things you liked about the speech—the qualities of delivery, content, and organizational structure that you want your other speeches to contain. Next, make a list of the characteristics you can change and you would like to improve upon. (Don't worry if your voice sounds strange to you; you are probably just not used to hearing it on a recording device.) Keep the two lists, and review them when you prepare your next speech. Mentally reinforce the qualities you like, and work on at least one item that you want to improve.

## QUESTIONS FOR DISCUSSION AND REVIEW

1. What is meant by the word *attitude?* How are attitudes formed, and how do they affect behavior?
2. How do you explain the fact that attitudes are generally not chosen intentionally?
3. What is meant by the term *self-concept?* How does self-talk affect self-concept?
4. What is meant by *self-esteem?* Why is a person with high self-esteem generally willing to take more risks?

5. What is meant by the *spiral effect?* What determines whether the self-esteem spiral goes up or down?

6. What is meant by *cognitive restructuring?* How can it affect one's attitude toward public speaking?

7. What does Maxwell Maltz mean by the term *psychocybernetics?* What would be an example of a psychocybernetic mechanism?

8. How do psychocybernetic mechanisms affect a player's performance in sports? What do champions do to make themselves winners? What is the disadvantage of doing what they do?

9. How does a narrow "comfort zone" reduce the richness of a person's life?

10. Why is it that New Year's resolutions are generally not successful in changing behavior?

11. What's wrong with having someone else set goals for you?

12. What advantage is there in recognizing your limitations as well as your assets while you are in the process of goal setting?

13. How might your previous experiences in communication situations affect your self-concept?

14. What is meant by an *affirmation?* Why should affirmations be written in the first person, present tense?

15. What are some ways to imprint affirmations? What is the value of imagining yourself going through the process of preparing and delivering a speech?

## PROGRESS MANAGEMENT CHECKLIST

### *How can you tell if you are making progress?*

_____ 1. You will begin thinking more about your subject matter than your fear of giving the speech.

_____ 2. You will not be in a hurry to "get it over with" and will become more concerned about wanting the audience to understand what you have to say.

_____ 3. You will make sure you are thoroughly prepared and will not have anxieties in the preparation stage.

_____ 4. You will not engage in "creative avoidance."

_____ 5. You will let go of negative attitudes that inhibit you from participating in experiences you can enjoy.

_____ 6. The messages you give to yourself will be positive rather than negative.

_____ 7. You will feel yourself developing a broader "comfort zone" and expanding your willingness to try new things.

_____ 8. You will begin setting realistic goals.

_____ 9. You will begin looking forward to speaking opportunities and regarding them as growth-enhancing experiences.

*Visit the book's Web site at www.mhhe.com/hasling8 for study tools such as practice quizzes, activities, and Web links.*

CHAPTER 11

# *Delivering the Message*

**AFTER READING THIS CHAPTER, YOU SHOULD BE ABLE TO DO THE FOLLOWING:**

- Practice using standard English when speaking to an audience for the sake of making your ideas clear and comprehensible; recognize that words have denotative and connotative meaning; use connecting phrases to tell how one thought is related to another; avoid offensive language.
- Know how to make a short, impromptu speech by responding directly to a question, developing your answer, and moving toward your conclusion; know the advantages and disadvantages of a fully scripted speech and a memorized speech; know how to prepare for an extemporaneous speech.
- Recognize the primary, auxiliary, and secondary dimensions of a message; be aware of what can and cannot be communicated nonverbally; enhance your articulation through volume, projection, pitch, vocal emphasis, and rate of delivery.
- Draw attention to key points in your speech by using the right amount of repetition, pointer phrases, oratorical emphasis, and visual reinforcement.
- Respond to questions from the audience.

*H*enry Higgins, a character created by George Bernard Shaw who appears in the play *My Fair Lady,* decries the linguistic characteristics of the people in his own country when he says, "Why can't the English teach their children how to speak?" He is critical of another character, a young woman named Liza Doolittle, who he claims will never be anything more than a miserable street peddler as long as she continues to corrupt the language with her Cockney accent. Higgins says to his friend, "If you spoke as she does, sir, instead of the way you do, you might be selling flowers, too."

Almost everyone has an accent of one kind or another. Yours may be one that identifies you as a person who comes from a particular section of the country, such as New England or the Deep South, or it may be that English is your second language and you reveal your national origin when you speak. The accent itself does not need to be a problem as long as your diction is clear. But if you run words together, leave out syllables that need to be sounded, mispronounce words, and use careless grammar, your audience will be as critical of you as Henry Higgins was of Liza Doolittle.

## THE USE OF LANGUAGE

I recommend to my students that they learn to speak standard English. Although this may not be necessary on every occasion, some audiences will expect you to use proper grammar and correct syntax, and you will lose credibility if you are unable to do so.

You probably never think about the grammatical construction of your sentences when you speak. If you had good models in your early childhood years, you perhaps learned correct usage just by example. Later, when you went to school, you were taught how to diagram a sentence and how to identify the nouns, verbs, adverbs, and adjectives. You learned that a sentence must have a subject and a predicate and must express a complete thought, and that you use a semicolon or conjunction to connect two clauses and place a period at the end of a sentence. You were also taught that the verb in the sentence must agree in person (I am . . . you are . . . he or she is . . .) and in number (he doesn't . . . they don't . . .) with its subject. You can probably recognize by sound that it is incorrect to say "I is . . ." or "he don't . . ." You may also remember that it is redundant, and therefore ungrammatical, to use double negatives when you are speaking English. (This is not the case in all languages.) People who say, "We didn't do nothin' . . ." reveal that there are gaps in their education and should make an effort to learn the basic rules of grammar in order to communicate in a style that does not detract from their message and credibility.

### Words and Their Meanings

Your primary vehicle for communication is verbal language. If you have ever played the game of charades, you know how difficult and frustrating it is to try to convey an idea without being able to use words. For everyday interaction

162

with people, we rely very heavily on language for communication, but we often develop careless speech habits. We frequently take verbal shortcuts when we speak, assuming that the listener will be able to fill in the blanks. For example, we may say, "You know what I mean." The other person might nod in the affirmative but not really know what we mean at all. In public speaking, we need to break our careless speech habits because the people we are talking to don't know us well enough to guess accurately at what we mean. We need to use the right word or phrase to express what we want to say, and we must arrange our words in a sequence that people can follow.

## Making Meaning Clear

Words have both *denotative* and *connotative* meaning. The denotative meaning is the one we find in the dictionary and forms the basis for our understanding. The word *forceful,* for example, is defined in the *American Heritage Dictionary* as "effective; persuasive." But there is also a connotative meaning, which is a subjective interpretation that is attached to the word. I might say that a speaker was very *forceful* in his delivery, meaning that his arguments were convincing and he was confident in what he was saying. But to you the word *forceful* might connote arrogance and abrasiveness. If you had to rely on a one-word description, you might misconstrue my meaning. For that reason, I build on my message by using other words for clarification. Perhaps you have had conversations with people who do not elaborate on what they are saying, such as the following example:

"How was the movie?" you ask.

"It was good," your friend replies.

"What do you mean, 'good'? Was it funny? Was it exciting?"

"No, it was good."

The point is that words are not absolutes. By themselves, they have limited ability to convey precise meaning. Expanding your vocabulary will open up possibilities for expressing more thought in greater depth.

## Connecting Phrases

In an earlier chapter we looked at phrases called *transitions* that are used to help the audience follow our progression of thought leading to our conclusion. A similar kind of rhetorical device is a *connecting phrase,* which points out the relationship of one thought to another. A connecting phrase is commonly used when you want to tell the audience how a specific instance relates to a generalization. Throughout this book I have frequently used the phrase *for example* to tell you that what follows is an illustration of the thought I want to convey. Here are few other commonly used connecting phrases:

- What this means is . . .
- This shows that . . .

- As evidence for this we can see that . . .
- This indicates . . .
- As one suggestion . . .

Just as transitions help the audience to know that it's time to move on to the next point, the connecting phrase provides a link between the abstract statement and concrete example.

## Offensive Language

Comedians who entertain at "roasts" for prominent actors, politicians, and sports figures generally try to avoid "stepping over the line." That expression has come to mean the use of offensive language and crude references that are more embarrassing than they are funny. Once in a while entertainers will violate this code for the sake of gaining headlines, but when they do so, they alienate themselves from audiences that have a regard for good taste.

### Obscenity

In many social circles obscenity seems to be a common part of everyday conversation. Because it is so, we may have come to believe that it is equally acceptable in public address. We need to understand, however, that obscene words and references that are often merely tolerated in discussions with our friends sound coarse and degrading when spoken from the podium. Obscenity is not only crude, it is also generally sexist and racist, characteristics that make it even more offensive. People who rely heavily on the use of vulgarity identify themselves as being callous and insensitive, and consequently suffer a loss of credibility. Those who are offended by it may become distracted and may fail to comprehend any legitimate point that the speaker might be making. Certainly, there are some audiences who will find such remarks to be humorous and colorful, but seldom if ever does the use of obscenity in rhetorical dialogue contribute to the clarification of an issue.

### Slang

What about the use of slang expressions? If they are used in moderation and are part of your own speaking style, they might keep a speech from sounding too "stuffy," but they do also tend to lower the intellectual tone of the speech. However, sometimes a slang expression has more impact than the standard English equivalent. For example, saying "I was blown away" has greater intensity than "I was very surprised." Given the right circumstances, the authentic use of slang can bring you closer to people who are comfortable with that kind of language and who appreciate your ability to speak it correctly. The danger is that a slang term used in the wrong way can make you sound rather foolish. The primary criterion is that the expressions you use must be understandable to the audience. Another drawback is that slang is often spoken as a means of excluding outsiders, and that's not what you want to do when you are on the podium. Yet another problem with slang is that it tends to oversimplify complex concepts. To say that a particular event was "awesome" does not tell a great deal about the specific characteristics of what is being described. People who rely heavily upon slang often neglect standard English terms that would be more precise and frequently wind up saying such things as "you know" and "you really had to be there."

## MODES OF DELIVERY

Sometimes we watch experienced orators at work on the podium as they express themselves with power and clarity, and we tend to think that it looks easy. It seem as though the words are simply flowing with complete spontaneity. When Daniel Webster made his famous "Reply to Hayne" on the floor of Congress in 1830, he was asked how he could have made such an eloquent speech on the spur of the moment. His answer was "I've been preparing that speech all my life."

Fortunately, you do not have to spend your whole life in preparation, and no one expects you to give an eloquent presentation on the spur of the moment. You generally will have a reasonable amount of time to prepare for a speech, and you'll be able to practice before you deliver it.

### Impromptu Speaking

On some occasions you may be asked to speak without preparation; this kind of speech is called *impromptu*. People who give the best impromptu speeches are those, like Daniel Webster, who have anticipated the opportunity to speak and have made their preparation in advance. An impromptu speech should be given only by a person who has some understanding of the issue under discussion; it is pointless to take up the time of an audience when you have nothing of significance to say. It may be better to decline politely than to make a valiant, but meaningless, effort. But if you do anticipate that you might be called on to speak, here are a few things to keep in mind:

> *Pay attention.* Whenever you attend a meeting or gathering of any kind, stay alert and pay attention to what is being said. Think in terms of how you would respond if you were asked to comment on something the speaker had just said.

> *Give a direct response.* Often, the impromptu speech will be a response to a question. Begin by answering the question as directly as you can; then qualify and develop your answer. Don't leave your listeners wondering what your position is, so that they have to ask the question a second time.

*On some occasions you may have to speak without preparation.*

*Keep it short.*  No one expects a full-length speech on the spur of the moment. If the chairperson had wanted you to give a major address, you would have been included on the program. Keep your remarks short and to the point, and don't deviate from the central idea.

*Move toward a conclusion.*  The hardest thing about giving an impromptu speech is ending it. Remember that all speeches, whether they are prepared or not, must have conclusions. In order to make sure your speech doesn't just wither away and trail off into silence, plan your concluding statement as soon as you begin talking, and start phrasing it in your mind before you come to it.

Impromptu speaking is not easy. The people who do it well are the ones who do it often and have a large fund of ideas and information to draw upon. In this respect, good impromptu speeches are not really spontaneous. They reflect ideas that have been given considerable thought and have probably been expressed before in less structured communication settings.

## The Fully Scripted Speech

Don't feel defeated if you are not comfortable in giving impromptu speeches. You might be the kind of person who has a lot to say but needs to spend time in preparation before expressing it. That's quite understandable, and there are alternatives for you. You can, of course, write the speech out word for word and then either read it or deliver it from memory. There are advantages and disadvantages to each of those two choices, as we shall see.

### Speaking from a Manuscript

This kind of speech is difficult to prepare but easy to deliver. The advantage is that you can include as much detail as you want and not have to worry about forgetting something. You can polish each phrase with just the right words, and if you read well, you can make yourself appear to be an eloquent orator. Political speakers like to use this mode of delivery because it reduces the danger of their saying the wrong thing. The delivery, with practice, can be made smooth and articulate, and an advance copy can be made available to the press.

The manuscript speech does have disadvantages, however. It tends to diminish audience contact, because speakers have to direct their attention to the script rather than to the listeners. If a speaker does not read well, the speech can sound stilted, and it often becomes boring. Furthermore, there is a loss of credibility when the speech is read from manuscript. The audience may wonder whether the speech was actually written by the person reading it.

### Memorizing

Committing a speech to memory can be a worthwhile method if you plan to give the same speech on a number of different occasions. You can make sure the language is precise, the content is detailed, and the organizational structure is flawless without losing audience contact, which happens when you read a speech from manuscript. The problem is that if the speech is a long one, you may have a hard time memorizing the whole thing. Even if you can do so, you often find yourself thinking in terms of the sequence of the words rather than the meaning of the ideas, and if you forget a word, you may lose your composure. Another problem with the memorized speech is that it often *sounds* memorized, and the audience may wonder if you are really giving thought to what you are saying.

## Speaking Extemporaneously

The best alternative for making a prepared presentation is to deliver the speech *extemporaneously*. Make sure you understand what that term means and how it differs from the impromptu speech or the fully scripted speech. An extemporaneous speech is one that is *prepared* but not written out word for word. As the speaker, you would work from an outline—getting the main ideas and specific information from the printed page, but choosing the actual words from your own vocabulary in order to express what you want to say. There is a very important difference between extemporizing from an outline and reading from a manuscript. A person can read a speech word for word and make it sound eloquent, yet have no idea of what the words mean. When you deliver a speech extemporaneously, it is necessary that you engage your brain as well as your voice. Having the outline in front of you to provide the structure makes it possible for you to utilize your time efficiently, while expressing the ideas in your own words conveys sincerity and enhances your credibility. The audience is more likely to believe that the ideas are your own and that you have an understanding of what you are saying.

The extemporized speech is the kind most frequently emphasized in public speaking courses because it provides students with the best learning experience. Preparing for the speech helps you develop skills of research and critical thinking, and knowing that you are prepared builds your confidence. The most important thing is that you *feel* prepared. A great many of the anxieties people have about public speaking can be significantly reduced by thorough preparation. If you are confident that you have gathered the information you need, have organized it in a way that makes sense to you, and have practiced out loud what you want to say, you will begin to feel much more comfortable.

## Using Note Cards

A common source of anxiety about public speaking is the fear of forgetting what you are going to say. Don't feel that you have to rely on your memory—provide yourself with materials that will assist you in remembering what you want to include in the speech. Note cards are perhaps the most reliable memory aids. You can carry them with you and use them wherever you happen to be. They are inconspicuous and do not create a distraction because listeners are generally accustomed to speakers' using notes. You can keep them in one hand and not have to put them down when you move around or gesture. If you are working without a lectern, you can hold them at a comfortable level (for example, eye level) without having to lower your head and break eye contact with the audience. Another advantage is that cards don't rattle the way a sheet of paper does if your hand happens to shake a bit. When you are preparing note cards, there are a few things you should remember:

1. Type or write legibly. The print should be dark enough so that you will be able to see the words clearly at a glance. Underline or highlight important words. It's also a good idea to put quotation marks around direct quotes and to include the source of the quotation.

2. Write on only one side of the card. If you have to turn the card over, you may forget whether or not you have already covered the material on the other side. End each card with a completed thought; don't carry a sentence or a phrase over to another card. You may also find it advisable to number each card.

3. Include only necessary words and phrases. If you write the whole speech on the note cards, you will be tempted to read rather than extemporize. Don't make your notes so detailed that the speech becomes one that is read from manuscript.

**Practicing the Delivery**

The hours you spend gathering material and organizing it into a workable pattern will pay off when the time comes for you to deliver the speech. Confidence results from knowing that you have done your "homework." The delivery of the speech is the part of public address that you will probably find the most gratifying because you will have a sense of really having accomplished something. When you write an article for a magazine or newspaper, you seldom know whether or not anyone reads it. But when you give a speech, you can see the response of the people who are hearing your ideas.

An important part of the preparation for a speech is practicing the delivery. This does not mean that you have to memorize every word and every gesture. What it does mean is that you should try out the speech on someone else before you deliver it to the audience. Hearing the sound of your voice expressing your ideas will help you become familiar with them.

Try to anticipate as much as you can about the situation before you step into it. If it's possible to do so, visit the room where you will be speaking. Note the size and decor of the room, the seating arrangement, the ventilation, and anything that might create a distraction. Walk up to the front of the room and see what the perspective is from the place where you will give the speech.

When all your preparation is completed, the time will come when you will see what the audience looks like from the speaker's platform. It's then that you have a chance to apply all that you have learned and see if the theory really works for you. If it does, remember what it is that you did. If what you do falls short of your expectations, don't be disheartened; learn from the experience, and do better next time.

# THE DIMENSIONS OF THE MESSAGE

You can improve your chances for success if you try to anticipate how the audience is going to receive you. From the moment you step up to the podium, your listeners will be forming in their minds an impression of the kind of person you are, how well they like you, and whether or not they are inclined to believe and accept what you have to say. The impression they receive is important because it will affect the way they react to what they see and hear. One way to analyze an audience's perception of a speaker is to look at the three dimensions that every speech contains: (1) the primary message, (2) the auxiliary message, and (3) the secondary message.

## Primary Message

The term *primary message* refers to the verbal content of the speech—the words that the speaker uses to express the ideas, the information, and the opinions that form the substance of the message. This is the meaning the audience would get if the channel of communication were the printed page rather than the spoken word.

## Auxiliary Messages

By *auxiliary messages* we mean the dimensions to communication that can be added when the message is delivered orally. We refer here to what the speaker can do deliberately to enhance the reception of the primary message. Auxiliary messages include tone of voice, vocal inflection, posture, gesture, rate of delivery, eye contact, style of dress, and other delivery techniques that the speaker can employ to reinforce what he or she is saying.

## Secondary Messages

Messages that are projected to the audience but are not part of the speaker's plan are called *secondary messages*. They are impressions created by characteristics over which the speaker has no control, such as age, sex, race, nationality, or physical appearance. They could also come about as a result of unconscious behavior patterns. Secondary messages can work to the advantage or to the disadvantage of the speaker. If they are mannerisms that indicate nervousness, uncertainty, or insincerity, they can be quite detrimental. For example, the speaker might have a distracting twitch or may be toying with a pencil. These are secondary messages that would interfere with the audience's receiving the message that the speaker wants heard. On the other hand, secondary messages can have a positive effect. The speaker may have attractive facial features, natural poise, or an empathetic expression. Qualities such as these would contribute to the audience's willingness to accept and believe what the speaker is saying.

## Nonverbal Communication

The visual impressions that we call *nonverbal communication* could be in the form of auxiliary or secondary messages. Whether such communication is intentional or unintentional, it has a lot to do with the establishment of the speaker's credibility. Consider your own perceptions: What is it that you, as a member of the audience, like to see when you are listening to a speaker? Generally, people say they like to observe a posture that conveys a feeling of confidence, gestures that seem natural and at ease, direct eye contact, and friendly facial expressions. Although these characteristics are by no means proof of sincerity, audiences do tend to make judgments based on them. We no longer teach students to rehearse gestures in front of a mirror, as teachers of elocution used to do in previous generations. Today, we believe that what you do on the podium should develop naturally out of your own style and personality. There are, however, some conventional behavior patterns that might be appropriate for you to consider.

## Posture

The basic posture for the speaker is to stand. When you stand, you are in a better position to gain and hold the attention of the audience—which is, of course, what you want to do. Keep your weight on both feet. Don't slouch, and don't lean heavily on the desk or lectern. Avoid shifting your weight from one foot to another or pacing back and forth across the room. Try not to look as if you are tired; your audience wants to see you awake, alert, and displaying a reasonable amount of vitality.

You probably will want to establish yourself behind a lectern, if there is one. But remember that this piece of equipment is designed to rest your notes or manuscript upon—not your body. Don't grip the sides of the lectern too tightly. A speaker with white knuckles tends to lose the confidence of the audience.

## Gesture

If you are motivated to gesture, do so. Allow your hands and arms to help you communicate your ideas. It is probably better to stick with conventional speech gestures rather than to try to transmit elaborate descriptions in the air with your hands. Several simple gestures are easy to use and will look natural to the audience: holding up fingers to indicate a number of items, drawing the hands toward the body in a welcoming motion, turning the palm out toward the audience to suggest *enough,* using a rolling motion with the hands to indicate an idea in process, and pointing to a chart or visual aid. All of these are referred to as *motivated* gestures. They are not to be inserted artificially or at random; rather, they should contribute naturally to the emphasis of the thought.

## Movement

Feel free to move around if there is a reason to do so. You may want to walk to the whiteboard or to a flip chart. You might wish to change your position in order to have better visual contact with your audience. Another reason to move is to communicate intensity in the thought you want to convey. Closing the distance between you and the audience is a nonverbal way of saying that the next point is very important.

## Eye Contact

Maintaining eye contact with members of the audience is the speaker's way of saying, "I am aware of your presence, and I want to establish communication with you." Looking at faces is important for the sake of establishing rapport with the audience. Don't look over the top of the listeners' heads or stare at your notes; let people know that you are interested in the feedback they give you as you deliver the speech. Eye contact is one of the factors people use to determine the sincerity of a speaker. You are less likely to be trusted if the audience members believe you are not willing to look them in the eye. Your eye contact is also perceived by the audience to be an indicator of your confidence level. Looking at people's faces tells them that you are sure of what you are saying.

## Vocal Communication

Although a great deal of communication occurs at the nonverbal level in public speaking, the voice is the primary instrument for conveying messages. How well you are understood depends on your ability to verbalize what you want to say. You will find that using your voice for public speaking is somewhat different from using it in ordinary conversation, particularly in terms of volume.

### Volume

Beginning speakers sometimes have difficulty in determining the volume level that is required when they are speaking to a large group. Probably you are used to talking to 2 or 3 people at a time; if you use that same volume level for 20 or 30 people, you will most likely not be heard. If speaking up is hard for you, you will need to practice. Before you make the speech, have a friend stand 30 or 40 feet away from you. Deliver the speech to your friend, increasing the volume until he or she is able to hear you easily. Make note of the way your voice sounds at that volume level. When the time comes for you to give the speech, you will know how loud you have to talk. Adequate volume is one of the most fundamental requirements in public speaking. Unless people can hear what you say, your message will not be communicated.

### Projection

Volume is not the only factor responsible for audibility. The extent to which you *project* your voice will also determine whether or not you can be heard. Projecting the voice means aiming the words directly at the people who are the targets of your message. The best way of doing this is to *extend* the sound of your voice to reach the people farthest away. That works much better than talking loudly to the people in the front row.

### Pitch

The word *pitch* refers to a speaker's tone of voice. What you want to achieve is a *modulated* pitch—one in which the vocal tones rise and fall, giving emphasis to your meaning. If you are not modulating your voice, you are said to be talking in a *monotone*. Although this problem can be difficult to overcome, you want to work on it—a monotone can make a speech sound dull and tedious. Practice by speaking into a tape recorder; then play back the tape and hear how your voice sounds. If you perceive that you are speaking in a monotone, go back over the written material of your speech and *underline* key words and phrases. Now, record the speech again, placing vocal emphasis on the items you underlined.

A related voice problem is that of a *patterned pitch.* This means that your voice is modulated, but the highs and lows come at regular intervals without regard for the points you want to emphasize. This problem is most likely to occur when you are *reading* from a book or manuscript. An audience can generally tell when you have stopped extemporizing the speech and have begun reading—the rise-and-fall patterned pitch is a dead giveaway. If you have to read portions of your speech, try to maintain the same modulated vocal inflection that you use when you extemporize.

## Vocal Emphasis

Vocal emphasis is important, not just for the sake of making what you say sound interesting, but also for the sake of making your meaning clear. It is possible to modify the way your audience perceives your meaning without changing any of your words. For example, the following sentence could convey several different meanings, depending on the words that are emphasized:

I didn't say he stole my book.

Try saying this sentence seven times, emphasizing a different word each time. You will find that there are seven different meanings:

1. *Someone else* said he stole my book.
2. I *deny* that I said he stole my book.
3. I might have implied it, but I didn't *say* he stole it.
4. Someone stole it, but it wasn't *he.*
5. He might have borrowed it, but he didn't *steal* it.
6. He stole someone else's book, not *mine.*
7. He stole something else, not my *book.*

From this illustration, we can see that it is not the word that conveys the meaning but the way the speaker uses the word. Words are tools that a speaker uses to communicate, just as a hammer is a tool that a carpenter uses to drive nails. The hammer does not drive the nail; it's the way the hammer is used that drives the nail.

## Rate of Delivery

How fast should you talk? That's a question that is hard to answer. A lot depends on your own personal style. The best thing to do is to speak at a rate that is comfortable for you; however, a brisk pace works better than a slow one. By *brisk* we mean a rate that is rapid enough to hold the attention of the audience but not so fast that your words are running together. If you can speak rapidly and still enunciate clearly, do it. But don't sacrifice clarity for speed.

Here is some quantitative evidence you might consider: The average conversational speaking rate is about 150 words per minute; a disk jockey on a rock station will probably clip along at about 170 words per minute; a fast-talking announcer doing a commercial for a used-car company may hit 200 or 210 words per minute. Even if you could talk that fast, you probably would not want to. At that rate, words begin to become indistinguishable, and listeners are unable to comprehend what is being said. Speaking too fast also results in loss of both vocal inflection and emphasis on key words and phrases. Therefore, deliver your speech at a rate that allows you to modulate your voice, and pause for the sake of emphasis.

## EMPHASIZING KEY POINTS

Speakers sometimes seem to have the idea that everything they say will be remembered. Classroom lecturers would certainly like to think that is so, but the results of final examinations do not always confirm that notion. Gaps in listening are also evident in the business world. A study conducted for the Unisys Corporation revealed that adults listen at only a 25 percent efficiency level.[1] There are, of course, a number of variables: the importance of the information to the listeners, the extent to which they will be held responsible for the information, whether or not they are taking notes, the time of day, the temperature of the room, the attentiveness of other people in the audience, and so on. But as a speaker, you must be realistic about how much people are able to assimilate.

If your listeners are only going to retain a small percentage of what you say, you have to ask yourself two questions: (1) "What are the important points of my message?" and (2) "How can I emphasize those points so that they will be remembered?"

### Repetition

Repeating key words and important points appears to be the most effective mode of emphasis. Instructors know that this is absolutely necessary when they have reason to believe that the word or the information is being heard by students for the first time. For example, as we noted in Chapter 9, an expression used in the theory of argumentation and persuasion is *cognitive dissonance.* This is a term that appears frequently in professional journals, but it probably does not come up very often in everyday conversation. The two component words are not really difficult to understand; *cognitive* means "knowing" and *dissonance* means "out of harmony." So, *cognitive dissonance* refers to the condition that may develop when you learn something that seriously conflicts with what you had believed to be true. As a teacher, I would not expect students to be able to remember that term unless I first explained what it meant, and then used

---

[1]Roy Berko, Andrew Wolvin, and Darlyn Wolvin, *Communication: A Social and Career Focus,* 6th ed. (Boston: Houghton Mifflin, 1995) p. 81.

it several times in my lecture. Let's look at another example and see how we might use repetition in emphasizing a key piece of information:

> Hybrid cars can double the gas mileage of some SUVs—they can get twice as many miles per gallon.

This form is called *concentrated repetition*. The information is reinforced immediately after it is said the first time. In this case, different words were used the second time, but that's not always necessary; the information could be repeated in exactly the same words. Repeating a phrase in the same words is a rhetorical device that skilled orators use to create a strong impact. Recall the words of Winston Churchill:

> We shall defend our island, whatever the cost may be. We shall fight on the beaches. We shall fight on the landing grounds. We shall fight in the fields and in the streets; we shall fight in the hills. We shall never surrender.

Word repetition is sometimes called *epistrophe*. Abraham Lincoln employed it when he said, "The government of the people, by the people, and for the people shall not perish from the earth."

## Pointer Phrases

Try to make it as easy as you can for your listeners to recognize what you want them to remember. One way to do this is simply to say to them, "Now here is an important fact . . ." We call this a *pointer phrase*; it's a device instructors often use to call attention to something they want students to remember. In class sometime you might have heard your instructor say, "Now this information is going to be included on the final examination." That's a pointer phrase, and it's designed to get your attention. Let's go back to the previous example regarding population. If you wanted to use a pointer phrase, you could preface your information in this way:

> One point stands out, and this is something that will affect us all within our own lifetime. Unless we can change the present trend, the population of the world will double in the next 30 years.

Always be sure, however, that the statement you are pointing to is truly significant and that it is stated in a way that is easily remembered.

## Oratorical Emphasis

The methods we have discussed so far apply to written statements as well as to spoken ones. However, there are some modes of emphasis that are available only to speakers. They include such things as dramatic pauses, vocal inflection, changes in volume, and the use of gestures. As a speaker, you have access not only to verbal communication, but to all the methods of nonverbal communication.

## Visual Reinforcement

Human beings probably first learned to talk by using visual aids. When you are shown an object and hear a sound, you establish a connection between the word and the thing. Once that connection is made, it's no longer necessary to show the object. Children learn to talk in the same way. As their vocabularies grow, children are able to communicate more of what they mean through language. But visual reinforcement is still a powerful teaching tool at any age. If you want something to stick in your listeners' minds, give them a picture as well as a verbal description. Modern learning theories tell us that people store events in two ways—through visual images and through verbal codes.[2] The more vivid you can make the visual image, the more likely it is that the idea will be remembered. Not every point you want to make can be projected pictorially, but when you have access to visuals that illustrate your words, use them. Here again, the principle you want to remember is that your chances for success in public speaking have a lot to do with your ability to make it as easy as you can for the audience members to comprehend the message and then retain it after they have heard it.

## RESPONDING TO QUESTIONS

Most of the time, your communication with the audience does not end with the conclusion of your speech; it's very likely that there will be a question period afterward. This is a time you should welcome as a speaker, because when the audience members ask questions, you can learn what they were thinking while you were talking. The interaction that takes place at this time provides an opportunity for you to clarify any misunderstandings and to elaborate on points of interest. If the topic is controversial, you will get some insight into the objections people have to your thesis or to your arguments. Be sure to communicate to your listeners that you are interested in their reactions and welcome their comments. Regard their questions as evidence that they were involved in what you were saying and want to extend the dialogue. For the most part, the responses you make to questions will have to be spontaneous, but there are some things you can do to prepare.

## Know Your Subject

It is at this time that your audience will not only have a chance to clarify any points of confusion but will also be able to find out if you really know what you are talking about. You should be able to add new information and use different examples in your replies, so that you aren't simply restating what you have already said.

---

[2]Albert Bandura, *Social Learning Theory* (Englewood Cliffs, NJ: Prentice-Hall, 1977), p. 59.

## Anticipate Questions

If you are well-prepared, there should be few questions that take you by surprise. If your subject matter is controversial, try to think of what objections there might be to the claims you are making. Don't let the audience believe you have been caught off guard by a challenging question. Make the listeners think that you welcome the opportunity to clarify your point.

## Direct Your Answers to the Whole Audience

First of all, make sure everyone has heard the question; if you have any doubt about this, repeat the question so that the whole audience can hear it, and have the questioner confirm your paraphrase. By doing this, you make sure you understand what the questioner is asking, and you also buy a little time that you can use for thinking about how you are going to respond. When you give your answer, make sure that everyone knows you are addressing the whole audience. Remember, your response to the question is part of the speech.

## Be Succinct

Don't make the mistake of launching into another speech in response to the first question; that has the effect of discouraging others from participating. Answer the question directly, but make it brief. If the question calls for a more detailed answer, or if it is off the topic of the speech, invite the person to speak to you at the end of the presentation so that you can discuss the issue further.

## Encourage Involvement

The question period should move rapidly and involve as many people as time allows. There will always be those who will try to make speeches of their own from the floor or who will ask you one question after another. Don't let that happen. If a question starts getting too lengthy or has too many parts to it, you may have to interrupt. Do it politely, give the best answer you can, and then move on to someone else. If you get caught in a dialogue with one person, you will lose the attention of the rest.

## Maintain Control

The question period is part of your presentation; it is not a group discussion. You should try to get lots of people involved, but be sure they don't take the floor away from you and start addressing questions to each other. This can easily happen if you allow long questions or fail to reply to each one. Sometimes a person will make a comment that is not in the form of a question. Treat it as a question and make some sort of response to acknowledge that you have heard.

## Know When to Stop

Because the question period is an important part of your speech, be sure you allow enough time for it. The length of a question period depends entirely on the circumstances. Often, there are time limitations—other speakers may be scheduled, or your listeners may be on their lunch hour. If your time is not restricted, you will have to judge for yourself how long to allow questions to continue. Probably there will be a moderator who will let the audience know that the time is up. When that happens, have a final comment in mind that you can use to bring closure to the presentation.

After you have made your first speech, you are in a position to assess your progress. This is a good time to stop and reflect on what you have learned so far from the text, from the lecture material you have had in class, and from your actual experience of speaking. Review the criteria that were suggested in the first chapter and see how well you think you have observed them. You may have received some feedback on your speech from the other students in the class, and you probably also got a grade from your instructor. All of that is very helpful, but the important thing is for you to be satisfied with your own progress. Don't let a speaking opportunity go by without learning something from the experience.

## EXERCISE

Public speaking is a lot less difficult when you know what information your audience is interested in hearing. A good way to practice is to provide your listeners with a set of questions that you know you can answer. As a preparatory exercise, write three or four questions on small slips of paper and give them to several members of the class. Have those people sit in the back of the room while you stand at the front. The questions should be open-ended so that you have an opportunity to elaborate rather than giving just a simple yes or no answer. Number the questions so that they are asked in a logical sequence. This exercise will give you practice in phrasing questions, organizing material, speaking extemporaneously, and talking loud enough to be heard. In responding to a question, give a complete answer, but don't ramble. When you have finished your thought, drop your voice so that another person can ask the next question. Here are examples of questions you might want people to ask on the subject of family counseling:

1. What are the requirements in this state for becoming a marriage and family counselor?
2. How does a person receive the kind of experience needed to obtain a counseling certificate?
3. What career opportunities are there for a person who has the certificate?
4. What are some of the problems people have when they come to a marriage and family counselor?
5. How successful can a counselor expect to be in helping families deal with their problems?

You might notice that the questions above appear to be similar to what you might find as the main headings in the outline of a speech. You are right; they are. The only difference is that they are phrased in the form of questions. When you prepare your next outline, you might consider using this technique. There is nothing wrong with writing your main headings as questions.

## QUESTIONS FOR DISCUSSION AND REVIEW

1. What do we mean by *standard English?* Why is it recommended for most public speaking situations? What are the disadvantages of using slang expressions?
2. What effect might the use of obscenity have on an audience?
3. Who made the "Reply to Hayne" on the floor of Congress in 1830?
4. What do we mean by *impromptu speaking?* What are some ways you can "prepare" for an impromptu speech?
5. What are the advantages and disadvantages of memorizing a speech or reading it from manuscript?
6. How does an extemporaneous speech differ from an impromptu speech? Why is the extemporaneous speech generally the mode of delivery that is emphasized in most public speaking classes?
7. Explain the meaning of *primary, auxiliary,* and *secondary* messages.
8. What do we mean by *motivated gestures?*
9. Why is it important for a speaker to maintain eye contact with the audience?
10. Besides making the speech more interesting to listen to, what else is accomplished by vocal inflection?
11. How fast does the average person speak? About how fast can a really rapid talker speak?
12. What do we mean by *connecting phrases?* How do they differ from transitional phrases?
13. What are four ways to put emphasis on a word or a phrase?
14. How does concentrated repetition differ from distributed repetition?
15. What is meant by a *pointer phrase?*
16. What kinds of devices fall under the heading of *oratorical emphasis?*
17. How can you prepare for the question period of a speech?

## PROGRESS MANAGEMENT CHECKLIST

### *How can you tell if you are making progress?*

____ 1. Speaking standard English will flow naturally, and you won't make people wince because you are using double negatives.

____ 2. You will be able to think of more descriptive words and phrases to convey your meaning.

____ 3. You will find yourself more willing to ask questions and make impromptu remarks at public gatherings.

_____ 4.  You will not have to memorize your speech or write it out completely in order to deliver it effectively.

_____ 5.  You will discover that the more you practice the speech the smoother the delivery will be and the less nervous you will feel.

_____ 6.  You will be less likely to give distracting nonverbal secondary messages.

_____ 7.  Your gestures will be motivated and will come more naturally.

_____ 8.  Your volume will increase and you will begin using vocal inflection to emphasize your words and enhance your meaning.

_____ 9.  You will hear what you are saying as the audience hears it.

_____ 10.  You will welcome questions and be able to respond to them effectively.

 *Visit the book's Web site at www.mhhe.com/hasling8 for study tools such as practice quizzes, activities, and Web links.*

# *The Power of Visuals*

**AFTER READING THIS CHAPTER, YOU SHOULD BE ABLE TO DO THE FOLLOWING:**

- Know what to do and what not to do when preparing and delivering a PowerPoint presentation.

- Know that a specific audience that may have more background in a given field than a general audience will expect speakers to develop their subject matter in greater depth; be prepared to use physical objects or two-dimensional illustrations for visual aids; know how to generate graphics by using a computer; recognize what visual aids are able to accomplish.

- Be able to use visual aid equipment to project slides and transparencies; be able to use a whiteboard and flip chart while you are making a presentation.

- Know how to speak into a public-address microphone; know how to conduct yourself when you are giving a talk on radio or television.

*C*onfucius was probably right when he said that a picture is worth a thousand words. Advertisers who invest heavily in pictorial displays on television, billboards, magazines, and Web pages believe that it's true, and people involved in making business presentations would do well to follow their example. The fact is that there are many things that cannot be communicated in words. How could a fashion designer describe to an audience of buyers the latest Paris styles without using pictures or models? How could an architect convey to a group of contractors what a building was supposed to look like without showing them drawings and blueprints? Words alone are just not adequate for important presentations that require the audience members to reproduce in their own minds the same picture that you have in yours.

Computer technology has had a significant influence on public address and has given the speaker many important visual and verbal tools. One particular program created by Microsoft has infused the rhetorical arts with a whole new concept and vocabulary. When you need to give a speech that has maximum impact, you would probably want to make a *PowerPoint* presentation.

## POWERPOINT

The best-known PowerPoint presentation made to date is the one delivered by Al Gore called *An Inconvenient Truth.* It set a standard of excellence that will be hard to match, and contributed to the former vice president winning an Oscar and the Nobel Peace Prize. Of course, he had access to the best research scholars and technical directors that could be found, but more than that, he had what seems to be the most important subject matter of the century. If you ever doubted the power of public speaking, look to this presentation as one that

*Al Gore's speech changed the way we think about the effects of global warming.*

made a monumental change in the way people all over the world think about the impact of global warming.

PowerPoint is designed, as the name implies, to make a *powerful point.* It gives pizzazz to your presentation by allowing you to include special effects. You can add words to your photographs, dress up your visuals with attractive designs, highlight bullet points, use a variety of wipes and dissolves between slides, include music, and even create animation and moving pictures.

As you can imagine, making a PowerPoint presentation is not cheap. You will have to have access to some fairly expensive equipment. You will need a digital projector to put the images on a screen large enough for the audience to see. You will also need a laptop computer to run the program. So we're talking about a big investment in time and money. But when it is done well, using attractive visuals, the PowerPoint presentation can make a strong and lasting impression.

## Do It Right

The most difficult part in making a presentation with PowerPoint is gathering and assembling the graphics. They need to be of high quality. Software is not going to improve the look of a photo that is out of focus or a design that is poorly drawn. Better to leave out a slide that is not of high quality than mar the visual impact of the presentation.

- Don't make the slide too "busy" with elaborate shapes and complex designs.
- Don't try to dazzle the audience by using too many color combinations.

Remember that the purpose of the visuals is to gain and hold the attention of the audience and reinforce the message. Words on a slide are not designed to serve as a script for the speaker. Too many words are distracting. The speaker's job is to elaborate on the words and pictures that appear on the screen. Viewers should be able to read the slide at a glance.

- Don't include more than five or six lines of type.
- Don't have more than six or seven words in a line of type.
- Don't use more than four or five bullet points.
- Don't write all words in capital letters.
- Don't use too many different fonts.

Keep in mind that PowerPoint slides are *tools,* not *crutches.* It's possible for tech-minded presenters to become so caught up in the wonderment of a new toy that they become distracted by the glitter and lose the focus of the message.

## Practice, Practice, Practice

Once you have selected the slides you want and arranged them in the desired sequence, your next step is to practice the presentation. This is going to require more effort than you would normally put into an ordinary talk. Not only do you have to be familiar with the content and organization of your speech, but you must also be able to advance your slides with dexterity. All too often speakers lose the attention of the audience because of delays in getting the right slide on the screen. Remember the joke about the stranger in New York who stopped a man on the street who was carrying a violin case and asked, "How do I get to Carnegie Hall?" The man replied, "Practice, practice, practice." If you want to make a successful PowerPoint presentation, do likewise.

Because the preparation of a PowerPoint presentation is time-consuming, begin thinking farther into the future than just one talk on one occasion. If your speech is well received, you may want to make the same one several times in the future. PowerPoint gives you the opportunity to update your material and even change the order of the slides and the points you want to make.

## High-Stakes Presentations

With so much emphasis being placed on giving speeches in the classroom, you might begin to think that the purpose of learning the skills of public address is entirely academic. The fact is that your most important speeches probably will be given after you leave college. You might find yourself in the position of having to make a presentation to an influential group such as a city council. Possibly your opportunity to speak will come on the job, when a proposal needs to be made to a senior management–level committee. The stakes after college are likely to be much higher than they are now, and the success of your presentation may have a significant effect on your career.

Everything that has been said so far in this text applies to real-life situations as well as those that occur in the classroom. There is, however, a difference that should be taken into consideration in regard to the way you will be evaluated. In the classroom, your instructor is going to give you a grade based on how well you fulfill the assignment, prepare the outline, develop the topic, and deliver the speech. In a real-life situation, the people in the audience are the ones who will be making the evaluation, and they are going to base their assessments on how useful the information is to them and how clear you are able to make it. Let's look at effective ways to proceed when it's really important that your listeners get the full impact of your message.

### Speaking to a Specific Audience

We have already discussed the importance of learning as much as we can about a *general* audience, but when you prepare a speech for a *specific* audience, it is necessary for you to sharpen the focus of the topic even more. In a classroom, you have a general audience composed of people with many different interests and levels of comprehension. The material you present to them cannot be highly technical, because they would not have the background to understand it. But an audience of people that have assembled because of a specific interest will expect you to go beyond their common knowledge and present material in greater depth and detail. If the speech is to be useful to them, they must be able to connect what you tell them to what they already know, and they must be able to *remember* what they hear. It may be that the purpose of your presentation is to get the audience to approve your recommendation, to buy what you are selling, or to take action based on your information. That's a real challenge, particularly when you may be limited to only 20 or 30 minutes. What we're talking about here is a speech that looks and sounds like a professional presentation.

The purpose of a speech to a general audience—one that would be appropriate for the classroom—might be to describe how a network of computers can perform a variety of tasks in a business office. But if you were speaking to a group of people who already use computers in their places of business, you would have to go into more depth and detail. For example, you might make a presentation on a particular program application that is designed for a specific accounting function, or recommend a way to provide security for confidential information that is stored in a computer. Before you make this kind of speech, there are several matters you have to consider:

- Does the audience have the technical background to understand the new information that you plan to present?

- Is it enough for the audience members to merely understand the information, or must they be able to retain it and apply it?

- Do you have all the facilities you need in order to make it possible for the audience to visualize the object of your explanation? And will the listeners be able to keep the picture in their minds?

- Will your explanation be a sufficient teaching tool for the audience members, or will they need to have "hands-on experience"?

- Are materials available for the audience to review after the presentation is over?

- Is it necessary for you to know whether or not the audience members have retained what you have told them?

## The Tools of the Trade

There are times when you may have to be more than just a speaker; you might need to be a teacher. Under those circumstances, you must anticipate what your listeners require to be able to learn. Holding an audience's attention is one thing, but now we are adding a new and much more difficult dimension to public speaking—getting people to fully comprehend and *integrate* what they have heard. To do this, it is necessary that you learn to use all the "tools of the trade." Language will still be your principal means of communication, but often you will find that it is not enough.

## Physical Objects

Of all the visual aids you can use, the physical object itself is perhaps the best. To teach a person to swim requires that you have a body of water; to help someone play the guitar, you must let him or her hold the instrument; to provide instruction on how to use a piece of software, you will need to demonstrate on a computer. In all of these cases, verbal description alone is not sufficient, and there is no point in going through the motions of teaching unless the listener is able to learn. There may be occasions when it is not possible to produce the physical object itself, and the speaker may have to rely on a model. This is a technique that might be used by an engineer who is describing a plan for a new suspension bridge or a dentist who is explaining how to do a root canal. The model helps the listener *visualize* what the speaker is saying, and we know that visualization is an important key to learning.

## Two-Dimensional Graphics

If you can't get the object itself and are not able to obtain a model of it, you can use two-dimensional visuals in the form of photographs, drawings, sketches, paintings, cartoons, exploded or cutaway diagrams, bar charts, pie charts, blueprints, maps, key words, or any combination of these. Illustrations in color are best, but black and white will do. They can be displayed by means of computer projection, overhead transparencies, slide projection, movie projection, or video

**FIGURE 12–1.**   Cost of higher education.

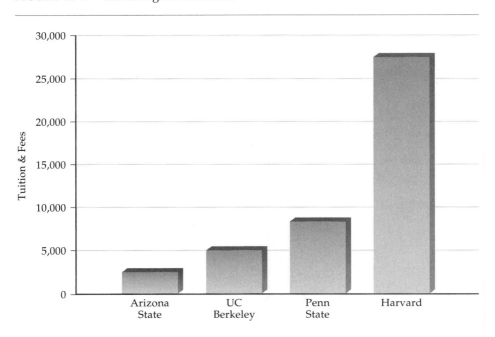

screen. And, of course, a method that does not require electronic equipment is simply to mount the visuals on the wall or on an easel. The important thing is that they be big enough and clear enough for the audience to see.

No longer do you need to be a talented artist or excel in calligraphy in order to produce professional-looking visuals for your presentation. Computer presentation programs designed for this purpose are readily available and easy to use. If you don't have such a program, you can find one online. Go to National Center for Educational Statistics at www.nces.ed.gov. It will take you through the steps of preparing any kind of graph you want.

The easiest form of visual aid is the line chart. It is helpful to both the speaker and the audience. You can print words on the pages of a flip chart with a dark felt pen. For example, if you wanted to talk about First Amendment rights, you could simply print the key words on a page.

```
┌─────────────────────────────────┐
│                                 │
│   FIRST AMENDMENT               │
│                                 │
│   •   Freedom of speech         │
│                                 │
│   •   Freedom of the press      │
│                                 │
│   •   Freedom of religion       │
│                                 │
│   •   Freedom to assemble       │
│                                 │
└─────────────────────────────────┘
```

## What Visuals Can Accomplish

Using visuals for important presentations will help you transform a casual speech into one that has a professional appearance. Consider the visuals you need for your speech in the same way you regard information and evidence. If there were a particular fact that you had to have to support your position, you would need to find it. By the same token, if there is a visual you need in order to make your point understandable, you will need to create it. Not every speech requires visuals, but if you try to do without them when they are needed, you will leave gaping holes in your presentation. Let's look at some of the ways that visuals can contribute to your talk:

- *Picturing what can't be described in words.* This is the most obvious contribution and one that has already been mentioned. But even when your thought is describable, keep in mind that visuals are more *succinct* than words; they reduce the amount of time you have to spend in elaborate explanations. People can see for themselves what you would otherwise have to spend considerable time explaining to them.

- *Giving the speech a professional tone.* Quality visuals convey the message that you know what you are doing and that you care enough to make an extra effort in helping the audience to understand. They set the speech apart from others and let people know that you have "done your homework."

- *Gaining and maintaining attention.* Your verbal facts and assertions may go unheard if your audience is not paying attention. Visuals keep the audience awake and focused on what you are saying.

- *Creating the "Ah ha" experience.* Every teacher will tell you that the best learning takes place when a light goes on inside the student's head and elicits the expression "Ah ha." That's when the listener literally "gets the picture."

- *Producing an emotional impact.* An audience can understand an issue in the intellectual sense, but still not feel the full impact at the emotional level. If the success of your presentation depends on your listeners' being able to internalize the feelings you want to convey, visuals will help to achieve that effect.

- *Appealing to the aesthetic senses.* If you were to rely on words alone to express pure beauty, you would have to speak in poetry. That may not be something you do easily, nor is it an appropriate vehicle for business presentations. You can gain a similar advantage, however, with visuals. For some kinds of speeches, such as travelogues and talks on architectural design, pictures are essential.

- *Imprinting an image for future recall.* Our hope is always that the material we present in the speech will be remembered. It doesn't need to be recalled word for word. What probably will happen is that images will be stored in the memory cells of the listener's brain. We can, of course, rely on people's creating their own images, as they used to do when they listened to drama programs on radio. That may work for the person with a good imagination; the problem is that everyone creates a different image, and some get no picture at all. If you want people to recall a specific scene or a complex idea, you need to provide them with a detailed illustration of what you have in mind. Explanations and descriptions may accomplish that, but well-prepared visuals often make a clearer impression and stay with the listener longer.

- *Providing an organizational structure for the speaker.* Visuals provide an advantage to the *presenter* of the material, as well as to the audience. When you speak, you can use visuals to help you recall what you want to say. Often, speakers find that they can dispense with notes altogether when they do this, allowing the visuals to give cues for both the substance and the sequence of the ideas. For example, the photographs you take of your vacation provide you with a means of recalling what you did and what you saw. If you were going to tell friends about your trip and show your photos, you would have no problem; the pictures themselves would provide all the recollection you would need. You would probably arrange the snapshots in a sequence that would give continuity to your story. This is precisely what you do when you use visuals in making a presentation.

# MAKING IT HAPPEN WITH VISUAL AIDS

At the same time that you study the possibilities in using visual aids, you need also to recognize their limitations. No visual is going to tell the whole story by itself. It is not advisable simply to run a film or a videotape. The fact is that there is no adequate substitute for personal contact, and in the final analysis, the persona of the speaker is the best of all visual aids. There is no chart, screen, or cathode-ray tube that will make people feel welcome, generate trust, or answer specific questions. The personality that you as the speaker project to your audience is the factor that will determine whether or not the message will be accepted. Visuals are simply tools that you can use to help make it happen.

## Projecting Images

Projecting slides and transparencies against a screen still works as well as it ever did. This method of displaying visuals is effective in gaining and holding attention, and contributes significantly to the impact of the message.

The content of the slide or transparency can be just about anything you want it to be. The slide projector is probably a better piece of equipment to use for displaying color photographs, although transparencies can also be used for that purpose. The overhead projector lends itself effectively to the display of charts, graphs, lists, diagrams, and key words, but slides can be made to do those things as well. Here are the generic functions of slides and transparencies:

- They can project an image on a screen so that it is large enough to allow all members of the audience to see the picture at the same time.
- They work equally well for large or small audiences.
- The pictures can be changed easily and quickly either by an operator or by the person who is giving the speech.
- The speaker can call attention to items on the screen with a pointer.
- The speaker can be facing the audience while describing the image or changing the picture.

### Speaking with Transparencies

Always make sure that the visuals you work with in making a presentation are set out in a way that facilitates the logistics of their use; you don't want to have to hunt for something when you are under pressure. The transparencies should have cardboard borders for easy handling, they should be titled, and they should be stacked in order. Here are some other suggestions for using transparencies:

- Have the first transparency lined up on the projector and in focus so that when you turn the machine on, it will appear without delay.
- Cover with cardboard any part you don't want displayed immediately. During the presentation, slide the cardboard down to reveal the figures

or diagrams you want the audience to see. This technique will focus the audience's attention.

- Display the transparency long enough for the audience to assimilate the information, but don't leave it there when you have gone on to another point.
- Have some comment about every transparency you display so that the audience will know what you have in mind. Don't expect the visual aid to speak for itself; your responsibility as the presenter is to help the audience understand the significance of each illustration.
- Be familiar enough with the material on the transparency so that you can direct your attention to the audience rather than to the screen.

Transparencies and slides each have characteristics of their own that may cause you to select one medium over the other: Transparencies have the advantage of being adaptable. You can change the sequence more easily than you can when you are using slides; the room does not have to be totally darkened in order to get clear resolution on the screen; you can call attention to items in the picture by pointing on the transparency itself; you can write on the transparency with a marking pencil; you can conceal part of the material on the transparency with a blank card or sheet of paper until you are ready to have the audience view it.

## Speaking with Slides

Slides have the advantage of producing high-quality images. Photographs can be projected with a realistic, three-dimensional look; the color in slides gives the presentation a highly professional appearance; the projected images can be changed quickly and easily, moving forward or backward with the press of a button. Be sure you know how the equipment works. Familiarize yourself with the kind of projector you will be using in the presentation. The best equipment would consist of a carousel projector with remote controls. Load the carousel yourself (slides go upside down and backwards) and run through them to make sure they are in the right sequence. Experiment with the switches on your remote control unit. You will be able to go backward and forward; you may have to focus manually, unless that function is automatic on the projector. Here are some other suggestions for using slides:

- Position the projector to accommodate the audience. Make sure the slides will be displayed so that everyone will be able to see. Try to avoid the "keystone" effect by keeping the projector on a straight line with the screen. Select a place where you can stand so that you are not blocking anyone's view. And be sure to bring a cord long enough to reach the electrical outlet.
- Practice using a pointer. There may be occasions when you want to call attention to a particular item on the display. The conventional speaker's pointer may work well enough, but if you are some distance from the

screen, a light-beam pointer might be necessary. If you have never used one before, try it out before you confront your audience.

- Consider how you will use your notes. Remember that the lights are going to be out when you show the slides. In a darkened room, you may not be able to see your note cards. It may be that you will not have to use them at all, because the slides themselves will help you recall what you want to say. But if you do have to use notes, provide a small light for yourself at the speaker's lectern.

- Designate a person to turn the lights on and off, and another person to start the slide projector. Remember that you are going to be in the front of the room facing the audience, and you don't want to leave your listeners in darkness with nothing to see or hear.

- Pace your presentation. There are too many variables to make a recommendation on how long to show each slide; you will have more to say about some than about others. But keep in mind the attention span of your audiences and the number of slides you intend to include. Averaging 4 slides a minute, you'll be able to show 120 slides in a half-hour presentation. Remember that the audience members are sitting in a darkened room. After the first 20 minutes, their attention may begin to decline. Don't let them fall asleep.

- Begin by establishing your own personal contact with the audience members. Use some introductory material to get their attention and provide enough orientation information so that they will know what you are going to talk about and what you will be showing them.

- When you are ready for the slides, signal the people who have previously been designated to control the light switch and start the projector. Don't try to do those things yourself.

- Control changing the slide by using your remote switching device. You can do that easily with your thumb. (Make sure you have the right button so that it goes forward instead of backward.) Have something to say about each slide that is projected.

- When the last slide has been shown, have the lights turned back on and the projector turned off. Don't finish the speech in darkness. Let the audience see you as you are delivering your conclusion.

As you can see, there are some logistical complications in making a slide presentation and more things to think about than there are in the unaided speech. You will need to do some planning and make advance preparation, but the impact on your audience will be significantly greater.

## Plain and Simple Visuals

An oral explanation, in my opinion, is more effective than a written one. There are, however, some advantages to information that appears on the printed page.

Complex material, particularly that which contains a great many names and numbers, may require some study on the part of the receiver. Sometimes oral presentations do not allow enough time for the listener to assimilate the material, and the message does not get thoroughly imprinted. When you believe that your listeners may need to review what you have told them after the presentation, you can provide a handout sheet for them. If you want them to follow along while you are providing the explanation, give it to them in advance. But most teachers will tell you that it's a better idea to give your information orally first; then, distribute the handout sheets.

Not all visuals need to be prepared in advance. There are times when you may want to create the visuals as you deliver the speech. The best example of such an occasion is when you are conducting a brainstorming session. You have several choices in selecting your equipment:

- *The chalkboard.* This is the old standby—possibly the world's first visual aid. It works well enough if you don't mind chalk dust on your clothes. I'm not fond of it for professional presentations, because it looks a bit funky and old-fashioned and tends to create a classroom atmosphere. It is also restrictive in terms of space, and your material cannot be saved.

- *The whiteboard.* This is a better choice. It eliminates the chalk dust factor and gives a more professional appearance to the presentation. However, there is still the restriction of space and the necessity of having to erase your material.

*Pictures and diagrams are more succinct than words and keep the audience focused on the topic.*

- *The flip chart.* This is perhaps the best choice. You have enough pages so that you are not going to run out of space, and you don't have to erase the material. The pages can be torn off and turned over to a secretary to be recorded, or possibly pinned up around the room so that the participants have a visual record of the ideas that have been generated.

The flip chart has other advantages as well as those just mentioned. I like to use this piece of equipment as a substitute for note cards. What I do ahead of time is to put my key words and main ideas on the pages in the sequence that I want to follow. As I move through the speech, I simply turn the pages—just as though I am revealing my notes to the audience as I go through the speech. The advantage of this technique is that I can give my full attention to the listeners without the need to be looking at something that they can't see. When I look at the page on the flip chart, they can see it too. Then, with my felt-tip pen, I can highlight items that I want to emphasize.

## Desktop Visuals

As we observed earlier, there are times when the best visual aid is the object itself or a representative model. Small pieces of equipment or artifacts can be held up or passed around if your audience is not too big. There are a number of ways you can display small, lightweight objects. The important thing is that they be visible to the audience while you are talking.

- Pin items to a corkboard.
- Hang objects from overhead clips.
- Place felt cutouts on a flannel board.
- Prop posters on an easel.

Don't put yourself in the awkward position of having to hold a large visual aid in front of you for a long period of time; either prop it up or have someone else hold it. For a small audience, a desktop easel can be used in the same way as a flip chart. A loose-leaf binder that can be mounted on a stand is also very convenient. It can also be carried easily and set up quickly.

Whenever you use visual aids, you need to take into consideration the particular circumstances of the speaking occasion. What works for a small audience may not work for a large one. The same is true in regard to your own voice and appearance. Let's consider what equipment is needed in order to extend your speech to a larger audience.

## MICROPHONES AND CAMERAS

The presentation you give to a small group should work well enough without amplification, but when you are speaking to a large audience, you may need a public-address (PA) system. As the speaker, the only thing you should have to be concerned about is the way you use the microphone, because the technicians will monitor the volume control.

## Public-Address Systems

There's no need to be intimidated by a PA system; all it will do is amplify the sound so that you can be heard without your having to raise your voice to an uncomfortable level. Use enough volume so that you can be heard 20 or 30 feet away, and the amplifier will do the rest. Just remember a few techniques.

- Speak into the microphone from about four to six inches away and at a slight angle. Try to keep the distance as constant as possible. You will know that the system is working when you hear the sound reverberation that is created by the amplifier.
- While the microphone is turned on, don't make any muttering or whispering sounds to yourself or to anyone else that you don't want the audience to hear. Microphones are sensitive and will pick up even low-volume noises.
- Handling the microphone will cause it to rattle. If it needs to be adjusted, let someone else do it for you. If you have to adjust it yourself, grasp it firmly, move it, let go, and then start talking. Never tap on the microphone or blow into it.

## Radio Microphones

If your speech is being carried on a radio broadcasting station, apply the same microphone techniques that were described for the use of public-address systems. The only difference is that you will not hear the sound of your voice amplified. There are two other very important things to remember when your speech is being broadcast:

- Don't start talking until you are given the *cue.* That will come in the form of a red light going on or a director's hand pointing at you. Once you have been given the cue, start right off with your first word, not a nonverbal sound such as "uh." And *never* begin by saying "Are we on?"
- As you get to the end of the speech, the director will give you a "wind-it-up" signal by making a circular hand motion in the air. This signal doesn't mean that you are to stop abruptly in the middle of a sentence; it means you are to finish what you are saying and drop your voice to indicate that you are through. Don't ignore the signal; there is hardly any point in continuing to speak when the mike is turned off.

## Television Cameras

Being televised is not so much of a novelty as it used to be. Local cable channels and broadcasting stations are able to take portable cameras almost anywhere to provide news coverage. Using a digital camera to capture the action of people and events is a common practice in schools, colleges, industry, and the home. It is quite likely that you will find yourself sometime facing a television camera and having a professional or amateur director point a finger at you to start. Here are some hints to keep you from getting completely flustered:

- If you are alone in the picture, talk to the camera. If there are other people with you, talk to them. Never look at the monitor screen, regardless of how tempting it may be to see yourself.

- Avoid sudden or unpredictable movements. If you stand up quickly or walk off to one side, you will move right out of the picture. If you move suddenly toward or away from the camera, you will go out of focus.

- Pay attention to your posture, whether you are standing or sitting. Avoid slouching, scratching your head, tapping your foot, and other ungainly and unnecessary movements that distract the viewer. Remember that those mannerisms will be amplified, because the television screen is able to bring you up close to the audience.

## PUTTING IT ALL TOGETHER

Modern technology has made public speaking a great deal more complex than it was in Aristotle's time—or in the time of Confucius. You can still give speeches the old-fashioned way, relying completely on your unaided voice and your personal image. In fact, that may be what you will be doing most of the time when you have the opportunity to speak. But be sure you know that audio and visual aids are available to you. Don't feel that you are restricted to any one particular kind; you can use a combination of those that have been mentioned. Think in terms of the effect that you want to create and what it is that you want to have stand out in the minds of the audience. Then select the object or the equipment that will do the job most effectively for you. Actually, it may be that Confucius underestimated—a picture could be worth a good deal more than a thousand words.

## EXERCISE

Prepare a visual of one of the kinds listed below. You can create it on a computer or simply print it by hand. It could be in the form of a poster, an overhead transparency, a slide, or a handout sheet. Stand in front of the class. Take three minutes to display the visual and make a short presentation telling what it represents and its significance. Be sure you plan the logistics: Figure out how you are going to display the visual and where you are going to stand. The visual you use could include any of these:

- A printed list of key words to indicate steps in a process.
- A bar chart, a pie chart, or a line graph showing percentages.

- A map of a geographic area that you can describe.
- A painting, diagram, poster, or large photograph.

Make sure that the visual is large enough to be seen. If you use a poster, the paper should be stiff enough to stand upright on an easel or chalk tray. Use a dark-colored felt-tip pen for printing and drawing. If you plan to use an overhead or slide projector, be sure to order the equipment in advance and come into the classroom early enough to set it up.

## QUESTIONS FOR DISCUSSION AND REVIEW

1.  In a real-life situation (as opposed to a classroom), what will probably be the audience's main criteria for evaluating a speaker?
2.  When your speech is being given for a specific audience rather than for a general audience, what changes might you have to make in the purpose and in the content?
3.  What new challenge is added to a presentation on the occasions when you have to be a teacher, rather than just a speaker?
4.  What are some of the ways visuals can be displayed? In terms of the audience's perception, what are the most important criteria for the display of visuals?
5.  How have computer presentation programs helped speakers make professional-looking visuals?
6.  Why would you want to use visuals in a speech? What are some things they can accomplish?
7.  What do we mean when we say that visuals communicate more *succinctly* than words?
8.  What do we mean by *appealing to aesthetic senses?*
9.  In addition to helping the audience understand and retain the message, how do visuals help the speaker in making the presentation?
10. Why is the persona of the speaker still the most important element in speechmaking? What can the speaker do that visuals cannot do?
11. What kind of visuals can you display using computer projection? What advantage does a computer-projected image have over a standard transparency?
12. What piece of equipment is probably best for displaying color photographs?
13. What piece of equipment would you probably want to use if you had several graphs, charts, and lists to display, but you did not want to be confined to arranging them in a particular order?
14. What advantages does a flip chart have over a chalkboard?
15. What is the value of handouts? At what point in the presentation should they be distributed?
16. What are some things you should not do when talking into a PA system?
17. What are some things you should not do while talking in front of a television camera?

# Progress Management Checklist

### *How can you tell if you are making progress?*

_____ 1. You will recognize the mistakes people make when they do a PowerPoint presentation.

_____ 2. You will start thinking about the talks you might be called upon to give after the speech course is over.

_____ 3. You will learn to use a graphics program well enough to make your own visuals.

_____ 4. You will recognize what can't be described in words and seek out the materials necessary to get the point across.

_____ 5. You will become aware of the limitations of visual aids and will not use them as crutches.

_____ 6. You will not make a slide show last so long that you put people to sleep.

_____ 7. You will come to know the flip chart as an aid to audience retention and a prompter for you as the speaker.

_____ 8. You will become familiar with the sound of your voice as it is amplified on a PA system.

_____ 9. You will get to like the image of yourself when you see it on television.

 *Visit the book's Web site at **www.mhhe.com/hasling8** for study tools such as practice quizzes, activities, and Web links.*

# Meeting
# Ethical Standards

---

**AFTER READING THIS CHAPTER, YOU SHOULD BE ABLE TO DO THE
FOLLOWING:**

- Understand what Aristotle meant by "ethos" as one of the modes of proof; know what Quintilian said about "a good man speaking well."

- Begin consciously clarifying your values; understand what is meant by "situation ethics"; compare and contrast categorical imperatives and utilitarian ethics; give thought to your own ethical code.

- Consider the implications of moral issues such as torture, and be able to apply an ethical code to the stand that you take; practice writing an ethical code for a club or organization.

- Understand the implications of plagiarism and know what you have to do to avoid it; consider the standards of "fair use" and know how much copyrighted material you can legitimately use in your speech.

- Know what is meant by social contracts and how John Rawls suggests they should be established; understand the practical, intrinsic, and social value of ethical conduct; consider how a speaker's code of ethics would affect the way you approach public speaking.

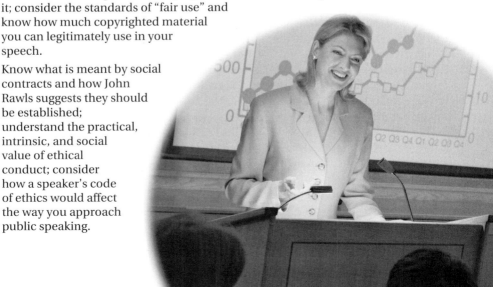

*A*ny criteria for evaluation in public address, as mentioned in Chapter 9, must include the ethical qualities of the speaker consistent with the "mode of proof" that Aristotle calls the *ethos*. The very essence of persuasion has its roots in the ethos, because the other two modes of proof, the logos and the pathos, fail to persuade unless the audience perceives the speaker to be a person of good character. When the integrity of the speaker is in doubt, listeners will question the validity of the evidence and will resist being moved by any attempted emotional appeal.

The Roman philosopher Quintilian (A.D. 40–118) regarded the speaker's moral integrity as an essential element in rhetorical evaluation. A speech of lofty purpose, he maintained, must be delivered by a "good man speaking well." Setting aside the obvious sexism of this declaration, we note that the character of the speaker in the classical view is inextricably tied to the quality of the speech itself.

When Aristotle used the term *ethos* as an element of evaluation, he was referring to the wisdom of the speaker, the validity of the message, and the extent to which the speaker addresses the needs of the audience. So how do you, as a speaker, make those qualities evident? How do you project sincerity and say to your audience, "I know what I'm talking about, you can trust me, and it's beneficial for you to listen"? Mostly it has to do with your being the person you say you are. There's no substitute for authenticity. If you, as a speaker, are going to maintain integrity on and off the podium, you must speak with honesty to yourself as well as to others. As Polonius said to his son, Laertes:

> This above all: to thine own self be true,
> And it must follow, as the night the day,
> Thou canst not then be false to any man[1]

## TELLING IT LIKE IT IS

The political ethic during the 1968 presidential campaign could be summed up in the popular phrase "Tell it like it is." These were words that were commonly shouted at political rallies, and candidates like Robert F. Kennedy responded to the cry. The trouble was that the meaning of the phrase was not always clear. What the crowd wanted was for the speaker to tell them what they wanted to hear. When Kennedy told his listeners that he did not believe in draft deferments for college students, he was booed. Kennedy replied that they wanted him to "tell it like it is," and that's what he was doing. There are several lessons in ethics that can be learned from this example. Kennedy's position was based on his own standards rather than those of the crowd. It was rooted in his fundamental belief that egalitarianism had more integrity than elitism. Those who supported the position of draft deferments for college students favored the notion that the "best and the brightest" should be protected from the ravages

---

[1]William Shakespeare, *Hamlet*, Act 1, Scene 3, lines 78–80.

*Students shouted to Robert Kennedy, "Tell it like it is!"*

of war. Kennedy, however, maintained that all had the responsibility to serve equally. In order to "tell it like it is," a speaker needs to have a solid ethical foundation that is shaped intentionally rather than randomly.

When Polonius said, "To thine own self be true," what he meant was that you should live up to the standards that you set for yourself. That can only be done if you have a clear idea in your mind of what your standards really are. The inclusion of ethics in the course of study for public speakers is certainly as important as learning about content or style. That's why taking a course in speech communication may be the best way to receive guidance in working out your own concept of right and wrong. There is no other academic discipline that is more relevant to applied ethics than public speaking. What you say when you stand on the podium should have behind it a moral and ethical philosophy. That is not to suggest that your code of ethics should be printed in your outline. But it should be something to which you could refer if you were challenged to defend a claim you were making in your speech.

## Values Clarification

No one can tell you what your moral philosophy should be, but there are books you can read that will guide you through the process of discovering it yourself. *Values clarification* is a method of helping you bring to the level of awareness a set of values that works for you and accommodates others. Most likely you have acquired your beliefs from family, friends, teachers, or institutions such as the church, Scouts, and social groups. You are fortunate if you have had healthy influences, because sometimes peer groups, such as urban gangs, can get young people into a great deal of trouble. College offers a good opportunity in your life to examine your moral beliefs to see if they are serving you well.

All too frequently people who have never considered a personal philosophy fall back on the simplicity of moral default. That is to say, they choose their behavior at the time the situation comes up. That may work out all right for those who have good instincts, but the danger is that moral default is generally restricted to that which is self-serving. The students in the earlier example who favored draft deferments for those attending college were not considering the value of fairness, but rather they were motivated by their own self-interest.

### Situation Ethics

*Situation ethics* is sometimes used to describe a philosophy in which moral judgments are based on the circumstances of the occasion. The term and the practice became popular in the 1960s when a book by that title was written by Joseph Fletcher. *Situation ethics* is actually a Christian theological term expressing the belief that love is the only moral criterion, and that everything you do should be measured by that standard. It became popular because it was flexible; it was also the subject of much criticism for the same reason. It's an attractive concept to some because it suggests that you don't have to learn any more rules of conduct other than loving your neighbor. One problem with this ethic is that the gap between your idea of expressing love and the way you behave in a given situation can be filled with self-deception and rationalization. The other problem is that situation ethics seems to imply that the morality of what you do is determined entirely by your motives. As long as your intent is to promote love, you can do what you want. In reality your motive may be pure, but your judgment could be seriously flawed. Extramarital affairs are often justified on this basis.

There is, however, a positive case that can be made for situation ethics. It frees you from acting in a rigid mechanical way that does not take possible exceptions into consideration. An example would be a judge who extends clemency to a remorseful culprit who shows signs of rehabilitation, rather than strictly applying the letter of the law.

### Categorical Imperatives

In the 18th century Immanuel Kant argued in support of what he called *categorical imperatives*—principles that are constant and not affected by changing social circumstances. Unlike situation ethics, the Kantian philosophy requires maintaining the constancy of a principle regardless of the consequences. There is much to be said for such a philosophy. Other people know that they can count on you. If your imperative is to tell the truth, it is certain that you will. The Founding Fathers applied a form of categorical imperatives when they wrote the U.S. Constitution. And when Thomas Jefferson wrote the U.S. Declaration of Independence, he said that people are "endowed by their creator with certain unalienable rights . . . life, liberty, and the pursuit of happiness." A religious creed could be seen in the same way. Imperatives are principles of certainty. If there is any question in your mind about the way you should behave, you can simply fall back on your fundamental belief to get the answer. Such a philosophy is comforting because it frees you from having to make a new judgment every time a situation comes up.

There is universality in categorical imperatives, the implication being that they should apply to everyone and in all cases. That could be seen as a good thing, or not. For example, medical science has raised issues that were not thought of when most moral principles were established. If you believe in the sanctity of human life, can you also believe that experimenting with human embryos is allowable for the sake of conducting stem cell research? You might want to make an exception, but, strictly speaking, categorical imperatives do not permit flexibility to accommodate scientific progress.

## Utilitarian Ethics

Utilitarian ethics, espoused by John Stuart Mill, calls for the greatest good for the greatest number of people. It maintains that there can be no universally accepted standard for moral behavior. If there is more benefit from a given action than there is injury, it would be regarded as ethical. Stem cell research would be permitted because the value of the human beings who would be helped is greater than that of the embryo that would be destroyed.

As a governing philosophy, the ethics of utilitarianism work well as a means of fulfilling the needs of the majority. However, the philosophy sometimes treads on the interests of the minority. It relies heavily upon contemporary cultural mores and consequently may permit social injustices. In the years before the U.S. Civil War, for example, advocates of slavery were able to maintain their position because in their local regions they had popular support. They could argue that a greater good was being served by the institution of slavery because slaves on the southern plantations were helping to ensure economic stability and provide prosperity for the whole population. Furthermore, they could assert that slaves in the South were generally treated better than the free workers in the northern factories. That reasoning, of course, was seriously flawed. It would have been more ethical for southern plantation owners to have applied the categorical imperative that slavery is an abomination, and there is no moral justification for it.

The greatest good for the greatest number carries with it a caveat: What group of people constitutes the "greatest number"? Is it the world? Your country or your state? Or by the greatest number are you referring to the people you know in your immediate neighborhood? Who and how many, for example, would be included in something called "a tax cut that is good for the middle class"? Who and how many benefit from farm subsidies that are designed to protect American agriculture and keep food prices low? What about farmers in smaller countries who can't compete with the low prices that farm subsidies create? Who are the people hurt by such policies? Where do they live and how many of them are there? At least you must know in your own mind where your loyalties lie and whose interests besides your own are being served by your rhetoric.

## Applying Your Own Code of Ethics

The good news is that you don't have to select from a given list of moral codes. But you do have to give some thought to them and shape them into a code that is useful to you in making moral choices. Most likely your judgments, and consequently the point of view you express in your speeches, will take into account more than one of the philosophies mentioned.

A classic example is the treatment of prisoners during time of war. Are nations justified in using torture as a means of gaining information from a prisoner? The nations that signed the Geneva Accords on August 12, 1949, said they were not. The United States, however, equivocated, wanting to leave open the right to use some pressure such as "waterboarding" to learn about possible terrorist plots. Supporters of that position applied the classical argument that "the end justifies the means": If we do, in fact, get the information that would prevent a devastating attack, we might save many thousands of lives. The opponents of torture maintained that such tactics should not be used because confessions obtained under torture were not reliable; in addition, the United States would lose the respect of other nations of the world. You might be able to apply the utilitarian argument of the greatest good for the greatest number, but would that be a satisfactory justification? What if torture did produce reliable information, and what if we did not lose the respect of other nations? Think this matter through and ask yourself whether, in this case, you would rather apply the categorical imperative that torture, under any circumstances, is unacceptable for a civilized nation.

# ETHICAL STANDARDS AT RISK

The collapse of Enron on December 3, 2001, brought into focus the consequences of a large corporation losing its moral compass. Thousands of employees lost their jobs and their retirement pensions. Investors lost the money they had saved in a company they trusted. The event itself was bad enough, but what made matters worse was the realization that much of the unethical behavior on the part of the top executives was not against the law—they simply failed to advise employees and investors of the financial health of the company and neglected to reveal they

*The arrest of Enron CEO Ken Lay demonstrates the consequences of not acting in the best interest of your audience.*

had been selling their own shares. Federal Reserve director Alan Greenspan told Congress during an investigation that it is not that humans have become greedier than in generations past, but that avenues to express greed have grown so enormously.

What we can see is that legal guidelines may not be the highest standard for ethical behavior. To say that you obey the law is no longer proof of right conduct. Most corporations attempt to fill that gap by writing and maintaining a code of ethics. What happened to the executives of Enron was that they failed to read and take seriously their own code, which said, "We treat others as we would like to be treated ourselves . . . We do not tolerate abusive or disrespectful treatment. Ruthlessness, callousness and arrogance don't belong here . . ."

## Political Ethics

The issue of ethics in public life is most conspicuous in the political arena. Many voters feel that the term *political ethics* is an oxymoron. Is it possible for anyone to hold an elected position and still be able to maintain high ethical standards? Politicians sometimes refer to the "rule of survival," which means that they have to save their seats before they can save the world. There are many intelligent, highly qualified people in this country who would make excellent legislators but do not wish to serve because of the compromises they believe they would have to make in their principles in order to get elected. Members of the U.S. House of Representatives must run for office every two years; that means a person in Congress needs to be campaigning almost all the time. Political campaigns cost a great deal of money, and politicians must gain the favor of large contributors in order to build up what they call their "war chests." This certainly does not justify making exaggerated promises or accepting fees for favors, but it helps us to understand the pressure that is placed on a person who makes politics a career.

Former U.S. representative Paul "Pete" McCloskey from California, who served for 20 years in Congress, advises young people who are considering running for office to wait until they have established their careers in the private sector before they subject themselves to the rigors of an elected position. By doing this, he says, representatives do not become dependent on the political office for their livelihood and are free to say no to those who try to buy their vote. Then if they lose an election, they have a career to fall back on.

The pressure on a politician to get reelected can be illustrated in the example of Richard Nixon's involvement in the Watergate scandal. Overzealous supporters of the Republican Party hired burglars to break into Democratic headquarters to learn about the political strategies of the opposition. It was a clumsy and unnecessary act because the polls showed Nixon leading his opponent, George McGovern, by a comfortable margin. The discovery that the president and his advisors had authorized the break-in had devastating consequences. It's true that the president lied about his involvement in the matter and the subsequent cover-up, but no lasting harm was done either to the nation or to the Democratic Party, so why the big fuss? It appears that the American public is offended to a greater extent by the act of lying than by the damage that is done by the lie. It also seems that the lie is much worse when it is told by a person who is in a high position of public trust.

## Avoiding Plagiarism

Every time you give a speech in class or outside of class, you have an opportunity to practice maintaining high ethical standards by avoiding plagiarism. I'm referring to the temptation that students often have of using someone else's words or original ideas in a speech or a paper and making them sound like their own. Sometimes this is done unintentionally, when students do not understand the guidelines for fair use or fail to recognize the seriousness of the consequences. The Internet and the vast network of information sources that technology has made available have certainly provided many new opportunities for accessing information, but they have also increased the number of unfair shortcuts students can take in selecting material for their speeches. Search engines such as Google and Yahoo! can call up Web pages that make it easy for students to lift long passages that compose an entire speech. However, students must remember that instructors, too, have access to those same pages. There is also software that makes it possible to trace plagiarized material to its original source.

Plagiarizing someone else's words and ideas is not only unethical: it can also be illegal. You probably have heard of cases when prominent politicians, writers, and historians have seriously jeopardized their reputations and their careers by carelessly allowing their speechwriters and research assistants to provide them with someone else's copyrighted material. In worst-case scenarios lawsuits of millions of dollars have been filed. For students it may just be a matter of a failing grade and an important lesson.

## Citing Sources

So, knowing the hazards, how can you use information you find in your research without plagiarizing? This can be a real dilemma when all you know about a topic comes from words that someone else has written. The short answer is that you need to cite your sources. But when and how often do you have to do this?

- Certainly you must give credit to the source when you are using a direct quotation from an identifiable person, or copying something word for word from a book, periodical, or Web site. Generally the claim you make should be in your own words, with the quote being used as supporting evidence.

- Give credit when you are paraphrasing the words of another person if the content includes expressions that are uniquely phrased. You might say, "What we are seeing in Washington, D.C., is an expansion of the military-industrial complex that former president Eisenhower warned us against."

- Cite the source of information that the audience may find hard to believe. You do this for ethical reasons, but also for the sake of your own credibility. The audience must perceive that the source is reliable in order for them to find the information acceptable. For example: "According to *Mother Jones* magazine, one study shows that a gallon of hydrogen contains nearly 25 percent less energy than was consumed producing it."

- Cite the source if it's exclusive information found only in one publication. The *Washington Post,* for example, was the only publication that ran the initial story of the Watergate break-in. Your audience will have to decide for themselves if they can trust the source.

- Give credit to the source when it comes from someone you have interviewed. Be sure to establish the person's qualifications for expressing their views.

You don't need to cite sources every time you give information. If your facts are general knowledge; if they have appeared in three or more publications or can be found in any encyclopedia or reference book, go ahead and use them. But be sure you phrase them in words that are your own. A good practice is to read first and take notes; then put aside your reference books and write what you want to say without copying word for word.

## Fair Use

According to the Library of Congress and U.S. copyright laws, speakers and writers are permitted to quote limited passages from works that are copyrighted under a provision called "fair use" if such use is limited to education, criticism, news reporting, scholarship, or research. The key word is "limited," however. You can recite a few lines from a poem or a play to highlight a point you want to make, but be sure to give name credit to the author. Do not read long passages from a novel or a reference book without giving credit. It's not only a violation of copyright laws, but it's also boring.

### Flagrant Violations

There are certain flagrant violations that every conscientious student of public speaking should avoid. Copying and reading a prepared speech that has been written by another person or taken from the Internet is definitely out of the question. Just as bad is reproducing multiple paragraphs from one or two or even three library sources and claiming them to be your own work. Such practices are serious violations of ethical standards. Furthermore, students who do this are depriving themselves of the opportunity to take full advantage of the educational experience that college has to offer. Cheating yourself is just as bad as cheating others.

In my own classes I can generally tell when students are playing fair. If they start to read their speech without looking up from the paper, I get suspicious. I always make them extemporize. So, before you step onto the podium, make sure you thoroughly understand the message you want to convey. Make the material your own. What you say to an audience must be a clearly established part of your own thinking.

## Sophistry

The philosophers in ancient Greece had a term for speakers who ignored the principles of logic, reasoning, good sense, and sound ethical practices. The word was *sophistry*. Originally, it applied to a person of great wisdom—a teacher of rhetoric. But, as those who taught the art began to instruct their students in ways to deceive the audience and to make, as Socrates said, "the worse appear to be the better reason," the reputation of the sophists became severely tarnished. Today, the word is used in an accusatory fashion in reference to someone who attempts to manipulate an audience into accepting superficially plausible, but specious, reasoning. Unfortunately, such manipulation is frequently successful.

A high ethical standard is not something you can turn on when you step onto the podium and turn off when you step down. It is a quality that must be consistent in the personality and character of anyone who intends to engage in public address. Whenever you face an audience, you reveal not only your point of view, but also your moral integrity. If there are flaws in your character that you are trying to hide, your public speaking experiences will begin to feel uncomfortable.

## Civil Disobedience

What about civil disobedience? Can a speaker ethically advocate breaking a rule in a society that is committed to creating an environment that makes the pursuit of happiness a God-given right? Henry David Thoreau wrote, "If the law is of such a nature that it requires you to be an agent of injustice to another, then I say, break the law. Let your life be a counter friction to stop the machine."

The consideration that civil disobedience could be included in the ethical criteria for public speakers is certain to draw objection from those who subscribe to law and order. Yet, the issue must be raised because of the integrity and prestige of the people who have espoused their right to protest legal statutes that violated their personal moral codes. The fact that Martin Luther King Jr. is a national hero and is honored with a day that commemorates his birth is testimony to the ethical status of protesting a law by breaking it.

Civil disobedience does not mean that you have a right to break any law you don't like without paying a price. Thoreau, King, and others who were principal players in civil protests took the action they did with full knowledge of the consequences and with the willingness to accept the penalties of the law. Furthermore, they were prepared to defend their actions in open forum, with reason and evidence.

When the civil rights movement is measured by the standards of utilitarian ethics, we see that the benefits did finally come to outweigh the disruption of the society. The fact that the laws restricting racial equality were eventually struck down vindicated those who brought about the change through their physical actions and rhetorical protests.

## SOCIAL CONTRACTS

Civilization depends on social contracts. Society cannot allow all people to follow their own interests at the expense of others; therefore, we establish laws, customs, and codes to govern and regulate individual behavior. But on what basis do we make those rules?

Harvard University professor and philosopher John Rawls wrote that, ideally, the rules of a society should be established by reasonable people who are acting in their own self-interest, but who do not know in advance what their position in the society will be. In his hypothetical scenario, the people chosen to set the rules do not know, for example, if they will be male or female, black or white, young or old, rich or poor. Being reasonable and acting in their own self-interest, they would not pass laws that would discriminate against any particular sex, race, age group, or social class because such discrimination might ultimately infringe on their own welfare. Rawls says, "The intuitive idea is that since everyone's well-being depends on a scheme of cooperation without which no one could have a satisfactory life, the division of advantages should be such as to draw forth the willing cooperation of everyone taking part in it."[2]

This perspective may help us to establish a basis for our moral values because, as speakers, we do make contributions to social contracts. It is not

---

[2]John Rawls, *A Theory of Justice,* from Manuel Velasquez and Cynthia Rostankowski, *Ethics: Theory and Practice* (Englewood Cliffs, NJ: Prentice-Hall, 1985), p. 138.

enough for us to think in terms limited to our own conduct; we need to look for a philosophy that pertains to *policy*. We know that when we step onto the speaker's platform, we are extending our values to others, and even if we declare that we are speaking for ourselves, we are at the same time modeling what we would prescribe for those we address.

## The Value of Ethical Conduct

But what is the real value of ethical conduct? If the audience likes the speech, why should we, as speakers, be concerned about whether or not it conforms to ethical standards? That's an important question for us to address, because altruism may not be sufficient motivation for those whose actions are normally governed primarily by self-interest.

1. *The practical value.* The speaker whose position is based on sound ethical standards will be perceived by an audience as someone who can be believed and trusted. Therefore, the speech has a better chance to succeed.
2. *The intrinsic value.* This is value for its own sake. It is not measurable in terms of rewards, but it generates confidence and self-esteem within the speaker, who can say, "In my heart I know I'm right."
3. *The social value.* Any society will work better if its people subscribe to and behave according to rules and principles that are just. Those who speak in public have an added responsibility because they influence the thought and behavior of others.

All of this may sound as though demands are being placed on public speakers to be perfect in all respects. Not so. We all make mistakes and fail from time to time to abide by even those moral principles we have established for ourselves. But the fact that we commit indiscretions does not mean that we should advocate them. If a man is unfaithful to his wife, he need not feel that he must stand on the podium and advocate infidelity. In public speaking, we profess what we believe *should* prevail. If we acknowledge transgressions in our own behavior, it would be only to illustrate the point that there is need for vigilance against future misconduct.

Public speaking differs from other forms of discourse in a very important way. In private conversations or in closed meetings, we can explore problems and perhaps try out ideas by expressing them tentatively, without having them become open declarations. But, in public address, we are standing on what we profess to be our considered and reasoned values and opinions.

## The Speaker's Code of Ethics

Almost every profession has its code of ethics; doctors, lawyers, broadcasters, journalists—all have established standards of ethical conduct. That is not to say that everyone in each of those professions abides by the standards to the letter.

There is no force of law that compels them to do so, only their own sense of moral obligation and regard for their professional reputation. Schools, colleges, and universities require that graduates have an understanding of ethical standards in their field of study in order to maintain the historical tradition and the integrity of the profession.

In 1972 the Speech Communication Association adopted a Credo for Free and Responsible Communication in a Democratic Society. It condemns physical and coercive interference in the free speech of others; it urges respect for accuracy in communication and for reasoning based on evidence. Although the ability to speak in public is not something that requires a license or a degree, it is a recognized academic discipline, and students who choose to study the art at the college or university level should have the same appreciation for a code of ethics that people who pursue professional careers have. Those of us who teach public address certainly have a professional responsibility to see that ethical standards are observed in the classroom. As someone who is beginning to practice the art of public speaking, you will have to work out your own code for yourself. Some considerations to take into account are as follows:

1. The claims of the speaker must be based on accurate information, and no false or misleading evidence must be presented to the audience.

2. No information that would have a significant bearing on the speaker's case must knowingly be withheld from the audience.

3. Recommendations made by the speaker must be in the best interest of the audience, and any personal gain for the speaker must be clearly understood by the audience.

4. The message must clarify what the probable consequences would be, and who, if anyone, would be adversely affected if the postulates of the speaker were to be accepted.

5. The speaker must be prepared to take responsibility for claims made and be willing to speak in their support if called upon to do so.

6. The information of the speaker must be presented with the intent to clarify the issue rather than obscure or confuse it.

The conditions of this code do not provide any guidance for positions taken on particular issues, nor do they specify what moral principles should be followed. The implementation of the code is the responsibility of the speaker, and the interpretation must be that of the critic. Furthermore, the code is by no means comprehensive; a number of significant questions are left unanswered.

## Moral Questions

1. *Does the end justify the means?* Students of philosophy continue to wrestle with this question. Is it ethical to set aside a moral principle if a greater good is the result of the action? Would you, for example, condone torture

as a means of obtaining information from a terrorist in order to save the lives of hostages? If you subscribe to the philosophy of categorical impera- tives, you would have to say "no." If you apply the principles of utilitarian- ism, however, you would need to weigh the harmful consequences against the benefits of the end results.

2. *Is omission as bad as commission?* Certainly, if you lie to an audience you are violating a basic ethical standard. But what if you are in a position to give needed information and you fail to do so? Is it a breach of ethics for the vic- tim of a crime or misconduct to abstain from pressing charges? Is a woman who has been sexually abused or harassed guilty of an ethical omission if she fails to come forward with information that would identify the offend- ing party? How does such omission compare to a false accusation?

3. *What is the best response to make to charges of misconduct?* Making a public statement to defend yourself against charges of misconduct is probably not something you will be called upon to do, unless you are a celebrity. But what would you do if you were guilty and in this position? Would you be open and candid, even if it meant jeopardizing the reputation of another party? If a person refuses to answer the charges, is he or she committing an ethical violation? Is honesty always the best policy? We can see from the past experience of high officials in government that attempts to cover up transgressions can sometimes be more damaging to a cause than the mis- take itself.

## Reason Is the Ultimate Ethic

In the final analysis, reason must be the basis for any ethical code. We strive to do the right thing, not for the sake of demonstrating altruism, but because we know that it is ultimately in our own interest and that of the society to do so. Oliver Wendell Holmes said, "Reason means truth and those who are not gov- erned by it take the chance that some day the sunken fact will rip the bottom out of their boat."

## EXERCISE

Discuss in a small group how you would handle each of the following hypothetical cases:

1. You have a good job working for a large, prestigious company that manufactures silicon chips. Your job description includes making presentations to community organizations about the work your company is doing. Recently, you have heard rumors that your company has been violating Environmental Protection Agency (EPA) regulations pertaining to dumping toxic wastes. You contact your supervi- sor and ask her if the rumors are true. She is evasive and says it doesn't affect your department and you shouldn't be concerned about it. Furthermore, she suggests

that your job might be in jeopardy if you continue to pursue the matter. In the next presentation you make, a member of the audience asks you about the rumors. How do you respond?

2. A close friend of yours is applying for a job at the company where you work. Your friend asks you if you would make a personal recommendation on his behalf to the human resources manager. You go in to see the manager, and she shows you your friend's résumé and letters of application. You notice that the résumé says your friend graduated from a university that you know he never attended. The manager says if you would like to make a recommendation you should speak to the hiring committee. What do you do?

3. You are about to make a major presentation to a top management group regarding the safety tests that have been made on a new windshield design for automobiles. If this management group accepts your proposal, your company will be awarded a major contract, and you stand to get a large bonus. You have studied this design for months and are thoroughly familiar with it. You have rehearsed the presentation a dozen times, and you are armed with a battery of handout materials and visual aids. Ten minutes before you go into the meeting, your assistant informs you that there appears to have been some mistakes in analyzing the test results. You know that a delay would mean that the order would go to another company. Your assistant tells you that the flaws are not very bad, and would probably go undetected, even if the car were in an accident. What do you do?

4. You are an instructor in a college speech class. A student shows you an outline for a persuasive speech he plans to give to the class the following day. The speech advocates white supremacy and calls for the organization of an Aryan club on campus that would have as its goal discouraging black, Asian, and Mexican American students from attending the college. You are not able to persuade the student to change the thesis in any way. Do you allow the student to give the speech? If so, what kind of evaluation do you make?

## QUESTIONS FOR DISCUSSION AND REVIEW

1. What was the point made by Quintilian regarding the "good man" theory?

2. What were Aristotle's three criteria for inspiring confidence in the orator's character?

3. What is meant by the term *sophistry?* Why are sophists often able to get away with specious reasoning and unsupported claims?

4. What is meant by *utilitarian ethics?* Who was the philosopher who espoused it?

5. Who was the American author who wrote the essay "Civil Disobedience"? Who was the civil rights leader who practiced the principles described in the essay? What do we have to understand about civil disobedience before we go out and break a law we don't like?

6. What did Immanuel Kant mean by *categorical imperatives?* How does Kant's philosophy differ from that of John Stuart Mill?

7. What is plagiarism, and how do you avoid it?

8. What is meant by "fair use" of copyrighted material?

9. Describe how John Rawls of Harvard University believes that the rules of society ideally should be created.

10. What are three reasons in the text that give value to having a code of ethics? What are the principal responsibilities that might be included in a speaker's code of ethics?

## PROGRESS MANAGEMENT CHECKLIST

### *How can you tell if you are making progress?*

_____ 1. You will begin to critique speakers you hear on the basis of their ethical qualities.

_____ 2. You will check your own speeches to see if they conform to the ethical standards you have set for yourself.

_____ 3. You will begin thinking of how your words will benefit the audience rather than how they will enhance your own well-being.

_____ 4. You will write for yourself a statement of philosophy to support the position you take on a controversial issue.

_____ 5. You will consider the merits of utilitarianism, categorical imperatives, and social contracts.

_____ 6. You will find yourself discussing at length with your friends moral questions such as the end justifying the means.

 *Visit the book's Web site at* **www.mhhe.com/hasling8** *for study tools such as practice quizzes, activities, and Web links.*

# *Speaking Opportunities*

## SHORT SPEECHES FOR SPECIAL OCCASIONS

The expression *giving a speech* has an ominous sound to it. It suggests the need to spend hours in the library researching a topic, writing an outline, making notes, and practicing the delivery. A long speech certainly may require all of that. But many times, a talk you are called on to give will be short and need very little preparation. The principles that have been described so far in this text are still going to apply; the only difference will be that what you say can be compacted into what we might call a "minispeech." Although that term sounds easier and a lot less demanding, there are still a great many people who make contorted efforts to avoid giving even the shortest announcements if more than a dozen people are listening. Having a willingness to speak to groups makes it possible for you to provide a valuable service to others, and at the same time contribute to your own personal growth, self-esteem, and professional advancement. Let's look at a few of the opportunities you might have to make a minispeech.

### *Introducing a Speaker*

When you are called on to introduce a speaker, you need to consider that you are performing two functions: You are giving a brief speech of your own, but you are also part of the presentation that is to be made by the major speaker. Your own speech must have an introduction, a main idea, specific details, and a conclusion. At the same time, you must remember that what you say is designed primarily to help the person you are introducing gain the attention of the audience. Your most important purpose is to pave the way for the main event by generating interest in the topic and establishing the credentials and expertise of the speaker. Here are some ways you can accomplish that:

- Begin by welcoming the audience. Let the listeners know you are glad they could come.
- Relieve the speaker of any mundane responsibilities such as asking them to turn off their cell phones.
- When you start your introduction, use the speaker's full name and title; make sure your pronunciation is correct.
- Tell what position the speaker currently holds and what recent accomplishments he or she has made that pertain to the subject matter of the speech.
- Relate a bit of the speaker's personal history and perhaps an anecdote that conveys some of his or her endearing qualities. You want to portray the speaker as being a likable person.
- Don't say, "Our speaker today needs no introduction." It's trite, and it may not be true.
- Don't exaggerate the speaker's wisdom or capabilities; it will embarrass the person and may cause the audience to become disappointed.
- Conclude your introduction with a cue for the audience to applaud. You can say simply, "Please welcome Mr. So-and-so," and then yield the podium.

Always remember when you are giving a speech of introduction that it's not you who are the featured attraction. You may be very interested in the topic and perhaps even know a lot about it. But be sure you don't preempt the speaker's remarks by making your own editorial comments about the subject matter. Doing that is intrusive and may, in fact, conflict with the speaker's message.

## Expressing a Word of Thanks

Special occasions such as large dinner parties, business conventions, class reunions, weekend workshops, or daylong seminars require a great deal of planning and preparation on the part of the people who organize them. Often that work is done on a volunteer basis, and the individuals who put in their time need to be recognized for their efforts. At some point during the occasion, either at the beginning or at the end, take the initiative to give a word of thanks to those who made the event possible. When you do this, make sure you get the attention of everyone, have the people who are receiving acknowledgment stand, know all of them by name, if possible, and make sure you don't leave out anyone. After you have expressed your thanks, start the applause so that others in the audience will follow suit. The main thing is that you want the ones being honored to feel affirmed.

## Presenting an Award

An award presentation is a short occasional speech that you might need to give when someone achieves something special, such as winning a tournament, receiving a scholarship, or graduating with honors. Again, start by getting the attention of the group; then call up the one who is to receive the award and have the person stand beside you. Next, describe the reason the person is being honored and what he or she was required to accomplish. You might want to give a bit of the history of the award itself so that people will appreciate the significance of the achievement. After that, tell the audience about the qualifications of the person receiving the award. Make the presentation short, and be sure that the focus is on the recipient rather than on yourself.

## Announcing a Coming Event

If you are a member of a club or an organization, you know that there are many occasions when announcements have to be made about coming events. You may wonder why such an effort is necessary. It seems as though we should simply be able to post a notice on the bulletin board and let people read it for themselves. The fact of the matter is that flyers or written memos do not have the same impact as the oral message. A speaker can generate interest and communicate a sense of importance that cannot be conveyed effectively by the printed word. To announce a coming event, make sure you have in your mind everything the audience needs to know. If you have any concern about forgetting, write the details down on a note card before you begin. Use the same methodology that journalists use: Tell *what* the event is, *who* is invited, *why* it is important, *how much* it will cost, *where* it is to be held, *when* it will start, and *how long* it will last. The audience members might also want to know whether it's a benefit for a cause, how often it will be repeated, and if they need to get tickets in advance. Try to be as well-informed as you can, and be sure to convey enthusiasm. After you have made the announcement, you can provide reinforcement by posting a written notice or giving handout sheets to people who are interested.

## Calling for Volunteers

Public speaking is an important part of leadership because it's a skill that makes it possible for you to mobilize other people to support a cause. You may be a creative and hardworking person, but if you can't recruit others to help, you will be limited in the amount you are able to accomplish. Getting people involved has multiple benefits. You as the initiator receive the help you need, the project gets completed, the burden of the task is distributed so that no one person is overloaded, and the people recruited receive the satisfaction of being part of a team effort. A mistake you want to avoid when you are asking for volunteers is to be apologetic about it. You are, of course, requesting that people take time away from their busy schedules, but you have to be sure in your mind that what you are having them do is worthwhile. Begin by describing the task that needs to be done and what results you expect to achieve; let the group know what skills are needed and how much time and effort is going to be involved. Be sure you are realistic. Don't say it's going to be easy if it's not. Don't minimize the skill level that is required if what you want is quality work. Let the people know how firm a commitment they are making and the extent to which you are counting on them. When you get your volunteers, write down names and phone numbers, and make a follow-up call to each without delay.

## Giving a Toast

Making a toast at a wedding or any special occasion is a long-standing tradition. To do this well you must have a close connection to the people being toasted and be familiar with the values of those who are to share in the toast. The most important element at this kind of speaking occasion is sincerity. The toast may have a humorous twist to it, but it also needs to be seriously affirming, with perhaps a touch of sentimentality. It does not have to be elaborately developed; it can be a single thought. However, you still need to gain the attention of the audience, identify the subject, express the main idea, and end with a concluding statement, just as you do in any other speech. For example:

> May I offer a toast—to my readers! They have mastered all the prerequisites to this course; they have endured discussions on the theory of oral communication; they have tolerated my occasional verbosity; they have placed themselves in harm's way as speakers at the lectern. May they receive the applause of their fellow students for their efforts.

## FORMATS FOR SPEAKING OCCASIONS

On some occasion, you may be the organizer of a public speaking event and will need to handle the logistics, such as setting up the chairs, placing the microphones, and so on. You may also be the one to establish the format for the program. There are a number of different ways you can arrange to have information communicated orally to an audience.

## Interview

A two-person interview is the simplest and most basic unit of interpersonal communication. It can be private, of course, but when we add an audience to the model, we have a format for public address. There are several reasons that it is valuable for us to examine the dynamics of an interview: It is a prominent format for newscasts and public affairs programs on radio and television, and it's an effective way to help knowledgeable people structure their comments when they have not had public speaking training. What you are doing when you interview someone is drawing out the information that interests you (and the audience) without letting the person go off on tangents that are not relevant to the main idea. In other words, the interviewer provides the organizational structure whereas the person being interviewed relates the information.

### You as the Person Interviewed

The interview format is a good place to begin your own public speaking training. Select a topic that is familiar to you. Then, sit down in private with the person who will be conducting the interview and work out a set of questions that pertain to the subject matter. The interviewer will do the audience analysis and will guide you into presenting the most pertinent information. You, of course, will also be able to suggest questions that lead into aspects of the subject you think are interesting. When you have your list of questions, arrange them in a logical sequence and think about how you are going to respond to each one. Now you are ready to do the interview in front of a real audience. In its entirety, the interview contains all the elements of a conventional speech. However, the only responsibility you have is to provide the substance in the body of the presentation; the interviewer will do the introduction and the conclusion.

### You as the Interviewer

When you are to be the interviewer for a public presentation, take time before you meet the audience to find out what questions the person to be interviewed wishes you to ask. During the interview, you can extemporize around your list of questions if he or she is reasonably experienced, but it would be discourteous of you to ask something that is going to cause the person embarrassment. The interview format is designed to allow people an opportunity to make the best case they can for the idea they want to express. Your job is to help them do that. Don't turn the interview into a debate, and don't start making a speech of your own.

## Symposium

One of the more structured formats is an arrangement called a *symposium.* In setting up a speaking occasion of this kind you would first decide on a topic—one that is clearly stated but fairly broad. Suppose you are considering "Alternative Energy Sources in a Petroleum-Based Society." A topic such as this gives speakers a general direction but enough latitude to pursue their own interests. Usually, a symposium consists of five or six people who prepare their remarks independently of one another and speak in turn on a given topic for a specific length of time. The topic may be either of an informative or a controversial nature, and the participants may or may not agree with one another's points of view. After all the speakers have made their presentations, they may be given the opportunity to respond to questions from the audience or perhaps interact in a less formally structured exchange of ideas. The symposium is not competitive; it is designed to offer information and, perhaps, arguments that members of an audience can consider and evaluate.

## Panel Discussion

A typical format frequently used on television is the *panel discussion*. This arrangement can also accommodate five or six speakers but is less structured than the symposium. Generally, the panel discussion will have a moderator who will introduce the topic and pose questions to the panelists. There is no set order in which the participants speak and no specified time limit for each one. They react to the questions as they are moved to do so, and they direct their attention to each other as well as to the audience. In many respects, the panel discussion is similar to a conversation; the difference is that the panelists know that an audience is listening and that they need to project their voices with enough volume so they can be heard beyond their immediate circle. Panel members may prepare for a discussion and may even bring notes, but they know that they are not going to express all of their comments from start to finish without interruption. They need to be flexible, to listen to what other panelists say, and to be able to respond in an impromptu fashion. The moderator is responsible for getting the discussion started and providing some closure at the end.

# PHOTO CREDITS